The Day of the Mugwump

X

THE DAY OF THE MUGWUMP

Lorin Peterson

RANDOM HOUSE

NEW YORK

First Printing

Published in New York by Random House, Inc., and simultaneously in Toronto, Canada, by Random House of Canada, Limited.
Library of Congress Catalog Card Number: 61-12151
Manufactured in the United States of America
Designed by Patricia de Groot

to

Joyce

and

Thair

Contents

Introduction

The author did not set out to write a book like this. I set out to buy one. It was only after fruitless roaming through bookstores and library catalogs that I concluded I would have to settle for a bit of information picked up here and a piece found there. I made the mistake of beginning to stick things into file folders, and the project grew insidiously from that point on.

It led me to quit a pleasant job with the American Broadcasting Company news and special events department in Los Angeles in 1957 and to take the first of two trips across the United States. The other followed in late 1960. These junkets to a score of large cities resulted in 330 interviews with politicians, public officials, newspapermen, civic agency employes, and citizens who involve themselves in local politics and government.

Some interviews lasted only fifteen minutes, others went on all afternoon, through dinner, and into the evening. Most of them lasted one to two hours.

Some took place in automobiles. Some in restaurants. A few

even had a cloak-and-dagger atmosphere in a hotel room with tape recorder going. The great majority, however, were prosaic affairs in a business office.

Nearly all had this in common: the people interviewed received me with unfailing courtesy, even though in most cases I arrived an unannounced and total stranger. Only three times did I find myself brushed off—once by the lieutenants of a Philadelphia political boss who said the boss did not trust writers, again by a southern newspaper editor who said he didn't want anybody picking his brain, the third time by a harassed New York labor leader who pleaded he was up to his ears in the 1960 presidential campaign. All these sounded like valid excuses at the time, and they still do.

The reason for so many kindly receptions is not merely that most Americans are nice people. They opened up because they find the political affairs of a great city a fascinating drama—one that runs day after day, year after year, with no final curtain and no two performances the same. And since they find it fascinating, they want to talk about it, especially with a listener who finds it fascinating as well.

In choosing the cities to visit, I used three criteria. Is the city of major importance to its region? Does it have a story that should be told, like that of Memphis and Boss Crump? Can it be squeezed into an itinerary of limited time and budget? I regret that the last restriction kept me from doing justice to such centers as Baltimore, Buffalo, Miami and Denver, which certainly deserve study.

Needless to point out, much of the information in the book is perishable. Affairs of politics and government move rapidly, and today's major fact may be only part of the record tomorrow. Some of the information may be misleading, too—the result of the author's ignorance or misinterpretation or naïveté. I can only hope that these slips have been kept to a minimum.

And I have a further hope—that this project will encourage, or irritate, other reporters and analysts to scrape together the time and money to produce their own versions of the political facts of life in America's big cities. The field has been woefully neglected. If *The Day of the Mugwump* accomplishes this, the four years it has consumed will seem eminently worth while.

It would be fitting to acknowledge debt to each of my informants in print. Some, however, exacted promises of anonymity. Others did not so specify, but common sense indicates a happier future for them if they remain unidentified.

Among those I feel free to proffer thanks to are: in Boston, Robert Bergenheim of the *Christian Science Monitor*, former city councillor Gabriel F. Piemonte, Professor Samuel H. Beer of Harvard, attorney Jerome L. Rappaport, and Joseph F. Turley of the Gillette Company; in New York, Paul Crowell of the *New York Times*, Luther Gulick of the Institute of Public Administration, Richard S. Childs of the National Municipal League, Allen Seed, formerly league field director, city councilman Stanley M. Isaacs, attorney Adolf A. Berle, Jr., Gus Tyler and Mrs. Evelyn Dubrow of the ILGWU, Morris Iuschewitz of the AFL-CIO; in Philadelphia, John Calpin of the *Bulletin*, Joseph T. Kelley and Edward Toohey of the AFL-CIO, Peter Schauffler and Walter Phillips; in Pittsburgh, Mel Seidenberg of the *Post-Gazette*, J. Stanley Purnell, James McClain of the Allegheny Conference, Dr. David H. Kurtzman, formerly of the Pennsylvania Economy League, former city planning director Frederick Bigger; in Cleveland, Wright Bryan of the *Plain Dealer*, Richard L. Maher of the *Press*; in Cincinnati, attorney Charles P. Taft, George Hayward of the Citizens Development Committee, former councilman Theodore M. Berry, city manager C. A. Harrell, William H. Hessler of the *Enquirer*, Mrs. Iola Hessler; in Detroit, Willis Hall and Arthur Hinkley of the Board of Commerce, Robert E. Pickup and Robert Queller of the Citizens Research Council, William H. O'Brien of the Citizens League, Robert Wells of the *News*, Edward Purdy and Carl Westman of the United Auto Workers; in Milwaukee, former Mayor Frank P. Zeidler, Perry Hill and Lloyd Gladfelter of the *Journal*, municipal librarian Gerald P. Caffrey, councilwoman Vel Phillips, Leo Tiefenthaler of the City Club; in Minneapolis, Brad Morison of the *Star* and *Tribune*; in Kansas City, Mayor H. Roe Bartle, former Mayor John B. Gage, Don Jones of the *Star*, Albert P. Mauro, William Lewis of the AFL-CIO; in St. Louis, Robert Duffe, Herb Trask of the *Post-Dispatch*; in Memphis, Dr. Henry Gotten, Dr. Stanley Buckman, attorney Lucius E. Burch; in New Orleans, Glen Douthit, James Gillis and Bernard

Krebs of the *Times-Picayune*, Robert Starnes of the AFL-CIO; in Houston, George Nichols, attorney Lee Sharrer, George Carmack of the *Press*, Emmett Walter and Walter Mansell of the *Chronicle*; in San Antonio, Charles Kilpatrick of the *News and Express*; attorney Maury Maverick, Jr., Ellis Shapiro; in Dallas, Kenneth Smart and Bob Hollingsworth of the *Times-Herald*; in San Francisco, Roger Lapham, Jr., former Mayor Elmer Robinson, Mayor George Christopher, Judge Frederick Hamley, Judge Francis McCarty, Earl Behrens of the *Chronicle*, Charles Mayer of the *Examiner*, attorneys William Orrick, Jr., and William Coblentz, George Johns of the AFL-CIO, Albert Meyer, Hunt Conrad, Louis Clisbee; in Seattle, attorneys Richard Riddell and the late Fred Catlett, Mrs. Eve Sandell, and the author's colleagues of Municipal League days, Tad Crosser and Paul Seibert. The librarians at the UCLA Bureau of Governmental Research and at Santa Monica public library deserve a special word.

Many others who were helpful are mentioned elsewhere in the book, and the debt to them is obvious.

Lorin Peterson

Santa Monica, California
August 1, 1961

The Day of the Mugwump

1

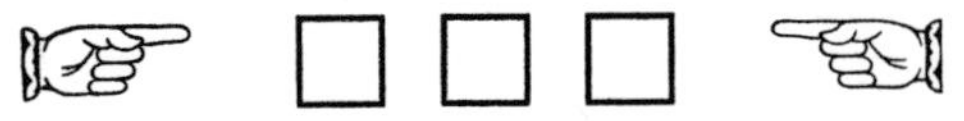

The Paradox

The great political body threshes and heaves, as if trying to haul itself erect. It strains to rise a few inches, then falls back, seemingly held in an invisible net. The muscles bulge, but the limbs barely move. The voice roars now and again in anger and frustration.

Plainly the creature has within it tremendous vigor, yet it cannot gain its feet and walk. Remindful of Gulliver bound, it struggles there, a mass of energy without power.

It is the American city.

2

The Setting

Like an aging actress who thinks she still looks as she did once long ago, America tends to see her political self as it looked in the school book: a collection of pink, yellow and green states—big rectangles in the west, smaller jigsaw pieces in the east—each state complete with a major seat of government, the capitol, and a flock of minor seats of government, the county courthouses and city halls.

This picture once mirrored reality. Back when the pieces numbered only thirteen, George Washington took his oath as president of a country where big cities were not only unimportant but nonexistent. Philadelphia, the largest, had 40,000 people, only five other cities had more than 8,000. Americans living on farms and in small towns outnumbered these urban dwellers thirty to one. When Washington and his colleagues were writing the Constitution, anyone who had suggested that the federal government should have some direct relationship with the cities would have been thought out of his mind. Cities and towns and counties were mere subdivisions of the sovereign state, creatures regulated by the state legislature and expected to do little but help collect taxes and maintain the peace. Many mayors were still appointed by the governor as they had been in colonial times. It was only natural that the Constitution should refer to the states more than a hundred times, and mention cities and municipalities not once.

A century later, British visitor James Bryce found conditions basically unchanged. In his classic *American Commonwealth* he wrote:

> The United States are the only great country in the world which has no capital . . . what Paris and London are to France and England, what Vienna and Pesth are to the Dual Monarchy . . . a city which is not only the seat of political government but is also by the size, wealth, and character of its population the head and centre of the country, a leading seat of commerce and industry, a reservoir of financial resources, the favoured residence of the great and powerful, the spot in which the chiefs of the learned professions are to be found, where the most potent and widely-read journals are published, whither men of literary and scientific capacity are drawn. The heaping together in such a place of these various elements of power, the conjunction of the forces of rank, wealth, knowledge, intellect, naturally makes such a city a sort of foundry in which opinion is melted and cast, where it receives that definite shape in which it can be easily and swiftly propagated and diffused through the whole country, deriving not only an authority from the position of those who form it, but a momentum from the weight of numbers in the community whence it comes. The opinion of such a city becomes powerful politically because it is that of the persons who live at headquarters, who hold the strings of government in their hands, who either themselves rule the state or are in close contact with those who do.[1]

That was seventy years ago. On paper, the United States still appears as diffuse and decentralized as it did to Lord Bryce; legally, it is still a collection of states, each with a capitol and a legislature that hold the reins of control running to every county and city within its borders—fifty little webs of power with a state house at the center of each.

But as diagrams of the real world of political power these webs have no more pertinence than the pathways on a game of Uncle Wiggily.

The energy that drives most political machinery of mid-twentieth-century America originates not in fifty state-systems but in half that number of cities—some two dozen densely settled areas consisting of a central city (or twin major cities) with their suburbs and satellite communities. Here in these clusters are the men who write and publish the major newspapers and magazines, who write and deliver the major newscasts, who raise the bulk of political campaign funds, who study governmental affairs and write books or reports about them, who handle government bond issues and large private financing, who decide where new factories will be built, who negotiate industry-wide labor contracts

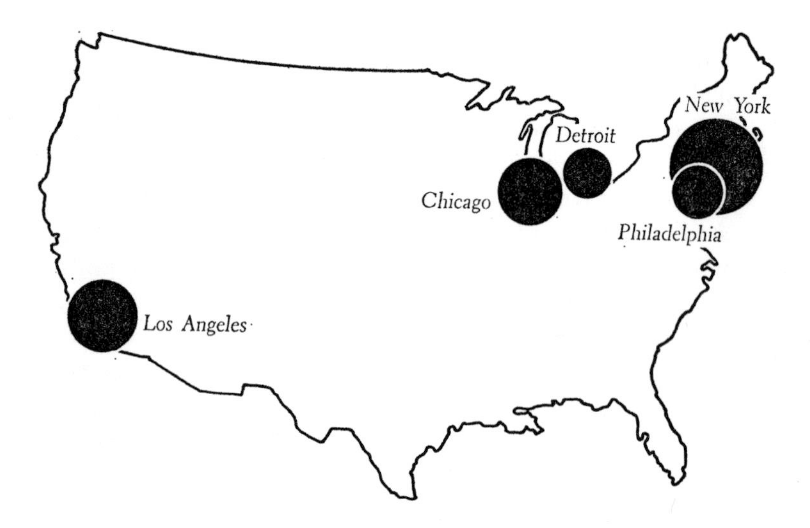

—men who by the very nature of things in a centralized industrial economy make the decisions that eventually shape the course of other men's opinions and actions.

Greatest by far of these decision-making centers is the New York City metropolitan complex, with a population close to fifteen million. Next come the four complexes of Chicago, Los Angeles, Philadelphia and Detroit, totaling over twenty-two million people. These five super-metropolitan areas—we might call them *super mets*—with an aggregate population of some thirty-seven million, dominate the American scene by sheer mass.

Next in weight are six major metropolitan areas, or *major mets*, ranging from three million down to half that size: Washington-

Baltimore, Boston, San Francisco–Oakland, Pittsburgh, St. Louis and Cleveland. This group has a total population close to fifteen million, about equal to that of the New York complex.

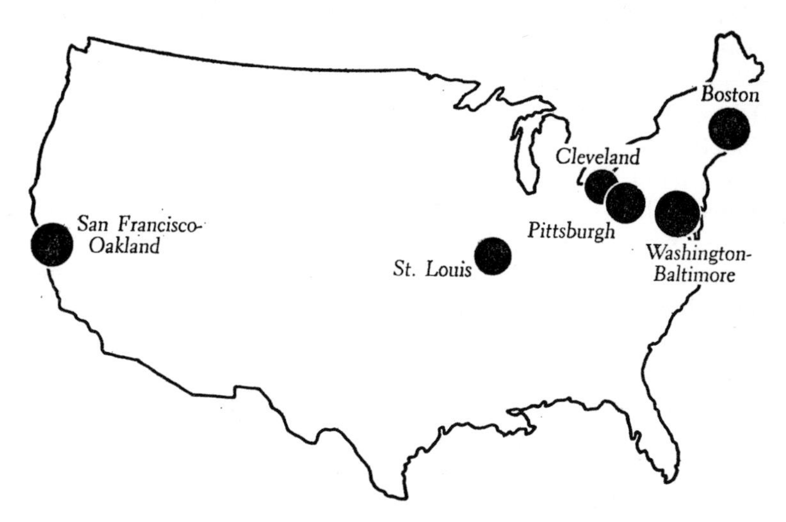

Nearly the same total population lives in fourteen middle-sized metropolitan centers. Most of them, distant from the super mets, dominate regions covering up to several thousand square miles, often thinly settled. These *middle mets,* varying from less than

a million to one and a half million in population, include the complexes of Buffalo, Cincinnati, Milwaukee, Minneapolis–St. Paul, Kansas City, Atlanta, Miami, New Orleans, Houston, Dallas–Fort Worth, Denver, San Diego, Portland and Seattle-Tacoma.

In addition, the federal census bureau lists some 160 minor metropolitan areas, each with approximately 50,000 to 700,000 inhabitants, which have a total population somewhat under the thirty-seven million found in the five super mets of New York, Philadelphia, Detroit, Chicago and Los Angeles. Most of these *minor mets* lie near a larger major or super met complex that overshadows them. The more isolated ones, however, like Memphis, Louisville, Phoenix and San Antonio, have become regional centers.

Yet for all their bulk, their concentrations of economic, social and intellectual influence, American cities are political prisoners. Since colonial days they have grown up in captivity and, like tame elephants, they are still confined by rules laid down for them in their babyhood.

When they were younger, the cities admittedly needed rules. In the nineteenth century a weakness for governmental corruption created a feeling even among their own inhabitants that the cities could not be entrusted with political responsibility. The citizens permitted themselves to be plundered by assorted plug-hat and silk-hat thieves until nearly all faith in big-city government was destroyed.

But even as the odor of corruption grew strong and the need to clean out the thieves and incompetents became unmistakable, surprisingly few volunteered for the task.

Fortunately it did not require many. And among the handful who did volunteer was one group of reformers who stuck with the job for more than half a century until, for all practical purposes, it was done. Not all whom these reformers accused as thieves were thieves. Not all they labeled incompetent were incompetent. In their housecleaning zeal they sometimes swept out the good with the bad. But these were incidental casualties in a drive that did finally overturn the old ways of governing American cities and brought a new age to municipal government across the land. This, in an era that extended from the 1880s through the 1950s, was the first revolution in the cities.

The men who fought it were an improbable-looking lot of revolutionaries whom we shall call here, because no one has given them any other name, the mugwumps.

Their interest to Americans is more than historical. For it seems quite likely that in the remaining decades of the twentieth century they will lead another kind of uprising—a second revolution of the cities.

This revolution seems unavoidable because the nation's centers of energy, its political and economic muscles, have become concentrated in a few dozen metropolitan areas; yet these scattered power centers have only the most rudimentary communications among themselves. They are like bundles of muscles unconnected by a nervous system. Lacking pathways of communication, the cities cannot formulate action. They produce little but isolated random motions and feeble flickerings of ideas about the direction in which they should all move.

This anomaly of strength without communication contains a critical threat to the United States, for strength without communication means strength without purpose. Since America's power centers are in the cities, it is from the cities that the momentum for change must come—the momentum and the plans, the programs, the statements of objectives. To obtain an effective consensus on these matters requires a system of intercommunication among the cities. We have no choice but to create it.

The material that will flow over this communication network will deal with the people of America—how they live, what they want to do, what they want to build, changes they wish to make in their society, how they prefer to make these changes; and, conversely, what things in society they wish to preserve, what institutions they want to strengthen rather than discard, what values they want to reinforce. This communication system, in other words, will constitute an instrument of national purpose.

Americans recently have been talking quite a bit about "national purpose." Why don't we have one? Where did it go? How can we find it again? There has been much digging around in the Federalist papers, the speeches of Abraham Lincoln, the writings of Emerson, and other likely sources, searching for the missing ingredient.

This disquiet arises from the growing realization that, while the country does have a degree of national purpose, it covers only a part of the American horizon. It can do no more because it rests upon an only partly completed system of political communication.

The communication system that has developed in America so far works something like this:

A few men—paid staff, elected officials, or eminent volunteers—develop a possible course of action. They submit it to a larger group for approval and perhaps modification. Then the agreed-upon result is floated as a trial balloon before various opinion-making groups, publishers and other "national leaders." If it passes this test without evoking unfavorable majority reaction, it becomes "policy."

The members of this jury include certain prominent individuals, spokesmen for economic interest groups, congressional and other major political leaders, organizations like the Foreign Policy Association in New York and the San Francisco Commonwealth Club, and a few publications of influence such as the Luce magazines, the New York *Times*, the Hearst, Knight, Scripps-Howard and other newspaper chains. Sociologist Floyd Hunter, in his *Top Leadership U.S.A.*, estimated that in 1958 there were 199 top national leaders on matters of public policy. He classified them as including twenty-three industrial leaders, fifteen United States senators, five congressmen, four assistants to the president, ten cabinet members, four cabinet assistant secretaries, the president and two former presidents, the chief justice of the United States, the vice president, the ambassador to the United Nations, five bankers, five publishers, three labor leaders, three attorneys, two governors, two airlines presidents, two professors, and a scientist, railroad president, radio-television executive, religious leader and utilities executive.

Regardless of who actually belongs to this cult of the consulted, it has become clear that they can shape national purpose in only partial terms. They can more or less agree on military-diplomatic policy—on maintaining close ties with Western Europe, supporting the United Nations, granting foreign aid, spending so many billions for weapons and armed forces. On these things an effective consensus is achieved, effective in the sense that it leads to tangible action.

But on internal policy, on matters closer to the day-to-day lives of the people, particularly people in the cities, the system breaks down. Here there is seldom an effective consensus and, consequently, seldom any action. In these broad areas the country lacks both purpose and performance.

This aimlessness is something the nation can hardly afford. Its internal affairs, the affairs of its big cities, are too important. These power centers, like any pieces of vital machinery, must be cared for—and they must be utilized. Otherwise, the United States faces a long slide into impotence.

The first essential, we have said, is a system of intercommunication among the big cities so that they can arrive at a consensus, can agree on a set of objectives, and can go about attaining them. Somebody must create this system of communication and decision-making. Who will the creators be? What will motivate them? Where and how will they start?

A century of history points to one logical nominee. This group, more than any other in the field of big-city government, has shown a talent for creating a sense of purpose, for articulating objectives, and for translating these objectives into reality. This group is the mugwumps.

3

Activists, Men of Property and Mugwumps

Most Americans look at politics the same way the frontiersman used to regard a bath: as something to be indulged in only every year or so. It may be just as well for the sake of public peace and order that the great majority contents itself with an annual or biennial trip down to the polling place. The political process has become confused enough with only some five percent, more or less, of the citizenry actually trying to influence what government does.

This five-or-so percent can be subdivided, for convenience, into:

the *activists*, who work at politics and government full time as elected officeholders, or appointed administrators, or as hired help in a party headquarters, a citizens league or the political section of a labor union, Chamber of Commerce or other organization;

the *men of property*, who intervene in government and politics because they have to, for business reasons;

and the *mugwumps*, for whom politics and government is a personal interest—they intervene because they want to.

Like any attempt at classifying people, this one becomes fuzzy around the edges, but describing the core members of each group may help make clear whom we are talking about in the chapters that follow.

The man of property operates a railroad, brewery, cement plant, gas company, department store, office building, fish market, construction firm, or whatnot. He copes with government as he copes with such problems as labor unions, transportation and the weather. Each is something to be controlled wherever possible so that it does not get in the way of running the business. Government is a cost to be kept down (unless the new street, sewer or water system it builds will aid the business). Government also is unavoidably a friend to be cultivated if one expects to obtain an occasional zoning variance, a franchise, or a permit to unload trucks in the street.

For the man of property, government and politics are means to an end: that of making a profit and keeping the stockholders happy. This entails campaign contributions to help keep "sound" men in office, a periodic bottle of Scotch to underlings in the planning or purchasing or building departments, and annual checks to the Chamber of Commerce and trade organizations that may stand up for him in time of need. The man of property usually does not spend much time on politics. He buys his way.

For the *activist*, government and politics are an end in themselves. He works at them full time, partly for the money, otherwise for the fun of playing the game. The activist tends to see himself as an idealist, but this is a delusion. He is essentially a mercenary, a political fighter for hire. If he is a politician, he will campaign for office on any issue that will win, provided it is not so shabby that it violates the rules of good long-range politics. If he is a political researcher or writer, he will work for any citizens organization, newspaper or magazine that is not entirely despicable. Given the choice, he might prefer to run on a platform, or work for an organization chiefly concerned with, promoting justice and bettering the lot of the downtrodden, but if such a platform cannot win, or if no such organization exists to pay his salary, the activist will settle for the next best thing. Only in the last extremity will he give up the field of government and politics completely. (The mass of civil service employes are not considered activists in this sense. Their duties as clerks, meter readers, gardeners, rubbish collectors and so forth are technical and nonpolitical like similar jobs in private industry.)

The *mugwump* is the gentleman-citizen who thinks he should do something about the government. He forever feels that government could be better than it is, and he usually has specific suggestions for making it better. What is more, he works to see his suggestions adopted—works persistently, doggedly, year after year.

It is this willingness to work, to form organizations and keep them alive, that distinguishes the mugwump from those who are merely mugwump sympathizers. The sympathizers may share the mugwump outlook, they may sound like mugwumps around the luncheon table or the cocktail bar; but it is the mugwump who belongs to the reform organization and supports it with time and money.

The mugwump has a maddening habit—maddening, that is, to the professional politician and the practical businessman—of judging political issues in terms of morality. The mugwump always asks first: Is this thing right or is it wrong?—rather than will it win votes, or will it work, or will it get something built, or will it prevent a political blowup. To the pre-Civil War mugwump, for instance, slavery was a moral issue and nothing else. That this issue might lose an election or destroy a political party was irrelevant. Slavery was wicked, and wickedness must be cast out. To the mugwump of a later generation, corruption and graft were the cardinal sins. Anything tainted with graft—a streetcar system, an electric-power franchise, a garbage contract, a new city hall—became an object of repulsion. It mattered not whether the streetcar system, the electric power, the garbage collection or the new city hall was needed, or whether the graft amounted to a minute fraction of the money involved. If there was any taint of corruption at all, the whole project stank, and it was fit subject for attack.

To attack, of course, has always been normal behavior for the mugwump. He criticizes constantly; that is to say, he unceasingly tests, examines, searches for what he considers defects in government and, whenever he finds any, proposes repairs.

Thus the mugwump is a reactionary in the literal sense. Incurably critical, he is always looking for something to react against; and he perforce can only react against the status quo. His causes are of necessity molded by existing conditions and institutions. These determine, in any given period, what he will crusade for or against. Politically, the mugwump is a hammer with a single function: to pound. And he must pound against whatever is there to be struck.

This point must be kept in mind. Otherwise the mugwump becomes a baffling figure. He is not to be understood by isolating him on a slide and trying to trace *in vacuo* how his attitudes, beliefs and crusades evolved. He does make sense, however, if one regards him as a counterpuncher, fighting back against his political environment.

For instance, at the turn of the century, and as late as 1920, the mugwump fought big business, particularly the traction, gas and electric utilities that were then openly corrupting city governments; in the 1960s, with the environment changed and the utilities better behaved, this feeling is almost extinct. The mugwump campaigned tirelessly for civil service a few generations ago when there was none and every jobholder was the vassal of a political boss; today, with civil service solidly established in most cities, the mugwump is one of its critics, suggesting ways to make it less rigid. Mugwump organizations in the 1920s and 1930s preached the virtues of pay-as-you-go financing for public buildings and other government construction; yet in the 1950s, aware of American cities' accelerating decay, the same mugwump organizations were urging government to go into debt and float multimillion-dollar bond issues for reconstruction.

The mugwump, in other words, is a pragmatist in politics, as well as a moralist, inconsistent as that may sometimes seem. With his do-good talk and legalistic arguments, he may often sound doctrinaire. But the mugwump usually has a hard, specific goal in mind—breaking up an opponent's political organization, rooting out a gang of corrupt officials, enacting a particular program or piece of legislation. Whatever his objective, the mugwump generally has plenty of doctrine around to fit the situation. And if not, he quickly manufactures some.

To be a mugwump, of course, takes time. He must have freedom to attend long luncheons, go to afternoon or evening meetings, carry on lengthy conversations in his office or elsewhere about mugwump affairs. This rules out most auto mechanics, store clerks, newspaper reporters, bank cashiers, dentists, television engineers and anyone else tied closely to his job. Thus the great majority of mugwumps are lawyers, independent businessmen, or executives in a bank, utility, insurance company or other firm—executives at a high enough level that they can detach themselves for civic duties during working hours.

It has been argued that these business and professional people have inherently a greater feeling of community responsibility than mechanics or clerks. The point is academic. The business and professional men are the ones who have the opportunity to be mugwumps. Most others do not, whatever their inclinations. And this preponderance of the business-professional element has led to a preponderance of Republicans in mugwump organizations.

Since he is most likely to be a business or professional man, the mugwump usually has a presentable appearance and at least a modicum of social position. He cannot be spotted, however, by his looks or by his rating in the business world or on the society pages. Nor is he necessarily a patron of the arts, a member of the symphony board, director of a tennis club, trustee of a foundation, or perennial chairman of charity drives. Many citizens indulge in these things, yet are not mugwumps.

The mugwump is the one who belongs to an organization that intervenes in government. Through the organization, he keeps track of what officials are doing, inquires into the problems they face, frequently dishes out criticism, sometimes offers solutions, and periodically berates his fellow citizens for their indifference to these matters.

A natural question is—why? What impels the mugwump to all this effort?

Some men join a mugwump organization to advance their own careers. A young attorney, insurance man or securities salesman may hope to drum up business or to launch himself in politics. These joiners, however, soon find that the mugwump code prohibits using the organization openly for personal gain. Discovering this, they may drop out and pursue their goals more directly. Or by this time they may have become emotionally involved with mugwumpism and stay with it as true practitioners.

Others join a mugwump group hoping to advance the cause of the Republican or Democratic party by influencing the organization. These encounter the same barrier as the personal-gainers. While most mugwumps are nominally Republicans or Democrats, while they may send in campaign contributions now and again, they are not basically party men. Their first loyalty goes to the mugwump cause. The party comes second. Indeed, blind party loyalty ranks as a major sin in the mugwump creed. Anyone guilty of it is usually eased out of the mugwump organization, or at least shunted to the sidelines.

An appreciable number of mugwumps, probably somewhere between five and ten percent, are hereditary members. Their fathers, and even their grandfathers, worked in mugwump organizations. These scions of reform are found in Boston, Milwaukee, Cleveland, Philadelphia, Seattle and other cities.

In the great majority of cases, however, the mugwump is recruited by a neighbor, a friend, or a law partner or other business associate. This friend detects in him the mugwump spark, or virus or whatever it should be called, and asks him to join. Later, he himself recruits others. It is largely in this way that the mugwump movement has survived and grown.

All this, of course, still begs the question, Why is a mugwump?

Perhaps, using Calvinistic terms, we could say he is driven by a desire to do good works.

Or his motivation might be called patriotism.

Or a feeling of noblesse oblige.

Or perhaps a Nietzschean will to power—a will too small to send him charging into the political arena as a full-time activist, but too big to be ignored.

Certainly there is something of the Adams in every mugwump, the high-intentioned, aristocratic, egoistic, withdrawn yet forward-pushing something described by one of the noted clan, James Truslow Adams:

> No Adams was ever a politician. They cared little enough for mere office in itself. They had little respect for the mind or opinions of the common man merely because he was a man. They always got their own light from their own guiding stars and not from the will o'the wisps of the marsh of "public opinion." But

> they did care intensely for power, power to serve their country and to direct events toward what they considered the right goal.[1]

Richard Hofstadter and others seem to believe the mugwump's chief stimulus, at least in the late nineteenth and early twentieth centuries, was wounded vanity. Accustomed to occupying a position of genteel, passive leadership in his community, the mugwump was stung into political action by discovering after the Civil War that he had been shoved into the background by two new forces—the Irish-dominated big-city machines and the captains of industry, most of whom had scrambled up from obscure family backgrounds.

This upsurge of the uncouth may well have stimulated the mugwumps to their great Progressive crusades before World War I. They reacted strongly, that is, because, from the mugwump viewpoint, they had a lot to react against.

Regardless of what phrases we use—wounded vanity, will to power, noblesse oblige, good works, patriotism—we really explain nothing. Nobody has yet found a way to lift up the lid and look inside an Adams or a mugwump and describe what fire burns there to drive him, any more than anyone has yet determined what makes this man a stamp collector, that one a beer drinker. We know only that there are stamp collectors, beer drinkers, Adamses and mugwumps. And we can observe that the mugwump is a form of political energy, always in motion, exerting pressure, forcing others into motion. Like other energy forms—sunlight, electricity, a running river—he may be diverted from one direction to another. But he does not rest.

We might describe the mugwump, using current phrases, as an inner-directed man, equipped with a full set of critical standards, given to analyzing things, reducing them to principles and sticking labels on them. He is self-possessed, but often shy when not among his own kind. He would almost rather go to jail than run for public office—not that he necessarily dislikes the idea of being mayor or senator, but he recoils from the prospect of a hurly-burly campaign that may end with his public rejection. (For that matter, the idea of the mugwump as an elected administrator of government, the mugwump in power, is an anomaly. The mugwump by definition is the congenital critic, not the wielder of authority. Once in power and running the show, he ceases to be a mugwump. He becomes something else—an office-holder, a political boss. He becomes the kind of person mugwumps train their sights on. Instead of the sniper, he becomes the target.)

While the mugwump avoids presenting his person for public acceptance or rejection, he does not hesitate so to expose his brain children. Indeed, he shows an almost masochistic readiness to throw his ideas into the political arena, where he knows they often will be torn apart. He prefers, of course, that they survive and win. But if the unthinking masses or their civil servants turn thumbs down on his proposed reform, the mugwump takes a certain bitter satisfaction in feeling that he is right and they will realize it some day. This willingness, almost eagerness, to remain constantly on the short end reveals itself in a few paragraphs done some years ago by one of the most articulate mugwumps, Richard S. Childs, who played a leading role as promoter of the short ballot, the city manager plan, and other causes. He wrote under the title "The Reformer":

> A reformer is one who sets forth cheerfully toward sure defeat. His serene persistence against stone walls invites derision from those who have never been touched by his religion and do not know what fun it is. He never seems victorious, for if he were visibly winning, he would forthwith cease to be dubbed reformer.
>
> It is his peculiar function to embrace the hopeless cause when it can win no other friends and when its obvious futility repels that thicknecked, practical, timorous type of citizen to whom the outward appearance of success is so dear.
>
> Yet in time the reformer's little movement becomes respectable and his little minority proves that it can grow, and presently the statesman joins it and takes all the credit cheerfully handed him by the reformer as bribe for his support. And then comes the politician, rushing grandly to the succor of the victor. And all the crowd!
>
> The original reformer is lost in the shuffle then, but he doesn't care. For as the great bandwagon which he started goes thunder-

ing past with trumpets, the crowd in the intoxication of triumph leans over to jeer at him—a forlorn and lonely crank, confidently mustering a pitiful little odd-lot of followers along the roadside and setting them marching, while over their heads he lifts the curious banner of a new crusade.[2]

4

The Curious Banners

The political archeologist probably could go poking through what we know of Rome, Babylon, Ur and most cities since, and find evidence of mugwumpish citizens who intervened in their governments. These organized political amateurs are no doubt a type both ancient and almost universal. One might even undertake to trace a mugwump line of descent from the Sumerian ziggurat through the Athenian assembly down to the Kansas City Citizens Association.

In this country, the trail would undoubtedly lead to people who were in the Continental Congress, in the Constitutional Convention of 1787, in both the Federalist and Jeffersonian Republican parties, and certainly among the Whigs who in the 1830s fought President Jackson and his successor, the New York machine politician Martin Van Buren. There would be a mugwump element in the splinter Liberty party that ran James Birney for president in 1840 and 1844 on an antislavery ticket; and, a decade later, in the antislavery men who met at Ripon, Wisconsin, to found the Republican party.

The mugwumpish strain would be discernible, too, among the "practical Christianity" reformers of New England, New York and Pennsylvania who begat scores of organizations in the first half of the nineteenth century—societies to aid the poor, to repeal imprisonment for debtors, to ban whipping, branding, mutilation and capital punishment, to urge temperance, to care for the insane, to promote education.

There would be evidence also of how mugwump thinking was

shaped by English and French rationalism of the eighteenth century, by Calvinism and the Protestant ethic as filtered through the chill screen of New England Puritanism, by the Manchester school of laissez-faire economics and individual enterprise, and even by the utopianism of Charles Fourier and other early nineteenth-century communalists.

All this composed the philosophical heritage of the American mugwump as he emerged after the Civil War. It made him a person who believed in individual freedom, individual effort, strict honesty, dignity, human progress, an orderly universe, and perfectionism.

These are the nice words. But each nice quality has its reverse side, and one must admit that the same heritage also made the mugwump something of an intolerant, narrow-minded, self-righteous, snobbish, irritable, inflexible fuss-budget.

Each description is accurate in its way. And each is inadequate, like any chain of generalities. The mugwump takes on three dimensions only as one observes his actions—what he did in the past, what he is doing today.

There have been, and are, mugwumps at all levels of government. Some have intervened only in federal affairs, some at the state capitol, some at city hall, some only in their local school boards or weed districts.

Some mugwumps work on several levels—local, state and national. This has been especially true of mugwumps in the biggest cities, the super mets, where lines of power tend to run beyond local boundaries. Back in the 1870s, for instance, many of the New York men who were fighting Tammany and Boss Tweed also led in the Liberal Republican revolt that failed to block President Grant's renomination in 1872, but did succeed four years later in preventing the railroads' friend, James G. Blaine, from heading the ticket. When the Republican regulars forced Blaine's nomination in 1884, the Liberals bolted to Democrat Grover Cleveland, who had been a clean-up mayor of Buffalo, an anti-Tammany governor of New York, and a staunch advocate of civil service.

And it was in this 1884 Cleveland-Blaine campaign that "mugwump" became a household word. The term itself, evidently taken from the old Algonquin Indian *mugquomp* or *mogkiomp*, meaning great man or chief, had been heard in northeastern United States for several decades, usually as a term of derision connoting someone "stuck-up" or self-important. The Indianapolis *Sentinel* called the Liberal Republicans "mugwumps" in 1872 when they nominated Horace Greeley to run against Grant. The name was launched into wide use by Charles A. Dana's New York *Sun* in June, 1884, when Dana used it in attacking the independent Republicans for supporting Cleveland. As often happens in politics, the intended victims fastened onto the name and adopted it as their own.

Describing this "new group which goes by the name of Mugwumps," Bryce wrote in *American Commonwealth:*

> At the presidential election of 1884 a section of the Republican party, more important by the intelligence and social position of the men who composed it than by its numbers, "bolted" from their party, and refused to vote for Mr. Blaine. Some simply abstained, some, obeying the impulse to vote which is strong in good citizens in America, voted for Mr. St. John, the Prohibitionist candidate, though well aware that this was practically the same thing as abstention. The majority, however, voted against their party for Mr. Cleveland, the Democratic candidate; and it seems to have been the transference of their vote which turned the balance in New York State, and thereby determined the issue of the whole election in Mr. Cleveland's favour. . . . The only organization they formed consisted of committees which held meetings and distributed literature during the election, but dissolved when it was over. . . . The chief doctrine they advocate is . . . reforming the civil service . . .
>
> They are most numerous in New England and in the cities of the eastern States generally, but some few are scattered here and there all over the North and West as far as California. It is, however, only in New York, Massachusetts and Connecticut that they seem to have constituted an appreciably potent vote.[1]

These post–Civil War independent Republicans, allied with northern Democrats, drummed steadily against the Radical Republican leaders in Congress and their captive President Grant. The mugwumps pointed indignantly to the land grants to railroads, the Jay Gould–James Fisk gold conspiracies, high tariffs for politics-playing industries, colonial policies toward the South so as to keep Democrats out of Congress, whiskey-tax-fraud collusion between distillers and revenue officials, and other fast shuffles.

Meanwhile, in the cities, a parallel war was developing between the mugwumps on one side and the professional politicians and their business allies on the other. It began when the mugwumps suddenly awoke to the fact that they were living in an age of robber barons, and the barons were taking control of city halls and state capitols, as well as Congress.

In retrospect, the rise of these barons of finance, land, rails, coal, oil, gas, timber, steel and traction, and their collaboration with political chieftains who commanded corps of paid followers, may appear as a normal stage of development in a fast-growing raw country. But the mugwump was not viewing these things in retrospect. He was living in the midst of the Tweeds and Boss Buckleys, the Charles Yerkeses and Jim McManeses. And his pride and stiff-necked Yankee belief in what was proper would not permit him to accept such men as directors of government.

Nearly every major city in those days before 1900 had its boss or bosses and its machine or machines. In some places one man held the reins of power; elsewhere two, three or more rival bosses divided the city among them. A typical machine, and one of the most effective, was the one put together by James McManes in Philadelphia.

This smart and strong-willed operator got his start when the city council appointed him one of the twelve board members of the Gas Trust. The Trust (what we now would call an authority) ran the publicly owned gas utility as an independent commission. It was required to send annual reports to the city council but actually was responsible to no one but its bondholders. McManes gained domination over the eleven other gas trustees and thus over the utility's 2,000 employes, its income, its construction contracts and other aspects of its multimillion-dollar operations. McManes and his friends then bought a controlling interest in the city's largest street-railway company. This gave him another army of employes to use as political workers. Having become indispensable to the ruling Republican party organization, McManes extended his influence over the city water department, streets department, tax department and others. McManes' Gas Ring soon had an estimated 20,000 municipal employes dependent upon the ring for their jobs.

By cracking the whip over this legion, McManes was able to nominate majorities in the council and to send his men to the state legislature. Since Philadelphia was a one-party town, the Gas Ring needed merely to manipulate the Republican primary nominating convention to assure its men election. Lord Bryce in *American Commonwealth* describes a typical Philadelphia convention:

> The Convention of 13th January, 1881, for nominating a candidate for mayor, consisted of 199 delegates, 86 of whom were connected with some branch of the city government; 9 were members of the city councils, 5 were police magistrates, 4 constables, and 23 policemen, while of the rest some were employed in some other city department, and some others were the known associates and dependents of the Ring.

Bryce also described the financial advantages of belonging to the Gas Ring:

> The possession of the great city offices gave the members of the Ring the means not only of making their own fortunes, but of amassing a large reserve fund to be used for "campaign purposes." Many of these offices were paid by fees and not by salary. Five officers were at one time in the receipt of an aggregate of $233,000 or an average of $44,600 each. One, the collector of delinquent taxes, received nearly $200,000 a year. Many others had the opportunity, by giving out contracts for public works on which they received large commissions, of enriching themselves almost without limit, because there was practically no investigation of their accounts.[2]

Similar conditions were to be found in other American cities of the era. And not only in that era. As late as the 1930s Tom Pendergast was running Kansas City in much the same fashion as McManes had exploited Philadelphia a half-century before.

In New York, mugwump outrage at local political conditions was expressed by young Theodore Roosevelt in the *Century* magazine in November, 1886. He wrote:

> In the lower wards where there is a large vicious population, the condition of politics is often appalling, and the boss is generally a man of grossly immoral public and private character. In these wards many of the social organizations with which the leaders are obliged to keep on good terms are composed of criminals or of the relatives and associates of criminals. . . . The president of a powerful semi-political association was by profession a burglar, the man who received the goods he stole was an alderman. Another alderman was elected while his hair was still short from a term in the state prison. A school trustee had been convicted of embezzlement and was the associate of criminals.

The reformers decided by the early 1890s that a nation-wide association might help. The Philadelphia Municipal League took the initiative and called an organizing convention. The invitation was signed by forty-three men from Philadelphia, twenty-four from New York, thirteen from Boston, and six from other parts of the country. It included the names of Theodore Roosevelt, publisher Edwin L. Godkin, planner Frederick Law Olmsted, Charles Francis Adams of Boston, Robert Fulton Cutting of New York, Marshall Field of Chicago, and William Dudley Foulke, a leader in the federal civil service reform movement. The group that met in Philadelphia on January 25 and 26, 1894, launched the National Municipal League, which was to become the leading information center among promoters of big-city reform.

At its beginning, however, the new league produced little more than hope. On the political battlefield it proved to have the same shortcomings as its components—a collection of start-and-stop reform organizations typical of the era, pushing for an occasional charter change, or coming to life at election time to fight the local machine.

The gulf between the mugwumps of Teddy Roosevelt's day and the political machine men was not only wide, it had been a long time developing. The case of the Irish immigrants offers an illustration.

The friction could be traced back to the early years of the Republic, when many Irish arrived in the country as political refugees from their chronic rebellion against the British. They hated England, championed the French Revolution and loudly urged United States aid to the French in their war with Britain, all of which angered the upper-middle-class forefathers of mugwumps in Philadelphia, New York and Boston. The phrase "wild Irishmen" became current, and some Federalists even demanded their exclusion from the United States.

Those early Irish, noisy and irritating as they may have been, were not a major political factor. But their countrymen continued to arrive. By the thousands they crawled off the ocean packets, often half-dead from the long sailing voyage and with only a few coins in their pockets—not enough to strike out as farmers even if they wanted to. They remained in the cities. They got what jobs they could, mostly low-paid, backbreaking labor, lived in shanties and tenements, and found themselves popular with almost nobody except the city politicians.

This comradeship was especially warm just before elections. Diligent ward workers rounded up the newcomers and marched them before pliable judges, who "naturalized" them in wholesale lots. Sometimes those taking the oath had been on United States soil only a matter of hours. The proceedings usually had a happy finale with drinks at a neighboring saloon—a custom repeated on election day after the casting of ballots for the right man. Since voting was not secret in those days, there was no trouble knowing who had voted for the right man.

At first the Irish and other immigrants were the pawns in this game. But by the mid-nineteenth century the Irish, who had a language advantage over other immigrants, had learned the tricks themselves and were taking over control of the machines. Irish names began to appear not only in city councils but in state legislatures and Congress. With most professions and businesses closed to them and many factory gates bearing signs "Irish Need Not Apply," they had gathered in their saloons and political clubs and city halls and had created a little economic world of their own where a clever man could rise to become ward leader, alderman or boss, and an unclever one could at least get a job as policeman or sewer digger.

The Federalists and their successors, the Whigs, believing that the unpropertied poor had no place in politics, made little effort to woo the Irish. And so the immigrants gravitated into the friendlier Democratic camp, especially after the Jackson era, when the party made a more open appeal to the comman man.

As the Irish gained in political skill and numbers, the Irish politicians and their blocs of loyal votes became key factors, often dominant ones, in Democratic forces in New York, Boston and other cities.

It will be recalled that waves of anti-Catholicism and anti-immigrantism swept New England and other sections of the north during the 1840s and 1850s, and again in the '80s and '90s. Boston crowds were known to insult priests on the street and stone the homes of Irish Catholics. Several Catholic churches were burned or wrecked. The Know Nothings agitated for laws permitting only native-born Americans to hold office, and forbidding foreigners to vote or own land until they had lived in the country twenty-one years and then been naturalized. The Know Nothing majority in the Massachusetts legislature authorized an investigation of moral conditions in Catholic convents and broke up militia companies composed of the foreign born. One lawmaker even introduced a bill to prohibit organ grinding so as to eliminate foreign street musicians.

These goings-on frightened Irish politicians and welded them closer to the Democratic party, especially as the Know Nothings in the 1850s succeeded in electing governors, gaining majorities in several state legislatures, and sending some seventy-five congressmen to Washington. In certain sections the Republican party campaigned jointly with the Know Nothings after the Civil War.

While the bulk of mugwumps were Republicans, and while they habitually looked down their noses at the Irish immigrants, there is little evidence that many mugwumps supported the Know Nothing crusades. Neither is there evidence that the mugwumps did much to shield the Irish from the attacks. To the beleaguered Irishman it must have seemed that every Yankee hand was raised against him; and like the settler facing the Indians, he did not have much time to distinguish between good ones and bad ones.

There were other sources of friction. The northern Whigs and later the Republicans antagonized the Irish with their talk of aiding the Negro. To the immigrants, Negroes were competitors in the job market, willing to work on riverboats, docks and ditches for low pay. The New York *Tribune* described in 1850 how the Irish, intent on voting down proposals for greater Negro rights, marched to the polls shouting, "Down with the Nagurs! Let thim go back to Africa where they belong!"

The Irish and other newcomers had difficulty understanding what most mugwump crusades were all about. As Richard Hofstadter says,

> . . . the reformer was a mystery. Often he stood for things that to the immigrant were altogether bizarre, like women's rights and Sunday laws, or downright insulting like temperance. His abstractions had no appeal within the immigrant's experience —citizenship, responsibility, efficiency, good government, economy, businesslike management. The immigrant wanted humanity, not efficiency; and economies threatened to lop needed jobs off the payroll. The reformer's attacks upon the [political] boss only caused the immigrant to draw closer to his benefactor.[3]

Yet another issue divided the mugwump from the Irish: labor agitation. The violence of the Molly Maguires in the Pennsylvania coal fields, the Haymarket Square bombing in Chicago, the mushroom growth of union membership around 1900, the rash of 20,000 strikes in that period starting with the great Homestead steel conflict in 1892 and the Pullman strike two years later, the obvious part played by Irish organizers and sympathetic politicians during these labor outbreaks, all proved to the mugwumps that here was an evil force that could destroy decent society. And so the mugwumps endorsed the use of labor spies, anti-picketing ordinances and other union-busting tactics, including the use of city police to break strikes.

The mugwump around the turn of the century tended to regard people as falling into two categories—the better element, and others. The better element were easily recognized. Their clothes, their speech, their manner indicated they had come from the proper type of home, had attended a good school and were, in a word, gentlemen. Their fathers had been gentlemen before them, and so had their grandfathers in most cases. They were not necessarily wealthy, but they were in comfortable circumstances, as their family had been for at least a couple of generations back, and preferably longer. The mugwump's standard of personal conduct was uncompromising; it was largely that of the New England Yankee who, in Max Lerner's words, was "spare, austere, shrewd, Calvinist, individualist, with a ramrod down his back, tenacious of his dissents as he is confident in his affirmations."

It might be instructive to turn back the clock to 1900 and see the world through the eyes of a composite mugwump—a young attorney, say, in his thirties, graduate of Harvard or Cornell, possibly a Democrat but more likely a Republican, a nice-looking chap even if a bit stiff in his wing collar and starched cuffs, high-buttoned waistcoat and black shoes laced above the ankle. He looked out through his pince-nez on an environment that contained many things he did not like. These included:

professional party politicians—a fundamentally immoral group, he believed, who would steal votes or money whenever they felt the need of either, open to bribery, always ready to approve contracts that would put money in their own pockets;

trusts, utilities and captains of industry—a grasping band of parasites, the allies and more often the masters of the politicians, a predatory crew who ladled out bribes so they could have a free hand at milking the public with their railroads, transit lines, power companies, timber lands and monopolies;

the Irish and other immigrants—a noisy, brawling, largely Catholic, illiterate mass, devoid of civic principles, who had seized control of the political machinery in too many American cities;

saloons—disreputable places frequented largely by Irishmen who used them as political headquarters, while at the same time encouraging simple workingmen to drink up their wages;

labor union organizers—a group of rabble rousers dangerously ignorant of economic laws and unaware that the able individual should rise by his own efforts, not by organized brigandage such as strikes.

Arrayed against this assortment of selfish groups, in our composite mugwump's view, were the Good Citizens—a mixture of clerks, cobblers, grocers and other respectable folk, led by the better element. They had no selfish interests. They sought only the public good. Their views on all issues were moderate, middle of the road and, in the long run, best for the community.

Something of this outlook can be found in a letter written in 1910 by Henry L. Stimson, then a young New York mugwump, later to be secretary of war under Presidents Taft and Franklin Roosevelt and secretary of state under President Hoover. The letter was sent to Theodore Roosevelt, urging him not to break with President Taft and form a third party. Stimson wrote:

> . . . the Republican party, which contains, generally speaking, the richer and more intelligent citizens of the country, should take the lead in reform and not drift into a reactionary position. If instead the leadership should fall into the hands of either an independent party or a party composed, like the Democrats, largely of foreign elements, and if the solid business Republicans should drift into new obstruction, I fear the necessary changes could hardly be accomplished without much excitement and possible violence.[4]

As for the mugwump concept of how to have good government, Stimson and his collaborator, McGeorge Bundy, summed it up thus in Stimson's autobiography (speaking of Stimson in the third person):

> He believed that . . . there was always a policy which was best for all the people, and not good merely for one group as against another. . . . The best political leadership, as he understood it, was that which appealed not to class against class

> or to interest against interest, but above class and beyond interest to the good of the whole community of free individuals.[5]

That statement could stand today as a fair summary of the mugwump philosophy of government.

Stimson and other mugwumps did not regard themselves as a class. The first- and second-generation immigrants were a class, the labor union members were a class, the Socialists were a class, the tycoons and monopolists were a class, the professional politicians were a class. But they, the mugwumps, were free individuals.

It must have struck some mugwumps, however, in moments of self-appraisal, that for a collection of individuals they were remarkably alike. George Mowry in his study of the California Progressives, and Alfred D. Chandler, Jr., in his nation-wide survey of 260 Progressive leaders of 1912, found them to be mostly prospering young attorneys, editors, real estate men or owners of moderate-sized businesses. Nearly all were Protestants with a heavy sprinkling of the New England religions—Congregationalist, Christian Science and Unitarian. Most were college educated, some had studied at European universities. The overwhelming majority regarded themselves as Republicans, even if they did not always vote that way.

Now, a half-century later, the make-up of most mugwump organizations has changed little. Members include more insurance men, accountants and others whose professions have grown up since the early 1900s. A few more Jews and Catholics belong, as well as more who have no religion in particular. The great majority are still Republicans. In a 1957 poll, the Seattle Municipal League, which with more than 4,000 members has the broadest base of any group of its kind, discovered that 72 percent of its members called themselves Republicans, 21 percent were Independents—many of these said they had Republican leanings —and only 7 percent were Democrats. (In some southern cities, of course, one must read "conservative Democrat" for "Republican." And in New York City, the proportion of Democratic mugwumps runs higher than elsewhere.)

Neither has the social composition of mugwump groups changed greatly in the passing generations. On a six-class scale of standing within the community, the membership of the Seattle Municipal League, were anyone to make a detailed study of it, would look something like this: [6]

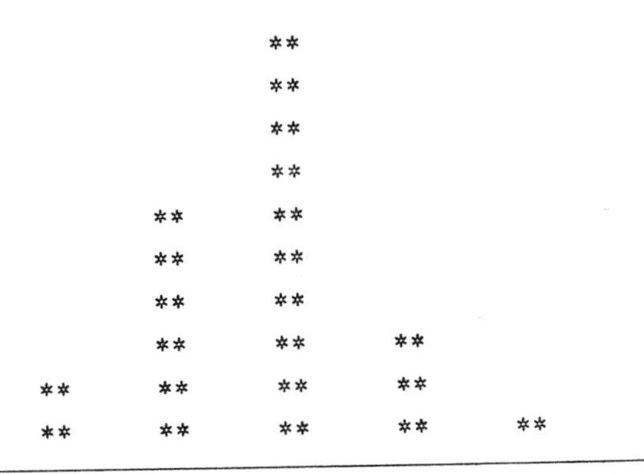

Citizen leagues and bureaus in Cleveland, Detroit, New York (Citizens Union), Minneapolis and Houston probably would show a social profile similar to Seattle's. Bureaus in Chicago, Pittsburgh, Philadelphia, New Orleans, Boston, San Francisco, St. Louis, Milwaukee and others with a narrower base of support would show more pronounced weight toward the upper end of the scale.

The old-style professional politician might have been willing to make a deal with the mugwump, to work out some division of power in the big cities. That, after all, was the way the professional operated. But the mugwump was no deal maker. To him, the machine politician was not a competitor to be accommodated, but the devil to be exterminated.

This battle the mugwump finally won, for all practical purposes. But along the way he made many false starts and campaigned up several blind alleys. Among these were the drives against big business and monopolies, against prostitution, against liquor and saloons, against tenements and slum conditions, and against sin in general.

These crusades were false starts and blind alleys in the sense that they had little direct effect in accomplishing the mugwump's major political objective—to overthrow the big-city machine and its freebooting type of government. Psychologically, however, there was a close relationship between the social reform and political reform movements. Both centered in the big cities; and both drew their energy from the wave of moralistic evangelism that made many nineteenth-century Americans constantly ask, What is right? What is wrong? Why don't we do something about it?

And both movements included a number of the same faces. For instance, help-the-poor efforts and temperance drives went hand in hand during the nineteenth century, and both veered off into political reform. As early as 1817 the New York Society for the Prevention of Pauperism announced that seven-eighths of the fifteen thousand charity cases it found in the city were the victims of excessive drinking. The hundreds of temperance societies that sprang up in the 1830s and '40s concentrated not on drinking among the well-to-do but among the poor. The settlement-house movement that mushroomed in northern cities during the 1890s drew many young college men and women into working in low-income neighborhoods, and there they became enmeshed in a variety of social and political issues. As Arthur Meier Schlesinger describes it in *Rise of the City:*

> Whether engaged in putting up fences or providing ambulances, humanitarian workers could not avoid seeing that the social maladjustments with which they dealt were often conditioned by forces and influences of which the individual was a hapless victim. Their aggressive altruism thus caused them to support all movements for uplift—better working conditions, abolition of child labor, sanitary housing, public health reform, penal reform, campaigns against municipal corruption. In particular they perceived in the ubiquitous saloon a relentless foe; and without caring whether poverty caused intemperance or intemperance poverty, they cooperated with those groups in American society which had long been battling against the evil.[7]

Hofstadter also points out that when the Webb-Kenyon prohibition law came up in the Senate in 1913, most of its support came from the mugwump-backed Progressives. Further evidence of the link in those days between mugwumpism and temperance is found in Detroit. There the mugwump political revival in 1912 was led by an ardent dry, Cadillac-maker Henry Leland, and his aide, Pliny W. Marsh, lobbyist for the Michigan Anti-Saloon League.

The mugwump disliked the saloon, it will be recalled, not only for moral and sociological reasons, but because it served as the professional politician's chief base of operations. Here the ward leader made friends, bought drinks, lent a sympathetic ear to personal troubles, enlisted help and issued orders. Bryce reported that in New York City's 1884 election well over half of all parties' primaries and conventions—633 out of 1,007—were held in saloons.

Mugwumps also lent a hand to anti-sin campaigns like that of the Reverend Dr. Charles H. Parkhurst and his Society for the Prevention of Crime. Professing alarm over rising crime rates in the eighties and nineties, the Presbyterian minister exposed vice payoffs to police and other New York officials. This led to hearings by a state legislative committee under Senator Clarence Lexow, and its findings apparently cost Tammany Hall the 1895 city election. A committee of the New York Chamber of Commerce dug into the vice situation again in 1901, and the resulting publicity evidently contributed to a Tammany defeat that year, too. Again in 1905 the better element created a Committee of Fourteen to crusade against disorderly houses. And in 1910 John D. Rockefeller, Jr., headed a special grand jury to investigate the white-slave traffic.

These and similar virtuous sorties caused much tongue-clucking and newspaper editorializing. They even swung votes. Yet when each squall had passed, Tammany or its counterpart in another city was still there, a bit disheveled but essentially unhurt.

The mugwump's moralism extended into his economic beliefs. While he believed in a fair return for individual effort and ingenuity, he opposed an unfair return—and in the mugwump lexicon that meant any return that resulted from monopoly, speculation or political finagling. This feeling sharpened in the 1870s, '80s and '90s as the tycoons' influence over finance and government grew.

Today's concepts of "liberal" and "conservative," one must remember, had no meaning then. Mugwumps, being mostly small economic units themselves—lawyers, editors, merchants, professors, local bankers—believed in an economy made up of such units, an economy of individuals each doing the best he could. They distrusted and feared those who would create big economic units—the builders of giant corporations, the labor organizers who would weld individual workers into a monolithic mass, the Socialists who would transform government itself into the biggest corporation of all. The mugwumps tended to support anything that would strike at these agglomerations of "privilege," as they called them.

Most mugwumps had a copy of Henry George's *Progress and Poverty* around. And they took a leading part in the anti-monopoly movement of the eighties and nineties. The mugwumps fought for lower tariffs, feeling this would expose the monopolists to foreign competition and cut them down to size. When the capital value of trusts more than tripled in six years at the turn of the century, mugwumps joined with other groups in urging government action to "bust" them. Similarly, a dislike of the timber barons with their policy of cut-and-get-out led many mugwumps into the conservation movement of the early 1900s. Hiram Johnson and the California Progressives, when they took over that state's government before World War I, enacted employers' liability, minimum wages and maximum hours for women, and anti-child-labor laws not only for humanitarian reasons but to rap the knuckles of the Southern Pacific Railroad and other big employers.

Many mugwumps of this era had no distaste for government regulation of business or even for government ownership. The *National Municipal Review,* published by the National Municipal League, carried approving articles during and after World War I about municipal fuel yards in Denver and other cities; Omaha's municipal gas plant; the Lincoln, Nebraska, municipal gasoline station; North Dakota's state-owned grain elevators;

Allentown's municipal vegetable farm that sold directly to consumers; and Milwaukee's municipal fish market for the poor.

Ten days after the Armistice of 1918, the mugwumps' National Municipal League convention at Rochester, New York, unanimously adopted a platform which began:

> During the war, as measures of necessary national efficiency, numerous matters formerly within private control passed to the control of the people. Some of these things should undoubtedly be returned promptly to private enterprise; but the American people will miss a great opportunity if they allow certain of these temporary powers to slip through their fingers in the next few months.[8]

After urging the federal employment service be continued, the platform dealt with "corporations, particularly those doing an interstate business." Of them, it said: "Federal control and supervision of their practices should be continued and extended." The resolution continued:

> The government has assumed control of railroads, telegraphs and telephones, opening the opportunity for either federal ownership with private operation, or federal ownership with federal operation, or a reorganization by economical regional systems under a method of control that will protect private capital by insuring a reasonable return, yet removing speculative and anti-social features of the private ownership of the past. . . . Essential features of our present control should never be relinquished. . . .
>
> The federal government through its food and fuel administrations and its war industries board has acquired a command over basic resources which played a vital part in securing national efficiency. Every effort should be made to preserve the nucleus of these valuable agencies. . . .
>
> The federal government has . . . exerted its war power to influence the cost of living and prevent profiteering. It should continue to exert its peace powers toward the same beneficent end. . . .

The platform concluded with the sentence:

> In short, we, as a people during the next few months, must vigorously hold the ground we have gained during the war.[9]

Several weeks later, on January 3, 1919, the National Municipal League called a housing conference of fifty leading citizens at Philadelphia. Among those signing the invitation were League president Lawson Purdy, city planner Frederick Law Olmsted, and American Federation of Labor president Samuel Gompers. This conference advocated "some kind of federal agency to deal with housing, town planning or community planning" and "federal action . . . toward creating a comprehensive and systematic mechanism to facilitate the financing of housing."

To the participants, these conferences and their ringing resolutions no doubt seemed the call to a brave new postwar era. Actually, they were the dying gasps of Progressivism, which proceeded to succumb during the twenties. That decade of reaction against righteousness brought other mugwump causes to a futile end. The fervor of the anti-saloon campaign petered out in the prohibition fiasco. The outcries against bawdy houses and other assorted sin became ludicrous in the age of the New Frankness, rumble seats and hip flasks. The long fight for woman suffrage, which the mugwumps had aided because they believed women would vote for purity in government, proved during the twenties an illusory victory like prohibition; the women voted much as their husbands had all along.

The mugwumps, however, had not been spending all their time promoting women's rights and tilting at trusts, madams and Demon Rum. These, as it proved, had been mere side shows. The major action had taken place closer to the core of politics.

Mugwumps had been trying since the 1870s to beat the big-city bosses by chopping off their two main sources of strength: their cadres of disciplined, dependent public employes, and their income from graft and from salary kickbacks levied against the employes.

The obvious way to break the bosses' control over employes was through civil service reform. The mugwumps started their drive shortly after the Civil War. By the mid-1880s James Bryce found that civil service had become the chief aim of American reformers. He wrote:

> They are laboriously striving to bring their civil service up to the German or English level. If there is any lesson they would seek to impress on Europeans, it is the mischief of allowing politics to get into the hands of men who seek to make a living by them, and of suffering public offices to become the reward of party work. Rather, they would say, interdict officeholders from participation in politics; appoint them by competition, however absurd competition may sometimes appear, choose them by lot, choose them anyhow; only do not let offices be tenable at the pleasure of party chiefs and lie in the uncontrolled patronage of persons who can use them to strengthen their own political position.[10]

After sporadic progress in the 1870s, the mugwumps pushed the Pendleton civil service act through a shocked Congress in 1883, soon after a demented office seeker had assassinated President Garfield. The mugwumps simultaneously were agitating for civil service in the cities. They obtained state legislation in New York in 1884 requiring written examinations for all municipal employes. Massachusetts followed suit the same year, and thereafter the system spread rapidly.

As a political cause, civil service had almost everything. It was dramatic. It was simple—anyone could understand it. It was virtuous—who dared publicly oppose it? It was an effective political weapon—it hurt the anti-mugwumps. And, most important, it was a winner. It swept across the country, going into effect, at least on paper, in nearly every major city.

To make civil service something more than a paper policy continues even today to be a lively mugwump cause, notably in Boston, Chicago, New York, Philadelphia and a few other cities where party hacks still sabotage the merit system at every opportunity. The mugwumps probably will have to beat back these attacks as long as party organizations exist around city hall.

In the majority of cities, however, where civil service is by now largely free of partisan assaults, the mugwump has other causes to occupy him. Indeed, the mugwump always has a cause, if he can arrange matters that way. The cause, he tells his wife, his friends and himself, is why he concerns himself with politics. It is the reason for his long meetings, his absences from home or the office, his periodic check writing.

In truth, however, the mugwump wants to get into reform politics for its own sake. That is why he adopts the cause. It serves as an explanation more socially acceptable than merely saying, "Well, I just get a kick out of politics." The mugwump who insists he would really rather be home at his fireside but is sacrificing an evening just as his obligation toward good government, should be taken no more seriously than the horse player who professes concern for improving the breed.

The mugwump's procession of causes, or "curious banners," as Richard Childs called them—to the Madison Avenue brotherhood they would be "gimmicks"—has been long and fairly consistent.

An early favorite, still popular, is the charter campaign. In this the mugwumps may demand a wholesale rewriting of the city charter, perhaps to alter the city's form of government; or the proposed change may be a minor one affecting firemen's pensions or the library board.

In the 1880s and '90s, many charter campaigns had as their goal the strong-mayor form of government, exemplified in Brooklyn, which was then autonomous. Mugwump interest switched after 1903 to the commission form developed in flood-ravaged Galveston and in Des Moines (with five commissioners elected, each to run certain city departments, who sit together as the city's legislative body). This strange amalgam of administrative and legislative power enjoyed a decade of popularity. Then, as World War I neared, mugwump theoreticians fastened on the council-manager form (or "commission-manager" form, as they first dubbed it) as the ideal way to run a city; it was modeled after a corporation, with the elected council sitting as the board of directors, their hired city manager handling the active duties of administration.

For a while, some mugwumps dreamed of transforming all government—county, state and even federal—to the manager form. To this day, mugwump publications and mugwumpinfluenced textbook writers speak of the manager form in hushed tones, as if it occupied a slightly higher plane than the grubbier, more "political" mayor-council system. But even the devout have come to accept, albeit reluctantly, that the council-manager system may be best adapted to the middle mets and smaller cities, and the elected mayor may be a necessary political instrument in the major and super mets.

The mugwumps' endorsements of the strong-mayor, the five-man commission and the city-manager forms reflected their political situation. Few in number and averse to ringing doorbells anyway, they could not match the ward and precinct organizations of the professional politicians. Furthermore, most mugwumps lived segregated in upper-income neighborhoods; in large sections of the city they were both uncomfortable and unknown. On the other hand, most mugwumps were also intelligent, educated, charming gentlemen. In private conferences with newspaper publishers and high-level politicians and administrators they could be persuasive and influential.

It was only natural, then, that the mugwumps should constantly seek to remove policy-making power from the large city councils composed of obscure men chosen by the local ward machines, and to transfer that power to one or a few men whom the mugwumps could more easily approach.

In this effort to concentrate policy-making power, the mugwumps attained partial success. They helped give many mayors more authority to hire and fire department heads and to prepare the city budget. They got the city-manager plan adopted in many places. They led movements that eliminated the huge bicameral councils (Philadelphia, for instance, had a 145-member council as late as 1920) and replaced them with smaller bodies. The smaller size, however, proved no magic answer. A political boss, as Pendergast and others demonstrated, could handpick a nine-man council as easily as he could a bigger one.

The mugwumps also sought to hamstring the professional politicians by amending city charters so that the members of the smaller councils would be elected at large by all the city's voters, instead of by wards. This, it was hoped, would squeeze out the ward organization men on the council and permit the mugwumps, aided by friendly newspapers, to elect more prominent citizens. This theory was upset chiefly because (1) the prominent citizens did not choose to run for office, and (2) no army of the righteous rose up to help the mugwumps finance and wage city-wide campaigns. After this disillusionment some mugwumps began to complain that an entire city was too large an election district, that the good-government amateur running for office with no political organization could not cover it in a campaign, and therefore the city should be divided into four quarters like Cleveland, or slit into a dozen or so long thin "ribbon wards" like Detroit. The debates over little wards, big wards or no wards boiled on well into the 1920s.

The gimmick of making all municipal elections nonpartisan found the mugwumps divided. A strong-minded minority believed in working for reform through the Republican party. First clean *it* up, they urged, and then clean up government, using the party as the instrument. These advocates included Charles Evans Hughes, Henry Stimson and Elihu Root. Historian Charles Beard told the 1916 meeting of the National Municipal League:

> Nonpartisanship has not worked, does not work and will not work in any major city in the United States. . . . The causes of parties lie deeper than election laws. . . . The causes of parties being social and economic, we must expect the continued existence of party organizations in our municipal affairs. . . . The task before the reformer is not the enactment of nonpartisan laws but the development of legislation and public opinion that will make parties responsible for their conduct of municipal government. . . . Men who want wise and just government in cities are likely to do as much good by cooperating with the parties and insisting upon the establishment of sound party principles and genuine party responsibility as they are by running to the legislature for new nonpartisan election laws.[11]

But among the mugwumps, Beard spoke for only a handful. The majority preferred to attack the city machines of both parties head on. And in most cities the mugwumps succeeded in driving the machines with their party labels off the ballot.

The mugwumps' love of governmental gadgetry extended to voting. Since they were usually a minority themselves (and since it also was the moral thing to do), mugwumps showed great interest in election devices that would enable minorities to gain at least some seats on a city council, instead of being blanked out by full slates of candidates voted into office en masse by machine-dominated majorities. These proposals included:

limited voting—if three men, for example, are to be elected, each voter can vote for only two, thus giving a minority faction a chance to fill one of the positions; this system was tried in Boston and New York, and is still used for some city and county offices in Philadelphia;

cumulative voting—if three vacancies are to be filled, the voter can cast one vote for each of three men, or he can bunch his votes and cast two or three for one man; Illinois still uses this method for electing the lower house of its legislature;

preferential voting—with one man to be elected, the voter indicates a first, second and third choice among the candidates; if no one wins a majority of first-choice votes, the second-choice and sometimes third-choice votes are counted; this system enjoyed a vogue from 1909 until World War I; it was adopted for varying periods in San Francisco, Cleveland, Toledo, Columbus, Portland (Oregon), Spokane, Houston, Jersey City and nearly fifty other cities; Oklahoma installed it for primaries in 1925.

These voting devices, once the subject of excited discussion and campaigning, were in time largely forgotten by mugwumps and everyone else. But the flame still burns bright in some mugwump hearts for one battered gimmick—the Hare system of proportional representation, P.R. for short. Under this method, named for its English inventor, Thomas Hare, the voter indicates on his ballot a first choice, second choice and so on through the entire list of candidates for an office. What makes the Hare system distinctive is its "quota" method of counting ballots. In practice, the counting method is not very difficult, but to describe it verbally is a formidable project.[12]

Mugwumps succeeded in getting P.R. adopted in four major American cities and a score of smaller ones. Cleveland tried it for a decade preceding the depression. Toledo and New York voted P.R. in during the mid-thirties, voted it out again in the late forties. And in 1957, the mugwumps lost their last major showcase for P.R. when Cincinnati's electorate discarded the system after more than thirty years. In all cities where P.R. was adopted, the party politicians declared war on it almost at once and sniped away until they obtained its repeal.

The mugwumps in the Progressive era before World War I found themselves in rather an awkward spot with another group of gimmicks—the direct primary, recall, initiative and referendum. They knew they should favor them on moral grounds; or, more accurately, they were hard put to find any good moral grounds for opposing them. But the Boston-New York-Philadelphia school of mugwumps, with their aristocratic heritage from Burke, Hamilton and John Adams, had little faith in the mass of voters. One never knew when a demagogue or political boss would stir them up to something foolish. In addition, the direct primary and direct legislation tended to put more names and more propositions on the ballot, something the eastern mugwumps could not square with their campaign for shorter ballots. The upshot was that most of the effective agitation for the direct primary and the initiative-referendum-recall package came from western reformers such as William S. U'Ren in Oregon, Dr. John Randolph Haynes in Los Angeles, and Robert La Follette in Wisconsin.

The short-ballot movement was largely a one-man crusade started in 1909 by Richard Childs, then a young advertising man. From a small New York office financed by his father, Childs sent out thousands of pamphlets urging that minor or technical jobs like those of constables, clerks, coroners, auditors, treasurers and such should be eliminated from the ballot, since the voter had no way of knowing much about either the job or the candidates' qualifications. Childs argued that the citizen should never have to vote on more than five offices at a time; this was as many as he could reasonably be expected to give individual study. Faced with twenty or thirty decisions, he would either vote blindly or not vote at all, leaving control with the disciplined bloc of machine votes.

Childs' ideas attracted the attention of the president of Princeton University, Woodrow Wilson, who became the head of

Childs' little National Short Ballot Organization. Harvard president Charles W. Eliot spoke for the short ballot. The proposal was soon accepted in academic circles, and it became a permanent part of the reformers' creed.

In retrospect, the mugwumps' collection of political gimmicks is impressive, despite the fact that it all must have seemed a bit abstruse to the man in the street—civil service, smaller city councils, unicameral legislatures, strong-mayor form, commission form, city-manager form, short ballot, county-city consolidation, P.R. voting, nonpartisan city elections and the rest.

But the bulk of the mugwumps' reforms and attempted reforms had a common basic trouble: they were rooted in the old American illusion that it is possible to change things merely by passing a law—or by rising up for a sixty-day campaign and electing a new mayor. Many mugwumps viewed government as largely a static thing made up of statute books and organizational charts. And bad government they thought of as something like a bad woman; you could remove it simply by stirring up the good people and bundling it out of town on the next stagecoach. The burghers of Seattle, for instance, fed up with having their city policemen and firemen used as political infantry, organized a Municipal League in 1894. It lasted less than a year, just long enough to get legislation passed placing the two departments under civil service. Then it disbanded.

As long as the mugwumps had this old-time reformer approach of temporary one-cause organizations, they were no match for the regular politicians. The professionals merely battened down the hatches when the storm of public criticism got too heavy, lost an occasional election, and resumed normal operations as soon as the temporary coalition of mugwump groups fell apart and the part-time reformers went back to their law offices and cash registers and collection plates. Sometimes the mugwump coalition won. They pushed across their charter change or elected their mayor. After all, even the best political machine could swing only a solid minority of votes, and whenever the mugwumps succeeded in whipping up the body of citizens to indignation, they could overwhelm the machine minority at the polls.

But the key fact was that, win or lose, the coalition soon disintegrated. Not until another cause, another gimmick, came along would the coalition reappear. This left the field to the political regulars most of the time.

It was no wonder, then, that the men of property preferred to play along with the regulars instead of the mugwumps. Although the mugwumps might storm periodically through city hall disrupting things, like Carry Nation descending on a saloon with her hatchet, they, also like Mrs. Nation, seldom stayed around very long, and then one had to deal with the old management again. No matter how morally righteous these interludes might be, it seemed better to operate under the live-and-let-live arrangement that had grown up over the years between the regular politicians and the men of property: the regulars would leave business alone, keep taxes down and grant necessary favors; in return, businessmen would leave the politicians alone, make reasonable campaign contributions from time to time, and recognize that the professional politician was entitled to a fair profit on the products he handled—paving jobs, garbage contracts, street-cleaning contracts, vice pay-offs, and his employes' salaries.

Mugwumps early in the century were pained and puzzled by this lack of business support. It seemed so immoral. The president of the Pittsburgh Voter's League, A. Leo Weill, complained in a speech in 1918:

> Municipal leaguers have learned these many years that our greatest opposition, or the least sympathy, was encountered among those elements of the community from whom we would naturally have anticipated cooperation and assistance . . . the captains of industry, the manufacturers, the financiers. . . . Whenever and wherever advances in municipal government, experiments in social betterment have been launched, these interests were either openly opposed or dishearteningly complacent.[13]

But processes were under way that, regardless of morality, were radically to realign the power elements in American cities. The mugwump and the man of property were headed toward partnership. The plug-hat politician was headed for the ash heap.

5

Research—The Gimmick That Worked

The big-city political machine of the nineteenth and early twentieth centuries was no invention of Satan, even if the mugwumps thought so. It was a product of its time, a logical result of immigration, illiteracy and immobility.

The machine's operators, mostly first- and second-generation immigrants themselves, were about the only ones who showed any concern for the newly arrived Irish, Italians and Germans. Those in need could look to the local political leader for a job (usually on the public payroll), a loan to pay the rent, a basket of groceries, a sack of coal, a friend at court when father or one of the boys got into a scrape. The machine served as an unofficial welfare state, asking no repayment except votes on election day.

The machine also provided a medium of political communication. Illiterate workmen in immigrant neighborhoods who read no newspapers depended for political information on word of mouth, often dispensed at the neighborhood saloon by the local precinct or ward leader. Mugwumps liked to portray these local leaders as skulking characters with derbies and cheap cigars. Some of them were. But the leader who was any good at his job generally had the reputation of being an affable hard-working fellow who kept his word.

The local leader might have remained a major political factor even after mass media appeared, had it not been for the disappearance of the third factor—the static neighborhood with a relatively immobile population. As long as city dwellers tended to spend most of their lives in the same block, the precinct and ward leader could maintain his influence. He could become acquainted with everyone, make friends and render an occasional favor at city hall. Knowing the political opinions of nearly everybody, he could accurately forecast the vote in his bailiwick. These forecasts were important, whether the machine intended to win the election by honest means or otherwise.

But this pattern of neighborhood living, where people went out on the front steps after dinner, or down to the corner saloon, or over to the Murphys or Bettinios or Gottmeyers for the evening—all this faded with the advent of the automobile, prohibition, mass reading and mass entertainment. People stayed indoors with their newspapers and magazines and radios, or they got in the car and went out for the evening. As they thus snipped the roots that tied them socially to a particular neighborhood, city folk formed the habit of moving from one part of the city to another, or even from city to city, sometimes because of a new job, sometimes just for the sake of change.

In this environment the local leader could not function. He lost his most valuable assets—a monopoly on political communication with several hundred voters, and a monopoly on the understanding of their political reactions—assets which had made him both irreplaceable and, as far as the mugwumps were concerned, generally unbeatable. The coup de grâce came in the 1930s when the government took over as the dispenser of relief to the needy.

But as these technical and social changes in America downgraded the power of the local leader, they upgraded that of the mugwump.

The process was hastened by a handful of bright young men in New York in the early 1900s, who hit upon a gimmick that was to prove immeasurably more effective than the reformers' erstwhile "cause" crusades. The new device came to be known as "governmental research"—meaning research into the doings of government by a private agency.

Intellectually, the movement started as an obvious cousin to the movement for scientific management of industry, which was getting under way at the same time. Just eleven years before the first governmental research bureau was started in New York in 1906, Frederick W. Taylor, the "father of scientific management," had read his first paper to the American Society of Mechanical Engineers, urging the use of research methods to create performance standards for industrial workers—that is, standards to determine what should be considered a good day's work. Two years later, in 1897, the Frenchman Maercelin Bertholet caused a stir in intellectual circles with his *Science et Morale*, declaring that man could eliminate disorder from society by applying scientific methods. In 1905, Sir Norman Lockyer founded the British Science Guild "to promote the application of scientific method and knowledge to social problems and public affairs."

The following year the New York Bureau of Municipal Research was launched, with the announced purpose, according to Dr. William H. Allen, one of the original three-man staff, of providing "a current record of what society is doing; current interpretations of what society needs, does, leaves undone; and current aggressive action to utilize information that comes from currently interpreting the current record of organized society's current acts." [1]

Although Dr. Allen spoke in general terms of "society," he and his colleagues, Dr. Frederick Cleveland and Henry Bruere, had something more specific in mind—the Tammany-dominated city administration. It was this body's "current record" and interpretation of what it "needs, does, leaves undone" in which they were chiefly interested. Politically, the first governmental research bureau was largely an anti-Tammany instrument.

The moving spirit behind the new bureau was wealthy Robert Fulton Cutting, who for years had been fighting both the Tammany Hall Democrats and the city's Republican party bosses. Cutting was also president of the silk-stocking New York Association for Improving the Conditions of the Poor, which concerned itself with tenements, pure milk, summer camps for poor children, sanitation, public bath houses and relief work. One of the Association's donors was John D. Rockefeller, and Dr. Allen, a professional social worker, was its executive secretary.

Cutting and others had organized the Citizens Union in New York in 1897. Like so many political reform groups of that time, the Citizens Union was supposed to elect candidates—good men who would bring good government. In 1901, Cutting and the Citizens Union led the successful campaign to elect Columbia University president Seth Low as reform mayor. But when Low, like other reform mayors before him, lasted only one term, downhearted reformers were ready to listen to Allen's idea for a permanent bureau with a paid research staff, an organization that would not be subject to the vagaries of the electorate.

Cutting talked to two other philanthropists, Rockefeller and Andrew Carnegie, who, their industrial empires built, were now doing good works. They underwrote a $150,000 fund to operate the new bureau for three years. Cutting became chairman of the bureau board. Other directors included George McAneny, who was secretary of the New York Civil Service Reform League and was president of the City Club; magazine editor Ralph W. Gilder, active in tenement reform; writer and social worker Frank Tucker; and Columbia University's noted economist Edwin R. A. Seligman.

Money quickly ceased to be a problem for the new bureau. Allen, Bruere and Cleveland began poking around in city records and checking with sources outside city hall. In November, 1906, ten months after opening the bureau, they published a pamphlet quoting figures, dates and items showing waste in the office of John F. Ahearn, Democratic president of the borough of Manhattan. An investigation followed, and Republican Governor Charles Evans Hughes (like Theodore Roosevelt, a mugwump hero) ordered Ahearn removed from office for "failure of duty." Soon after this, the bureau had two more borough presidents on the pan. Delighted mugwumps began to pour contributions into the bureau office. By 1909, the staff had grown to forty-six accountants, engineers and other specialists.

Outlook magazine at this point described the bureau as "a private organization supported mainly by the contributions of a few wealthy men." [2] The big contributors were indeed few, but they did not carry the whole load. Tammany counterattacks on the bureau in 1909 led fifty monied New Yorkers to establish a five-years fund for it. By 1914 the bureau had spent close to a million dollars, of which Rockefeller contributed $125,000, Cutting $117,000, Carnegie $55,000 and Mrs. Edward H. Harriman

$52,000. The remaining $600,000 came from 600 other individuals and organizations.[3]

Had the New York bureau devoted all its time to pursuing Tammany men, it would have been of no more permanent importance than the many turn-the-rascals-out groups that had come and gone before it. But the political weapon that Allen, Bruere and Cleveland created was much subtler than that.

The basic philosophy behind it was at least twenty years old. In 1888, Seth Low, who had recently finished his terms as mayor of Brooklyn (ten years before it became part of New York City), was fulminating against the traditional checks and balances in American city government. "Charters," he wrote, "have been framed as though cities were little states. Americans are only now learning, after many years of bitter experience, that they are not so much little states as large corporations."[4] This view was widely shared among mugwumps; and from it the assumption logically followed that what was good for corporations was good for city governments. Just as Taylor thought there was a "best way" to run a steel works, the municipal researchers preached that there was a best way to manage a city.

Looking at industry's annual budgets, standardized financial forms, allotment controls on spending, centralized purchasing, auditing controls, personnel studies and classification of salaries, the New York bureau sent a steady stream of suggestions to city hall. Some administrators gave them a warm welcome—notably Mayors George B. McClellan, William Gaynor and Purroy Mitchel, and City Comptrollers Herman Metz and William A. Prendergast. With their cooperation, the bureau brought in teams of experts to install the new systems in city departments.

Mugwumps in other cities watched the New York experiment with excitement. For all their hundreds of reform organizations around the country, they were having a hard time penetrating city hall. Here at last seemed a way to reform government without having to go through the grueling and often hopeless business of trying to win elections. More important, its approach of working for installation of specific procedures was a direct kind of reform, surer than the indirect route of electing a candidate who might prove unable or unwilling actually to change anything after he got into office.

This discovery of the merits of direct action resembled the conclusion Samuel Gompers had reached several years earlier about labor unions—that "ten men organized for collective bargaining in a shop could pry more social benefits from the boss than two thousand citizens could pry from a legislature." [5]

Mugwumps in Philadelphia started their research bureau in 1908. Those in Cincinnati followed in 1909, Chicago in 1910. Within a decade most major cities in the East and Midwest, and San Francisco on the west coast, had governmental research agencies modeled after the New York bureau. They were smaller, of course. The Philadelphia bureau, about a third the size of the New York one, operated on a budget of $30,000 to $35,000 a year. The others spent $10,000 to $15,000 annually.

As the bureau movement spread, the New York bureau in 1911 set up the Training School for Public Service to prepare men for municipal research jobs. It was thought that hundreds, perhaps thousands, of specialists would be needed to staff the citizen agencies. Every city and every state would have its watchdogs of good government—perhaps six to a dozen or more men in each bureau, standing guard over all phases of administration and ready with ideas for improvements. The Rochester bureau, financed by camera-maker George Eastman, was regarded as the coming pattern; it had five engineers, two accountants, a personnel expert, and several assistants.

This bright enthusiasm lasted until World War I. Then the reformist wave that had powered the Progressive movement and, as an auxiliary, the municipal research movement, went flat. Public attention wandered off to other things, principally the war in Europe. Several research bureaus expired. The hard realization dawned on many mugwumps that they had been placing their faith in a nonexistent Good Citizen who they had supposed was sitting at home just waiting for the researchers to provide stacks of objective information so that he could study it, reach intelligent decisions and then throw his weight into the fight for good efficient government. As the *National Municipal Review* of November, 1919, observed unhappily:

> An important theory of the founders of municipal research ran somewhat like this: We will classify municipal expenditures

> crosswise and vertically like a chocolate layer cake, analyze them, clarify them, unit-cost them, and lay down automatic deadly parallels between each item of last year, this year and next. Then, when the whole budget is published and brought up for passage, the city hall will be crammed with taxpayers with fingers pressed accusingly against certain telltale mathematics, demanding, for example, to know why the street commissioner needs 186 new brooms when he cleaned the same yardage last year with 130. . . . The projected scene in the city hall failed to materialize. It is the great disappointment of the research movement.

When it became clear that the researchers would never be able to send thousands of aroused citizens storming into city halls, both friends and foes recognized the bureau's political limitations. Some contributors cut their financial support. The New York bureau, after its early success with cooperative officials, met increasing resistance from Tammany-chosen administrators until, after 1915, a state of continuous cold war existed, and bureau men seldom ventured inside city hall; the bureau, reorganized in 1921 as the National Institute of Public Administration, became largely a group of consultants who made surveys of governmental operations for other cities.

Difficulties of this kind did not kill the research movement, but they slowed its growth.

Yet while the bureaus had fallen short as instruments of open political power, their prestige as propagators of new methods of managing municipal government steadily increased, and this insured the spread of the movement during the 1920s. New bureaus with two- and three-man staffs were established, often at the instigation of local real estate boards or chambers of commerce, who liked the bureaus' emphasis on eliminating governmental waste. Among the older bureaus, those of Detroit and Philadelphia received additional help from their community funds and so swelled their budgets into the $50,000-a-year class. The San Francisco and Buffalo bureaus were spending around $40,000 a year. Eastman was subsidizing the Rochester bureau at about the same rate. Most others were running on $15,000 to $20,000 a year in this decade after the war.

Then came the depression, and its effects on the research bureaus and on mugwumps generally were decisive.

The first effect, of course, was financial. The budgets of all bureaus shrank. Some shrank right out of existence.

A second result was to drive many mugwumps, particularly those of the Republican faith, further into the conservative camp, in reaction against the New Deal Democrats. Conservatives became more active in mugwump organizations and assumed part of the financial burden formerly carried by well-to-do Progressives. Since Democratic victories at the polls deprived conservatives of much of their former influence with public officials, the conservatives turned to the mugwump bureaus and leagues as an alternative means of influencing government. More and more the bureaus emphasized tax saving. They could be counted on to oppose any pay raises for municipal employes, any increase in staffs, any new municipal services, and almost any bond issue. Their opposition, however, seldom reached the tight-fisted extremes of the many taxpayer associations dominated by real estate interests that sprouted in the thirties.

A third effect of the depression was less obvious but of basic importance. Thousands of able and jobless young men were driven into government service, not only in Washington, but in the major cities. This hastened the professionalization of public administration. The new men, as they rose in rank, substituted modern management methods for the pen-and-ink, stool-and-ledger, jot-it-down-on-anything-handy methods long tolerated by old-time political appointees.

By mid-century the young men of the 1930s had become middle-aged executives in municipal government. They ran their departments, in many cases, up to performance standards equaling those in large private corporations. In some cities like Chicago and Boston the process remained far from complete; but the general effect was one of almost total victory for the systems and goals that Cutting, Allen, Bruere and Cleveland had set out to promote a half-century before.

6

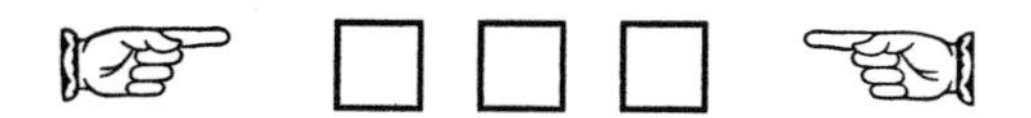

Four Instruments of Power

In the political life of every city is something we could call the mainstream of power. It is an intangible thing, but those in it can feel its pull and eddies as surely as a swimmer can feel the rush and twistings of a river. The mainstream is where political decisions are made. It is where policies are proposed, facts and arguments aligned, votes taken (if that is necessary) and agreements reached.

These things seldom take place neatly in one room at one time. Usually there are many meetings of many different men in many places—luncheons, committees, telephone calls, conversations in the corridor. But as these meetings of two, three or a hundred men take place, each one senses that he is playing a part, large or small, in molding the decision. He knows that he is in the mainstream of power.

Once he has experienced the mainstream, a man is seldom happy outside it. Whether he is an elected official, a career civil servant, a newspaper editor or a mugwump, if the fortunes of business or politics wash him out of the mainstream, he will nearly always try to get back in. He is "hooked."

The average citizen dimly realizes there is a mainstream of power somewhere and knows he is no part of it, but he does not particularly care. The mugwump feels differently. He does care.

And so he has invented a number of organizations to help inject himself into the mainstream.

We have mentioned these organizations as they existed in the latter nineteenth century and the early twentieth—the civil service leagues and other one-cause groups, the election-time coalitions to run or endorse candidates, the mixed welfare-and-reform groups, and the full-time municipal research bureaus.

From these have evolved today's array of mugwump power organizations. They can be grouped roughly into four types: the *research bureaus*, the *citizens leagues*, the *municipal parties* and, most recently, the *top-brass committees*.

Taken together, they contain mugwumps of all sizes and kinds—the little mugwumps who are schoolteachers, salesmen, junior executives, public employes, struggling architects and lawyers; middle-sized mugwumps who manage banks, real estate, utilities, major retail stores, insurance agencies and "name" law firms; and big mugwumps, few in number, who control nation-wide industries or otherwise rank as eminent Americans.

Since the research bureaus and the citizens leagues look much the same in operation, let's examine them together.

RESEARCH BUREAUS AND CITIZENS LEAGUES

Offices and Money

The building is usually old. So are the elevator operators. They let the visitor out at the third or fourth floor and he walks down the corridor, turns into another corridor, turns again, until just as it seems he must be almost back at the elevators he finds the frosted glass door lettered "Bureau of Municipal Research." He opens the door and walks into a little world of great calm. The middle-aged secretary may be placidly typing, or not doing much of anything. Through an open door a man can be seen telephoning. In another office a younger man bends over a work sheet of figures. None of the furniture is new. If the visitor guessed that half of it must be hand-me-downs from wealthy friends, he would be correct. There is usually a fourth room containing a mimeograph and old files; or it may have only a wooden conference table ringed with a dozen seldom-used chairs.

Such is the physical appearance of the average municipal research bureau or citizens league. To operate it costs $30,000 to $50,000 a year. The director receives a salary of $10,000 to $15,000, his assistant somewhere between $6,000 and $9,000, the one or two office secretaries commensurately less. The remainder of the money goes for rent, office supplies, mimeographing, printing of pamphlets, postage and so forth. Citizen agencies of this general type exist in Boston, Cincinnati, New Orleans, San Antonio, Houston, Detroit (Citizens League), San Francisco and many smaller cities.

The citizens leagues in Cleveland, Minneapolis, Seattle and New York (Citizens Union) have slightly larger budgets of $60,000 to $70,000. The St. Louis bureau spends $70,000 to $75,000.

In Chicago, the Civic Federation disburses around $120,000 a year. The New York Citizens Budget Commission lays out $150,000. The budget of the Citizens Research Council of Michigan, in Detroit, has risen to $220,000 annually. These bureaus have spacious quarters with staffs of five to seven researchers plus three or four clerical workers. The Michigan council also has a smaller office at the state capital, Lansing.

One organization, the Pennsylvania Economy League, ranks in a class by itself. With large offices in Philadelphia and Pittsburgh, each with a dozen or so research men plus clerical employes, and smaller offices at the state capital, Harrisburg, and in several other Pennsylvania cities, the Economy League's annual budget varies from $700,000 to $800,000. Like the Michigan Research Council, it divides its time between local and state matters.

At the opposite financial pole is the little Civic Club of Allegheny County, also in Pittsburgh, with a woman secretary and a total annual budget of $10,000.

Research, As It Is Called

The people one sees in these offices bending over figures or typing or telephoning are engaged in this thing loosely labeled "governmental research" or "municipal research."

Were a visitor to walk down the streets of Cincinnati or New Orleans or anywhere and stop people at random, asking, "What is the bureau of municipal research, and do you know what it does?" the chances are that four out of five would react with complete blankness. And the fifth might mumble something about the health department and test tubes.

The term "research" got stuck onto the movement a half-century ago by the New York bureau pioneers, who believed they were going to do things scientifically such as follow street cleaners around with stop watches, hoping to discover how the white wings could sweep and scoop with greater efficiency, just as Frederick W. Taylor had found ways to speed up steelmakers.

The idea of doing original research with time-and-motion studies of municipal employes did not last long. Nor did other plans for objectively studying the workings of municipal government and gradually developing broad principles to explain why things happen as they do. Instead of becoming political Newtons and Faradays, the bureau men were quickly caught up in a round of practical problems. The mugwumps supporting the research agencies wanted tangible results, preferably some that would embarrass Tammany Hall, the Socialists and other political foes. The activists employed by the bureaus became not inventors but borrowers. And so they remained.

At first they borrowed largely from private business, and from the British and German systems of municipal government. Since World War I they have been borrowing more from each other and from each other's cities. Whenever a problem arises in, say, a city water department, the local research bureau or citizens league finds out how water departments in other cities handle the problem, then pass on what seems the best solution to city hall. Of course, another city's solution can seldom be adopted bodily; the bureau generally has to modify it to fit local conditions. To that extent bureau men are able to call themselves inventors.

Probably more than anything else, the bureau men resemble management consultants. They ladle out advice on how municipal governments should be run. Sometimes public officials ask for the advice. More often they do not. They get it anyway.

From the beginning, most of this advice has concerned municipal finances. Some bureaus, like the one in San Francisco, declare that their *only* interest is in financial matters. But since few things in government are free, this blanket is large enough to cover almost any problem that arises.

All bureaus and citizens leagues pay close attention to the annual city budget. In some cases they even help write it. In Boston, for instance, the city council, which for some inexplicable reason had no budget staff of its own, relied for a time on two men of the Boston bureau to spend six weeks each year helping them review the city budget. In Pittsburgh, a staff man from the Pennsylvania Economy League worked on the budget with the mayor.

Most citizen agencies, however, lack such exclusive entrée. They have to content themselves with dropping suggestions throughout the year, then waiting for the preliminary annual budget to see how many of their proposed economies have been accepted.

Nearly all bureaus and citizens leagues prepare mimeographed statements commenting on the proposed budget, and give them to city officials and the press. The formula for these statements has become as cut and dried as a Western movie. The first page compliments the budget wherever it embodies one of the bureau's suggestions. The second page views with alarm selected increases in taxes or spending, especially for frills like pay raises, parks, playgrounds, libraries or welfare services. The third page singles out a half-dozen items that could be reduced or cut from the budget altogether. Finally, the statement expresses thanks to city officials for their cooperation and pledges that the bureau or citizens league will support any move for better government.

A bureau or league rarely sees all of its recommendations adopted. But a few may be. And the mere fact that the economy-minded researchers go over the budget and publicly lament any increases undoubtedly has had a restraining effect on free-spending officials. There is also little doubt that this anti-spending attitude has tended to starve certain city departments such as parks and libraries, whose friends may be many but politically amorphous. The citizen researchers, on the other hand, usually approve engineering improvements to streets, sewers and water systems.

In general, the bureaus' and citizens leagues' traditional attitude can be likened to that of a thrifty father—one who is willing to spend money to keep the house physically fit as to plumbing, wiring, furnace and sound timbers, but sternly disapproves such fripperies as a family book collection, a hi-fi set, or pictures for the walls.

As election time nears, the straight research bureaus do not openly endorse candidates and seldom give out even biographical information about them. That is left to the citizens leagues and others. But virtually all research bureaus, because of their concern with finances, issue a summary of the arguments for and against the bond issues that will appear on the ballot. Most bureaus write these summaries with reasonable objectivity, even though they sometimes conclude by recommending how the citizen should vote. Whatever their shortcomings, these bureau analyses are in most cities the best ones available, and newspapers tend to rely on them heavily. In only a few cities does the League of Women Voters or a conscientious editor or labor-union secretary take the trouble to make an equally thorough report on bond proposals.

Throughout the year the typical bureau or citizens league issues a slow, steady stream of reports on sundry subjects, averaging perhaps one every three to six weeks, depending on the size of the bureau staff and the scope of the study. Some are nothing but page after page of tabulated figures, showing tax rates and assessments, or the bonded indebtedness of the city or school district. It is not expected that anyone except a few specialists will ever peruse these close-printed statistics. Other reports deal with more everyday subjects: how many teachers are in the local schools, and how much they are paid compared with teachers in other cities; the record of the local fire department, and fire losses compared with other cities; the cost per patient-day in the county hospital.

Sometimes a citizen agency undertakes a study merely because it feels that certain information should be pulled together for the general use of public officials, library researchers, businessmen or anyone else who might find it helpful. The great majority of research studies, however, have a more specific purpose. They are expected to uncover inefficiency or corruption in a particular municipal department, or perhaps to help sell a proposal to local officials. The St. Louis bureau, for instance, reported on how fifteen major American cities were using one-man police cars, not because the bureau had an academic interest in police cars, but because it wished to persuade the St. Louis police board to use one-man instead of two-man cars, thus reducing the need for hiring more policemen. (The report served its purpose; the police board began experimenting with one-man cars.) Similarly, some bureaus issue reports suggesting how police cars could carry simple fire-fighting equipment and policemen could be trained to use it; this, the bureaus hope, will lessen demands for additional firemen and fire stations.

Frequently the bureau or citizens league men do not think up a project. It drops into their laps. The Seattle Municipal League had been paying no particular attention to the King County jail when, one afternoon, a sixteen-year-old boy prisoner was beaten to death in the jail's juvenile tank. Two other teenagers held the victim down on the concrete floor while a third slugged him with a metal shower handle. The press and public let out an indignant roar. While the editorials and resolutions flew, the league quietly sent a staff man over to the jail, where he practically lived for three weeks, talking with the sheriff and jailers and prisoners, eating jail food, moving from cell block to cell block, inspecting records, the kitchen, laundry, toilets, and the medical dispensary. Businessmen and lawyers serving on the league's law-enforcement committee dropped in unannounced to do their own inspecting. From the Federal Bureau of Prisons in Washington, the league obtained the names of seven jails in the United States it considered well run, then got in touch with the seven to compare their operations with those of King County jail. Finally the league issued a 7,500-word report urging twelve changes in the jail's administration. From month to month the league checked to see how many had been adopted. Within a year, most of them were in effect.

It would have been better, of course, if at the time the fatal beating occurred the league had had a plan ready for improving the county jail. Most citizen agencies have several of these sleeping projects on hand—plans which met public and official indifference when first proposed, and so have been shelved until some scandal or disaster comes along to arouse cries for action.

Politics being the opportunistic game it is, reforms must usually be preceded by a certain uproar. In the words of Harland Stockwell, director of Chicago's Civic Federation: "You have to do it when the time comes, and you have to be ready. We got through centralized purchasing when the time was right. We could not have got it through earlier, and not a year later. You wait until the right moment is there, and then you bang 'em with it." [1]

At times citizens organizations have indeed "banged" public officials with a proposed reform. In strong statements they demand a rascal be removed from office or a wasteful way of handling city business be changed. Back in pre–World War I days the reformers sometimes distributed printed cards on street corners denouncing city hall, or bought full-page newspaper advertisements exposing corruption. But such methods of open warfare became increasingly rare after 1920. Today one of the few mugwump agencies that still operates with the big stick is Philadelphia's Committee of Seventy, whose director, Harry K. Butcher, declares: "We like to sue them and prosecute them. We leave the research to the men in bifocals back in their cubbyholes."

Instead of open militancy, most directors of bureaus and citizens leagues prefer lobbying methods—building friendships around city hall, dropping quiet suggestions for the mayor and councilmen to pick up and adopt as their own, unobtrusively feeding information to newsmen, arranging for the city council or school board to invite the bureau to make a study for them or, more indirectly, arranging for the council or school board to appoint a citizens advisory committee which in turn will invite the bureau to handle its research.

These techniques of gently nudging officials into reforms do not always work. Yet even where more force is required, citizen-agency men prefer the hidden stiletto to the meat ax. There was the occasion, for instance, in Seattle when one of the county commissioners, a bit short of campaign funds, began urging that the county buy a parking garage for its official cars. Unfortunately, said the man who telephoned the league office (an attorney who was close to the deal), the county would be paying almost twice what the garage was worth, and most of the excess money was scheduled to filter back into the commissioner's pocket. League secretary C. A. Crosser first alerted a couple of trusted newspapermen to the plan. Then, at next Monday's regular meeting of the county board, when the commissioner moved, in a barely audible mumble, that the county buy the garage, Crosser arose and said in his sincerest manner: "Gentlemen of the board, the Municipal League recognizes the lack of parking space for county cars. A solution is needed and we are glad to see you attempting to find one. However, we are not sure the price suggested is proper. Some of our members believe it may be too high. Therefore, we have this suggestion. Why don't you ask the Seattle Real Estate Board, an impartial body, to name three good appraisers to look over the garage and give us their opinion? After all, I am no real estate expert and neither are you gentlemen. Let's call in trained appraisers for an objective report. None of us wants to waste the taxpayers' money."

The commissioner fumed a bit, but his proposition was dead and he knew it. And by using an indirect attack to kill the scheme, Crosser had protected his source of information so that telephone tips would continue to come into the league office.

The "Municipal Conference" Device

Most research bureaus, when speaking out publicly, do so in their own name. A few, however, have become parts of front organizations in which they submerge their identity when taking public stands on the city budget or proposed bond issues or state legislation.

The San Francisco Bureau of Governmental Research does most of the legwork and brainwork for what is called the San Francisco Municipal Conference, a coalition of nine business groups—the Chamber of Commerce and Junior Chamber, the Apartment House Association, the Building Owners and Managers Association, the California Northern Hotel Association, the Down Town Association, the Real Estate Board, the Retail Dry Goods Association and the Retail Merchants Association. Since 1938, delegates from these groups have met every month or so to hear reports from the research bureau director and vote what stand the conference shall take on civic matters. The conference boasts that it has never suffered a major defeat.

Boston's Conference of Civic and Business Organizations, born in 1953, operated in similar fashion. It was composed of representatives from the Greater Boston Chamber of Commerce, the Retail Trade Board, the Real Estate Board and the Boston Municipal Research Bureau. Unlike the San Francisco bureau men, who remain in the background as much as possible, Boston bureau director Joseph Slavet appeared at city hall and at the state house as one of the spokesmen for the Civic Conference. The conference functioned for six years, then broke apart in the late fifties after a series of internal disagreements involving the Chamber of Commerce.

Los Angeles has a Citizens Budget Committee, formed by conservative downtown elements in 1937 and headquartered in the California Taxpayers Association office in Los Angeles. The committee, largely a paper organization of some fifty business, service and community clubs, rarely meets. Its leading spirits call the executive committee together now and then to approve a statement on a bond proposal or on the annual city, county and school budgets. These statements are usually prepared by a Cal-Tax staff man who devotes a fraction of his time to Los Angeles local governmental affairs.

Who Picks Up the Tab?

While a research bureau may have anywhere from three hundred to a thousand contributors, the gross number means little. A handful of men and firms usually pay the bills, generally deducting it from their income taxes as an educational contribution.

Norman Gill, surveying fourteen bureaus in the late thirties, found that only 12 percent of the donors provided 73 percent of the bureaus' income. The same general condition holds true today. In 1960, for instance, the Citizens Research Council of Michigan in Detroit got half of its $220,000 budget from the Relm Foundation and seven large corporations; 300 other contributors gave the remaining half. In Houston, half of the 650 contributors gave five dollars a year, which accounted for only $1,625 in a total budget of $40,000. The Boston bureau lists 300 supporters, but many of these are five-dollar ones; for many years, one man—venerable former Harvard treasurer Henry L. Shattuck—took care of any bureau deficits.

Organizations with such narrow bases of support inevitably face charges of bias and special interest. Aware of this, many mugwumps have tried for years to broaden the number of bureau contributors. For a while the mugwumps sought recruits among the lower middle class. These little people and good citizens, it seemed, should be willing to add their mite to the cause of good government. But the little people remained supremely indifferent, and hope for their support gradually faded. Lent D. Upson of Detroit, the grand old man of research bureaus, told the Governmental Research Association in 1945:

> Unhappily, the ordinary citizen is little interested in the preservation of democracy. Too frequently he won't register, he won't vote after he registers, he won't be actively interested in a political party, he won't serve on juries unless compelled to. . . . What reason is there to believe that this ordinary citizen will be concerned in financial support of a professional agency? . . . It is difficult to imagine a million small home owners or small businessmen, concerned with their golf, their back-yard gardens or their appendectomies, rallying to the battle cry of economy and efficiency in public business.[2]

While the research bureaus met this blank wall, the experience of the citizens leagues in Seattle, Minneapolis, Detroit, Cleveland and New York, enrolling several thousand members at five to ten dollars a head, has shown that Upson was perhaps too pessimistic. The leagues have proved they can obtain help, if not from the little people, at least from some of the middle-sized people.

But even the citizens leagues have found that it requires as much work and expense to extract five dollars from the bank clerk as it does to obtain twenty times that amount from the bank president. It is not surprising, then, that even the broader-based citizens leagues now receive one-third to two-thirds of their income from big contributors, and the proportion is steadily increasing.

Big business is not always a big contributor. Huge industries such as oil, steel, auto, aircraft and others with national and international markets pay relatively little attention, or money, to local citizen organizations. Instead, the bulk of support comes from locally owned banks, utilities, retail merchants, real estate owners and managers, and others whose major stake is in the home town.

This stake involves not only profits but pride. The builder of automobiles or jet planes can win his prestige on a nation-wide stage. The local business and professional man must identify himself largely with his own metropolitan area. He can gain his self-respect and satisfactions only from what happens within a few miles of his office.

Boards of Trustees

Governing every research bureau and citizens league is a board of trustees, which hires the bureau director (and usually lets him hire and fire the remainder of the staff).

A board may be as small as the Detroit Citizens League's with fifteen members, or as large as the eighty-man board of the Houston bureau. The most common size is twenty to thirty.

There are window-dressing boards composed of the city's most eminent citizens, who as board members do nothing except meet two or three times a year, and permit use of their names on the bureau letterhead. And there are working boards like the one in Seattle, which meets every month and spends several hours threshing out policy. Most bureaus and leagues have found that the city's number-one citizens do not make good members for a working board. As the Houston bureau director says, "We don't try to get the top men. They don't have time to give us any attention. We try to get the executive who may be top man some day. We want the second or third men in major organizations."

The typical board of trustees is self-perpetuating. Whenever vacancies on the board are to be filled, the board itself or its president chooses a committee to draw up a list of nominations —and the number of nominations generally equals the number of vacancies. This slate is presented to an annual dinner or luncheon attended by a fraction, sometimes a very small fraction, of the bureau members; the chairman announces the nominations, saying others may be made from the floor; then, after a perfunctory pause, the chairman declares the committee's nominees unanimously elected.

Among the few exceptions to this gentlemanly procedure are the Seattle Municipal League and the Minneapolis Citizens League. They nominate two people for every vacancy, and the winner is chosen by the members' secret mail-in ballots.

Most board members, as might be expected, are conservative or middle-of-the-road Republicans, except in the South, where they are conservative Democrats with an occasional Republican. Several organizations have tried to make their boards more representative. In heavily Democratic Boston, for instance, the bureau has increased the Democrats on its board until they number ten out of forty. By special effort a bureau sometimes has a woman or a labor leader as a trustee. The Memphis Civic Research Committee has a Negro pastor on its board.

Oddly enough, groups that hand-pick their trustees have an easier time broadening their representation than those like Seattle and Minneapolis which use more democratic methods of election. In Seattle, for instance, the board's nominating committee in recent years has placed the names of several young Democrats, labor officials and women on the ballot mailed out to league members. But when the ballots come back, the league members, mostly Republicans, have voted for their friends—that is, other Republican business and professional men—and the unionists, Democrats and women, less well known among the members, seldom win a seat. Some boards partly offset this tendency by reserving two or three vacancies on the board to be filled by appointment.

Regardless of its make-up, any board of trustees has three main jobs to do: give the organization respectability, raise money, and employ a competent director.

The Director

The key man in any research bureau or citizens league is its manager, usually carrying the title of director or executive secretary. His ability determines whether the agency becomes an important political force in town or just another plodding organization.

Some directors are veteran war horses who entered the reform movement during the 1920s when remnants of Progressivism still clung to it. From that period, men like George Hallett of the New York Citizens Union, C. A. Crosser of Seattle, Alfred Smith of San Francisco, John Willmott of San Antonio and Calvin Skinner of Cincinnati have seen the citizens research movement evolve through the depression, World War II and the postwar era.

A man who got into the field during the twenties or thirties might have almost any background—engineering, accounting, newspaper reporting. Skinner, the dean of the group, once studied voice in Paris and was a professional singer. The newer generation of bureau directors, however, contains a heavy proportion of men with advanced college degrees in political science or administration and often some experience in government work. This "second generation" crop of directors includes Lennox Moak in Philadelphia, Norman Gill in Milwaukee, Robert Pickup in Detroit, Joseph Slavet in Boston, Val Mogensen in New Orleans, and others.

The directors tend to divide into two schools, when it comes to relations with their boards of trustees. The let-me-alone school regard themselves as specialists and the trustees as laymen who should not invade the specialist's field, any more than the lay board of a church should tell the pastor what to preach or the school board should tell the teacher what problems to put on the blackboard.

"They hired me as a professional, an expert," the director of a Texas bureau said. "It isn't up to them to tell me what to do. I'm like the doctor who tells them what is necessary. I have to lay out my program based on my experience and the evidence I have at hand."

The let-me-aloners give the impression of regarding the board as a necessary evil, at best a kind of hobble, much the same way as many government administrators feel toward the city council, legislature or Congress for which they happen to work.

The second type of director, belonging to the let's-get-together school, feels the same way upon occasion. But as a rule he operates on the principle that he and the board are a team. He gathers information, works out possible actions the organization may take, and submits the information and suggestions to the trustees. Then, at the board's monthly meeting, or the executive committee's regular Friday luncheon, or by means of a hasty telephone poll, the trustees make the final decision.

Pennies and Pounds

Most bureaus and citizens leagues, in the past, at least, have spent the bulk of their energies trying to tidy up the financial side of local government. Their concern with budgets and bonds and administrative waste gained them the reputation of penny pinchers. The agencies themselves, when appealing for contributions, have emphasized the millions of dollars they have saved the taxpayers.

Yet there is some question as to whether this reputation is deserved. Evidence exists that the bureaus and citizens leagues may not be nearly the successful scrooges they and others have believed. Furthermore, while conservatives in America are supposed to favor minimizing government, the bureaus and leagues, governed as they are by largely conservative trustees, seem in actual practice to have promoted not little government with minimum services but bigger municipal government with more services.

Tax rates have not dropped even in cities where the influence of mugwumps and their organizations has been strongest. Kansas City, for instance, was in the hands of mugwumps for twenty years after they ousted the Pendergast machine in 1940. Yet the city became mired in money troubles during the 1950s.

Lent D. Upson, after studying tax rates in large United States cities over a quarter-century period, concluded:

> The constant upward trend of these rates indicates that citizen effort at long range local tax reduction is futile. I doubt there is a citizens agency which can claim to have reduced taxes in the long run. . . . It has been my experience, and I believe that of many others in this field, that incompetent, grafting government is often, not always, cheap government measured in dollars spent.

This seeming paradox exists, Upson believed, because the people tend to trust an efficiently operated government, and so

> one sure way to increase taxes is to make government so effective that the public can trust it to do the things the public needs to have done.[3]

There is a further possible explanation. Mugwumps and their bureaus, as long as they are political foes of the local officials in power, serve as sharp critics. They automatically question every official action, scrutinizing it for flaws. The local newspapers, usually part of the mugwump team, do the same. This running battle between officialdom and mugwumps has the effect of making it difficult for officials to spend money for anything but routine running of the government. Even if an official has the imagination to propose a major improvement program for the city, it is almost certain to become bogged down in controversy.

But in cities where mugwump forces throw the opposition out, perhaps write a new city charter and install "efficiently operated government" (which to anybody, including a mugwump, means a government of which he approves), the situation changes.

The mugwumps and their bureaus no longer sharply criticize. They may have helped write the new city charter, so they cannot very well attack that. They may have helped recruit the bright, trained administrators brought in to modernize the creaky city government; indeed, the bureau director may have gone on leave to become the new mayor's right-hand man. Bureau trustees probably joined in persuading the good citizens now on the city council to run for office. And when the bright professionals begin proposing improvements—new equipment to modernize office procedures, more traffic lights and freeways to relieve congestion, sewage disposal plants, a modern police laboratory and police training school, a better public health program, a civic center with a steel-and-glass city hall, court building, pedestrian malls and a couple of fountains—when these and other proposals begin to appear, as they inevitably do, the citizens organization can raise little objection. It is the captive of its own success.

True, most of the political hacks who tended to run the city government like a billiard parlor, most of the petty crooks who thought in terms of stealing a thousand dollars, are gone. But in their place are professional administrators who know how to spend millions. The result may be more effective government. But not lower taxes.

The Middle-sized Citizen

From the outside, we have said, the citizens leagues and the research bureaus look much alike. But there is a distinction. The citizens leagues are where the lower bourgeoisie have their chance.

Historian John Geise has described their place in the community and how they got there:

> Modern Western civilization is largely a burgher civilization —a civilization of cities and the middle class. . . . The Commercial Revolution of the sixteenth and the Industrial Revolution of the eighteenth and early nineteenth centuries, combined with growth in numbers and wealth, produced a division of the middle class into upper and lower bourgeoisie. The first consisted of the great financiers and capitalists, the controllers of wealth. The second—a class of townsmen engaged on a small scale in industry and commerce but having only restricted control over its own activities—was the historical continuation of the original burgher class.[4]

Today a member of the lower bourgeoisie can join a citizens league merely by paying a five- or ten-dollar fee. He may work on a committee and help influence league policy. If he works hard enough and has the right personality, he may find himself on the league board of trustees, or perhaps appointed by the mayor to some honorary commission. The leagues offer the young unknown attorney, the retired hardware merchant, even the intelligent housewife an opportunity to earn a place in the city's mainstream of power. His or her influence may be indirect and marginal, but none the less real.

Of the numerous citizens leagues that have come and gone in the United States since the late nineteenth century, five major ones are now operating—the Municipal League of Seattle and King County, the Citizens League of Minneapolis and Hennepin County, the Citizens League of Greater Cleveland, the Citizens Union of the City of New York, and the Detroit Citizens League.

The two largest are the New York Citizens Union with nearly 4,000 members, and the Seattle league with 3,600 individual members and 550 contributing firms. The Cleveland league, along with its twin Research Bureau, has 3,000 members and 300 firms. The Detroit league roster contains 2,400 individuals and 200 business contributors. The youngest of the lot, the Minneapolis league, which was organized in 1952, enrolls 2,300 members plus 450 firms and organizations.

Pittsburgh's 650-member Civic Club of Allegheny County, although smaller, functions like the other citizens leagues.

Except for the Minneapolis league, these are old organizations. The Citizens Union in New York has operated without a break since 1897. The Cleveland league can trace its genealogy back to 1896 and the Seattle league to 1894, although both have undergone periods of hibernation.

All leagues have experienced cycles of growth and shrinkage. Cleveland attained better than 4,000 members and the New York Citizens Union nearly twice that number in the 1920s. Detroit's league reached a high of 5,000 members before World War II. The Seattle membership, only 300 in 1939, rose rapidly until it passed 5,200 in 1952; since then it has dropped to 4,200. The Minneapolis league, in a postnatal burst, grew to 3,500 members in its first five years, 1952 to 1957, but it has slid back since then to 2,300.

These rises and falls seem to depend upon two factors—the vigor of a league's membership secretary and its membership committee, and the presence or absence of a civic crusade capable of stirring the borderline mugwumps to join. Cleveland's league hit its high mark in the mid-twenties during the reformers' battles against Republican boss Maurice Maschke. The Seattle membership reached its peak in 1952 as the Municipal League was campaigning for a new county charter.

Reports on Candidates

Most leagues notice an upsurge of memberships during election years. This seems to result from the leagues' reports on candidates—the original *raison d'être* for the leagues and the one for which they still are best known.

The Cleveland and Detroit leagues invest approximately a third of their time preparing the candidate reports. The job absorbs somewhat less effort at the Citizens Union in New York, and in Seattle and Minneapolis the reports compose less than 10 percent of the work load.

Most voters in these cities are familiar with the reports through seeing them either in the newspapers or in the league pamphlets published before each election. The bulk of the report is devoted to thumbnail biographies of the men running for mayor, councilman, state legislator, sheriff and other offices. The following typical sketch is from a Minneapolis report:

> HOYER, Eric, 59, 1934 NE McKinley Street. Widower, two children. Minneapolis resident 38 years. Graduate high school, business and extension courses. Acting mayor 1948–49; elected 1949, 1951, 1953, 1955. Previously alderman 13 years. Active in numerous civic, fraternal and church organizations as well as business and labor groups.

The Minneapolis league adds no comments of its own on the candidates. It tried this once, in its first report in 1953, and created such an uproar that it has never used comments again. The Civic Club in Pittsburgh likewise gives only biographical sketches.

Other leagues, however, provide comments, some of them astringent. The Cleveland league may label a candidate "Preferred," which is its highest praise, "Well Qualified," "Not Recommended" or it may leave the space blank. The comments on even a "Preferred" candidate can be a bit sharp. For instance: ". . . completing his fourth term on the council; his commendable vigor is sometimes misdirected but he is better than his two opponents."

Nearly every local primary has a certain number of odd-ball

candidates—the dedicated promoter of Esperanto or the card who wants to give a few laughs to the fellows down at the service station. Most league reports dismiss these entries with a bare mention. Cleveland, however, leaves no room for doubt; thus, ". . . age 31, door to door salesman, attended grammar school, in our opinion completely unqualified for any office."

The Detroit Citizens League indicates its highest approval by calling a candidate "Preferred," designates others as "Qualified" or leaves a significant blank.

The Citizens Union in New York indicates its opinion of candidates by similar phrases combined with discriminating typography. If the Union feels enthusiastic about a man, his name will be printed in boldface capitals followed by "HIGHLY QUALIFIED AND PREFERRED." If the Union is not quite so enthusiastic but thinks he is the best of the lot, he will be "John Jones, Preferred," still in boldface type. Candidates bringing up the rear, however, get their names in only tiny lightface type.

The Citizens Union's comments, reflecting perhaps the Quaker background of its director, George Hallett, are gentler than some leagues'. Even candidates who receive the small-type brushoff are let down easy with phrases like "a candidate of agreeable personality" or "a lawyer of good character, education and intelligence." Sometimes, however, an edge shows; for instance, "Mr. Jepson favors a state lottery to aid education. He does not as yet appear to have given much thought to other issues." The Union is even more blunt in some of the press statements it releases before each primary. In these it usually backs reform-minded candidates running against Tammany hacks, whom the Union likes to identify as "a genial politician of the old school."

Seattle voters complained during the 1940s and early '50s that they had to read between the lines of their Municipal League's reports to figure out whom to vote for. After the usual brief biography, the league comment was clear enough if it read "lacks background for position." But voters had to scratch their heads a bit if one candidate was labeled "Sincere, well regarded in community" and his opponent was described as "Community leader, sincere." For a while the league attempted to fashion just the right phrase to describe each office seeker. The board of trustees, sitting as a panel of semantics experts, would debate for hours over the nuances of "adroit politician" versus "political opportunist." Only after years of verbal floundering did the league settle on the five-step glossary it now uses: "Superior," "Above average," "Average," "Below average," and "Unsatisfactory."

All leagues gather information for their reports in more or less the same way. The league office sends each candidate a form asking him to fill in biographical information and to give three or four references. The Civic Club in Pittsburgh does nothing further, printing the biography as given by the candidate. Explained the club secretary: "They have found it doesn't pay to give us false information. If a candidate does, an opponent or someone else exposes him and he is publicly embarrassed." One such unfortunate, in dictating his reply to his secretary, who reportedly was also his girl friend, sought to avoid disillusioning her by listing himself as single; when his wife saw one of the 25,000 printed reports, that piece of misinformation was corrected in short order.

Most leagues, however, have a policy of checking the candidates' answers. A league staff man or a member of the candidates' investigating committee telephones the references the candidate has given. This may lead to other telephone calls, especially to people who have worked with the candidate. Often the league checks the candidate's credit rating. If he is an unknown, one or two committee members may interview him; this is common with the Citizens Union in New York, where many candidates are unfamiliar.

If a man has run for office before, and most candidates usually have, the league's file on him simplifies the task of evaluation. Leagues sending observers to the state legislative sessions, like the Citizens Union and the Seattle league, keep an eye on local legislators' performance and add that information to the file. The Minneapolis and New York groups send each candidate a list of questions about current issues. The Minneapolis questions are relatively impartial in tone. Those, for instance, asked of each candidate for mayor in 1957 were:

1. What do you believe to be the single most important function of this office of mayor?

2. Do you favor or oppose each of the following ways of increasing city revenue: (a) an earnings tax (b) a wheelage tax (c) increased property tax?

3. Do you think the form of Minneapolis city government needs to be changed? If so, what changes would you suggest?

4. Do you think the liquor patrol limits should be cut down, kept as they are, expanded or removed altogether? Explain.

The candidates' answers are printed in the Minneapolis report.

The New York Citizens Union, however, "loads" its questions to serve as a sales piece for the Union's point of view. Even the most obtuse candidate has no difficulty seeing how he should answer a question like this:

> The City Board of Health and Health Commissioner have asked fluoridation of the city's water supply. There seems no question that this will protect our children's teeth as nothing else will and the overwhelming weight of medical opinion holds that there are no harmful effects, any more than from chlorination. The experience of other cities seems to bear out both claims. Are you in favor of fluoridation of the city's water? [5]

The Citizens Union, however, does not publish the replies, and it tells the candidates that "a reasoned difference with the Citizens Union's position will not necessarily affect the Citizens Union's judgment of a candidate adversely."

The Seattle league does its questioning in person, behind closed doors. The candidate enters the league's conference room to find himself facing twenty to thirty league members, each holding a mimeographed dossier of his record. Fifteen minutes or so of interview follows—courteous, sometimes even friendly, unless the candidate has come up to tell off the committee for unkind things it said about him last time. About three-fourths of the candidates keep their interview appointments. The absentees include not only perennial odd-ball candidates, who have learned to expect no favor from the league, but also many regular Democrats who regard the league as pro-Republican. The league has tried to refute this charge by pointing to Democrats it has praised in its reports.

Once the investigating committees write their reports and the wording has been approved by the organizations' trustees (sometimes with changes, much to the committees' annoyance), final copy goes to the printer. The Citizens Union and the Detroit league print 75,000 to 100,000 reports to distribute among members, friends, workers in factories and offices, church congregations and others. The Seattle league issues 25,000 to 120,000 copies depending upon the demand and the interest in the election. Cleveland releases 40,000 to 45,000 reports; in addition, the Cleveland *Plain Dealer* reprints it in full. The Minneapolis league prints only 3,000 reports for its members; for general distribution, it relies on the Minneapolis *Tribune*, which reprints the entire report in a special tabloid section. In other cities, too, the reports obtain their widest readership from newspaper reprints, although in some cases the papers boil down the report or leave out certain sections.

How much weight the leagues' reports carry is undetermined, and probably undeterminable. They are only one of many factors that contribute to victory or defeat for a candidate or a ballot proposition. No one doubts that the reports swing thousands of marginal votes, particularly among white-collar folk. On complex ballot propositions and in races for obscure offices, the reports exert great weight, since the voter has almost no other source of information.

It appears that the reports are slowly losing influence in some cities. One reason is the emigration of white-collar residents to the suburbs, where they no longer can vote in city elections. Another factor probably is the growing tendency of metropolitan newspapers to promote their own slates of candidates and ballot propositions, thus diluting the force of the leagues' recommendations. But in every city the leagues' endorsement is still a sought-after prize. And there is no record of anyone turning it down.

League Committees

The citizens leagues, as already mentioned, offer one of the few routes by which an average citizen can work his way into his city's mainstream of power. This route lies through the leagues' committees.

The route is most wide open in Seattle and Minneapolis (which modeled its organization after the Seattle league). In both places, any league member may join almost any committee he wishes. And if he demonstrates energy and good judgment in committee discussions of the city budget, city planning, crime rates or whatever, and if he seems willing to devote time to league work, he soon finds himself made a committee chairman. As such, he gets his name in the league's publication and sometimes in the daily newspapers. When a vacancy occurs on the league board of trustees, he may be selected. And when the mayor or county commissioners are looking for someone to head a citizens advisory committee, or perhaps to sit on the park board or planning commission, he may be appointed. If in addition he is willing to join other mugwumps in contributing to campaign funds for the right man for mayor, he will find himself consulted when it comes to choosing the candidate. In short, he can become about as deeply involved in civic affairs as his business and his wife will permit.

The New York Citizens Union, on the other hand, does not throw open its committees to all members. Instead, the officers and director hand-pick the thirteen committees, choosing specialists in law, finance, personnel or whichever field is allied to the committee's work. In talent-rich New York this system results in some imposing committees. It also results in a measure of inbreeding, with the same faces appearing around the committee table year after year. Serving on the Union's committee on legislation, for instance, has become almost a lifelong hobby for several attorneys, who meet to analyze bills for four hours every Friday evening while the New York legislature is in session. Walter Frank in 1961 was putting in his thirty-seventh year as committee chairman.

Minneapolis and Seattle staff workers admit that their wide-open committee system encounters a few problems—such as the conservatively dressed alcoholic who insisted on coming to committee meetings with several martinis under his belt and loudly denouncing the Seattle league's secretary as a crook. Despite such tribulations, the Seattle and Minneapolis leagues believe the constant infusion of new blood into committees is good for their organizations.[6]

It is generally agreed that league members do not join committees to work. They join to be consulted. A rare committee chairman may actually sit down at his desk and write something, look up a fact, or telephone a public official to get information. But 99 percent of such work is done by the league staff man who acts as the committee's secretary. He often condenses his findings into one, two or three mimeographed pages that are handed to committee members at the beginning of each meeting. The secretary usually suggests two or three possible courses of action. In most cases the committee approves one of his recommendations and sends it along to the board of trustees for its blessing.

The committee, in other words, play-acts as a little legislature. As the members sit over their coffee cups discussing whether the league should endorse a $20-million bond issue for new schools, they can feel the heady responsibility of political power. They realize that their action may decide whether the bonds pass or fail.

Like real live senators and representatives, the committee members often have limited personal information on what they are talking about, but they can draw on their experience and intuition in asking questions, arguing and finally voting. The level of debate is frequently higher than that heard in many city councils and state legislatures.

The Seattle league's secretary Crosser sums up the committee process in these words: "They'll come down for lunch and buy their own. They'll work from twelve-thirty until one-thirty giving their judgment to the matters at hand. The staff man must do all the rest of the work. But for that hour you can get the best brains in the city to concentrate on a problem."

THE MUNICIPAL PARTIES

Since earliest days mugwumps have sought to intervene in local government by running their friends for office. When the municipal research device appeared in 1906, it supplemented but did not replace the older practice. Some mugwumps kept right on in the candidate business.

The simplest and commonest procedure has been for a half-dozen or so mugwumps in town to take it upon themselves to gather informally and agree upon two or three possibilities for mayor or assessor or whatever the vacancy may be, then persuade one of the prospects to run, promising him campaign funds and newspaper support. Since few people in mid-career feel like chucking it all to run for office, the candidate usually ends up being a semi-retired businessman or a thirtyish attorney with a good appearance and a mediocre practice.

Once elected, of course, the draftee becomes a politician and may run for re-election again and again. This lightens the task of recruiting candidates, but even so the problem of finding enough men to run for the vacancies at each election—particularly on the city council—is usually more than these informal mugwump groups can manage. In many cities they try only to elect the mayor, and let it go at that.

In at least eight major mets and middle mets, however, mugwumps have put the recruiting and electing of candidates on an organized basis. They have created municipal parties.

The oldest and most fully developed of these is the City Charter Committee in Cincinnati, set up in 1925 by a group of liberal Republicans—mostly young lawyers and businessmen—to consolidate their victory over boss Rudolph Hynicka, who ran Cincinnati's regular Republican organization by remote control from his burlesque theater in New York.

Dallas mugwumps founded their Citizens Charter Association in 1931, and the reason was the same as in Cincinnati: to protect their new city-manager charter against counterattack by old-line politicians.

In the late thirties, Kansas City reformers organized their Citizens Association, overthrew the Tom Pendergast machine, and gained control of city hall.

A small group of one-time Willkie Republicans, returning from the wars to San Francisco, formed the Volunteers for Better Government in 1947. In recent years its candidates have occupied a majority of seats on the San Francisco board of supervisors.

San Antonio mugwumps revolted in 1949, tossing out the old commission form of government and replacing it with a council-manager form. They then created a Good Government League that has elected friendly city councils since 1955.

The story in Phoenix is the same—citizens rising up in 1949 against the old city-hall politicians and installing a new council and city manager, then protecting them with a Charter Government Committee that has since dominated local elections.

Mugwumps in Minneapolis, hoping to break the political hold of union boss Walter Cramond, established in 1957 a candidate-running group called CORG (Citizens Organized for Responsible Government). And in Memphis, the anti-Crump elements created a Citizens Association in 1959. Both groups have experienced victories and defeats.

Only the Cincinnati and Kansas City organizations operate year-round offices with paid staffs. The Cincinnati Charter Committee, as of 1961, was spending $32,000 annually for its office which has a director, a women's-division director and two clerical employes. The Kansas City association budgeted $25,000 for its office which has an executive secretary, a stenographer and a part-time woman consultant.

In most cities, the associations raise and spend $30,000 to $35,000 in each campaign for their slates of candidates. If the opposition is weak, however, as it has sometimes been in San Antonio, expenses may run half that amount.

By far the biggest spender has been the Kansas City association, which must battle through both a primary and a general election. Fortunately for the contributors, campaigns come only every four years. In round figures, this is the way the association's money was spent in a typical campaign (1955):

	Primary election	General election	Total for both
Administration and printing	$12,850	$14,180	$27,030
Newspaper advertising	3,200	4,500	7,700
Television	2,250	1,000	3,250
Radio	3,000	5,500	8,500
Postcard mailings	5,000	5,000	10,000
Operating four district headquarters	1,000	2,000	3,000
Public-opinion survey	2,000	—	2,000
Door-to-door precinct workers	4,430	—	4,430
Poll watchers, miscellaneous expense	3,520	5,820	9,340
Fund-raising cost	—	—	10,000
Totals	$37,250	$38,000	$85,250

The bill ran even higher in 1959, a total of $105,000, when the association found itself suddenly facing a strong coalition of politicians—a coalition that handed the association its first defeat in twenty years.

Raising money, however, is not the mugwumps' chief problem in Kansas City or elsewhere. The big worry is finding candidates. Among other qualifications, the man selected must be successful in his business or profession. He must be respectable; and he must be reluctant. If the man comes seeking the office, most associations want nothing to do with him. On the other hand, he must not be too reluctant; after a suitable amount of protesting and persuasion, he must be willing to succumb to his civic duty.

All associations go about unearthing these political nuggets in more or less the same way. The Kansas City association has a more elaborate procedure than most. Long before the election, the chairman of the association's executive committee names a candidate-finding committee of twenty-five, cross-sectioned among men, women, Republicans, Democrats, Jews, Protestants and so forth. This committee sends letters to the six thousand association members asking them to suggest candidates for mayor, councilman and municipal judge. These letters, plus stories planted in the Kansas City *Star* asking the public for suggested names, usually draw some two hundred replies.

The committee, aided by the association's executive secretary, gathers information about the proposed candidates, narrowing the field down to an average of five or six for each office. Committee members then interview them, asking if they are willing to run. About half say yes.

The candidates committee hands over this list of prospects to a 20-member screening committee, half Republicans, half Democrats. The screening committee then tries to assemble a full slate of thirteen—mayor, two councilmen from each of the four council districts (one Democrat and one Republican from each district), and four candidates for municipal judgeships. Sometimes, however, the slate has blank spots, especially for councilmen from the working-class First District.

With its proposed slate finally lined up, the screening committee presents it to a joint meeting of the association's twenty-nine-member executive committee and its thirty-one-member advisory committee. From there the names go to the association's ever-growing board of governors, which now totals nearly three hundred men and women. Someone in this massive gathering occasionally tries to alter the slate—in 1959 one change was made—but usually it is approved without fuss.

Once the slate is accepted, a volunteer campaign manager takes over and begins spending the $80,000 to $100,000 collected by the association's finance committee and its paid secretary.

In contrast to the Kansas City machinery, San Francisco's is perhaps the simplest candidate-electing organization to be found anywhere. It has no office, no telephone number, no staff, no dues, and hardly any members. The Volunteers for Better Government consists only of some three dozen young (under forty) lawyers and businessmen in the Montgomery Street financial district. At election time, a few of the older business leaders, such as banker Jerd Sullivan and Robert Hornby, president of the Pacific Lighting Company, raise $30,000 to $35,000 and give it to the Volunteers for campaign expenses. With this the Volunteers hire a campaign manager and run a slate of three or four candidates for the city-county board of supervisors. The Volunteers started in 1947. By the late 1950s they had attained a majority of six "graduates" on the eleven-man board.

Regardless of the size of an organization, how many thousand members it has or how few, the burden of organizing the slate, raising the money and masterminding the campaign nearly always falls upon—or is seized by—a small core of six to ten men. And the bulk of campaign funds generally come from not more than two or three dozen sources, although there is seldom evidence that these sources expect any direct, tangible return from the candidate.

Despite their remarkable record of success, the candidate-running organizations contain elements of danger to mugwump objectives (see Chapter Fifteen).

These, then—the citizens leagues, the research bureaus and the candidate-electing municipal parties—have been the chief instruments through which the mugwump played his part in the first revolution of the cities. It has been a half-century that saw the mugwump rise from the status of bothersome crank to that of dominant voice in the government of some cities, and a major influence in others. In only a few has he remained inconsequential.

This rise, to the moralistic minded, may seem the result of a staunch adherence to principles—sometimes narrow and intolerant, but principles based upon tradition and decency.

To the disciple of determinism, the mugwump's rise may appear largely fortuitous, much as Tolstoy considered Napoleon only "the figurehead on the prow of a ship," or "like a child sitting in a carriage, pulling the straps within it and fancying he is moving it along." The mugwump may seem to have hitched his political wagon to a rising star more or less by chance. Hoping to strike down those he despised—the hack politicians and the corrupting business barons—he espoused the cause of efficiency in government with its automatic impersonal controls, its fact-gathering, its budgets, formalized planning, rationalized administration and an engineering, legalistic approach to all problems. These were the weapons that would work in his favor politically. They happened also to be devices that were about to become an accepted, indeed a compulsory, standard for managing all large enterprises in an industrialized society. The old-time politician who opposed them was doomed. In an economy permeated with dehumanized norms, checks and record-keeping, the politician's dependence almost entirely on personal relationships appeared feudal. The managerial class who moved into the decision-making positions in the twentieth century could not take him seriously. The mugwumps, on the other hand, spoke the managers' language, and so the mugwumps won their support.

Whichever was true—whether the mugwump succeeded because of personal virtue, or because of lucky timing, or because of some combination of the two—the fact presently stands that he has gained most of his objectives. Pockets of resistance still remain in Chicago, Boston, Philadelphia, New York and a few other places. But in most parts of the United States, by the 1950s, the spoils system was little more than a memory. Wholesale vote frauds were gone. So were party labels in most municipal elections. Fewer officials were elected, more appointed. The carefree bands of open grafters had been reduced to a surreptitious handful. Behind most administrative desks sat a career technician instead of a ward worker or somebody's unschooled relative. While the mugwump might lose a direct contest at the polls here and there, his precepts and, usually, his friends prevailed at city hall.

And thus at mid-century the mugwump found himself becalmed. His old collection of gimmicks emphasizing honesty and efficiency in government had served their purpose. As Lent D. Upson of Detroit said in a 1945 speech, the research organizations henceforward "must have less and less truck with the procedures of government, certainly less with the specific installations of such procedures. The time for that should be past. Present-day officials know as much or more about those things than we do." [7]

What new banners, then, were there for the mugwumps and their hired activists to raise?

Some agencies, like those in Milwaukee and Seattle, tried dusting off an old gimmick in the 1950s by promoting administrative surveys of their local governments. They persuaded city officials to retain private management consultants to look over the operation of all city departments, hunting for waste. (In the 1930s and 1940s the bureau men had deprecated such surveys, declaring the thick survey reports only gathered dust.) The revival of surveys, however, was a mere stopgap. A mugwump organization needed more of a program than that if it was to maintain its momentum.

Of course, there would always be a certain amount of work for citizens bureaus in just holding the line—exposing the occasional thief or gross incompetent who is bound to appear in some city department, or preventing raids on the public treasury by organized city employes, real estate developers and other special interests. There would always be the annual city budget to pick at, and bond issues to analyze before each election. And the bureau men, by their very presence around city hall, would continue to have a salutary effect, like policemen walking a beat.

But while some activists in the bureaus and citizens leagues might be satisfied to earn their pay with such maintenance work, it was not enough for their employers, the mugwumps. The mugwumps needed, as always, a major gimmick, a crusade. For the mugwump, by definition, can never retire and contentedly leaf through past victories. He is driven forever to tinker with government. Other people may have a different concept of the central purpose of politics and of their part in it, but the mugwump participates to solve problems. He feels happy only when he has found one that, for some good middle-class moral reason, should be remedied. Having found this irritant, he must work out a method, a gimmick, for removing it. And then he must promote the gimmick. Once it is adopted, he has to discover another problem. In the hiatus between problems, he is lost.

The 1950s found him in such a hiatus. And the natural question was, how long would it last? And when it ended, in what direction would the mugwump move next?

Some thought there might be no next move, that the mugwump's day was over. He was lamented as a disappearing breed, his Yankee heritage grown thin and diluted. Eric Sevareid in a CBS broadcast after the death of former ambassador and presidential nominee John W. Davis spoke of him and his kind as a dwindling group whose minds and characters

> were formed in a quite different era. . . . Their principles of conduct and action, their faith in the American vision, were matured before the First World War, which began the present process of anarchy in personal and public principle. . . . There were eternal verities . . . always the principle was the thing, not the individual, not the pressing needs of the harried present nor the fleeting charms of popularity. . . . They proceeded from principle and hoped the needs of the moment would fit; they did not proceed from the needs of the moment, inventing or adjusting principle as protective coloration.[8]

Other observers, also in pessimistic vein, saw the mugwumps' future as that of a stubborn rear guard, like Roland at the pass, fighting back a growing horde of greedy public employes and ambitious officials. Try as they might to hold the line, the mugwumps had no choice but a slow retreat before Parkinson's law and inflation. Political scientist Wallace Sayre of Columbia University envisaged the coming big-city problem as "how to curb the bureaucrats, how to keep the experts under control, how to keep them from making all the decisions." [9]

It was indeed conceivable that the bright-eyed professionals the mugwumps had striven so hard to place in charge of government would evolve into fusty empire-building *fonctionnaires*, entrenched in their offices, resentful of ideas from the outside and secure behind a civil service mechanism that they themselves, in effect, controlled. There was evidence in some long-professionalized administrations—for instance, Los Angeles—that this process was taking place. Possibly the veteran civil servants, settled in their ways, would become just as truly hacks to be rooted out as were the professional hard-hat politicians against whom the mugwumps campaigned in the first half of the century.

But other events seemed to be shaping a more sweeping assignment for the mugwump. These events could be described in a phrase: new population and old cities.

Millions of farmers, miners, lumberjacks, small-town dwellers, hillbillies, Negroes and Puerto Ricans were streaming into the metropolitan areas where jobs were to be had. Millions of high school and college graduates were heading for the big centers in search of excitement and a chance to reach the top. Millions of new families needed enough space for a child, a car and a dog. Thousands of new industries were demanding water, power, level acres, a sewer main, a rail spur, and unclogged streets for trucks to roll in and out.

All these pressures converged, and cities run down after fifteen years of depression and war, kept gaunt by an old belief that municipal government should have to beg for every dollar, frozen within boundaries set a half-century ago and within legal strait jackets much older than that, jammed morning and evening with a crawling horde of cars and buses, and afflicted with decay, obsolescence and neglect which spread like a fungus over downtown sections, neighborhoods, parks, playgrounds, into schoolhouses, libraries, through water systems and sewers, through cracked pavement and sidewalks. In the air, pollution; in lakes and rivers, pollution; and above all, in Washington and the state capitols, a blank-eyed indifference to the cities' travail.

For this indifference the cities had only themselves to blame.

Government is, after all, largely a matter of communication. Public officials must communicate plans and problems to the people; the people must communicate back their reactions, criticisms, desires and approval. Not all plans and problems, of course, and not all the people. Such total communication is impracticable and inconceivable. But a certain minimum of communication is required. If communication falls below the minimum, government ceases to function. Likewise, as communication shrinks closer to the minimum point, government slows down and loses more and more of its capacity to act. Officials become isolated from the community's sources of energy. They become ineffectual prisoners in their offices, occupying them more or less in a state of siege.

This situation has been not the exception but the rule in most large American cities in the past century. The fault has lain partially with the professional politicians themselves. Many have been louts, crooks or incompetents with nothing worth communicating. Part of the fault has rested with the business and social leaders who have taken their city for granted, ignoring its government while they bustled around making a success of their banks, shoe factories and churches. Even public officials with something important to communicate have had difficulty finding anyone who would listen. There was no way, in other words, of arriving at an effective consensus—a massing of enough political force to overcome community inertia and work together toward a major objective.

This semi-paralysis of the cities did not bother the mugwump too much. He worried less about how to attain effective consensus than he did about efficiency. He sought not multimillion-dollar programs of improvements, but neatness, economy and decency in government.

As World War II ended, some mugwumps began to sense that this was not enough. They saw that the critical problem had become not how to keep things neat but how to get things done.

This change in signals emanated chiefly from places high in the business world and from mugwump agencies that have close connections with them. From there the new psychology began slowly filtering down to the more middle-class levels of the citizens leagues and the smaller research bureaus, and to the mugwumps who supported them.

It was an expansionist boom-time psychology, based on the belief that America will grow and grow, and a city that hopes to survive must keep up with the pace. Instead of the old gospel of tax saving, the new text was, you've got to spend money to make money. If a city wanted to attract new industries, it could not expect to do so with a pinch-penny municipal budget, a patched-up water system and dingy buildings on narrow streets —any more than a grocer with a run-down store could expect to attract customers away from the new supermarket by firing a clerk and cutting prices a few cents a can.

More lay behind this movement, however, than a desire to merchandise one's city as a site for new businesses. The complex of motivating factors included:

economic fear felt by downtown property owners and merchants as suburban shopping centers sprang up and downtown property values skidded—a fear communicated to metropolitan newspaper owners; combined with this was a feeling of shame that one's home city was sinking into shabbiness like a neglected house,

political fear among mayors, councilmen, top administrators and others whose fortunes would rise and fall with those of the central city,

enthusiasm of city planners and architects, who leaped at urban redevelopment like hungry men at a steak, turning out sheaves of plans for clearing out old sections and replacing them with towers and plazas,

encouragement from the construction industry, for obvious reasons,

encouragement from the building trades and other labor unions, for the same obvious reasons,

a change in businessmen's esthetic standards, so that a new glass-walled building with paneled offices, air conditioning, potted philodendron and sleek secretaries became badges of prestige, de rigueur for any self-respecting firm,

a change in businessmen's economic thinking, especially among the rising class of corporate bureaucrats, rejecting the old Yankee idea that the sound society is one of scrimpers and savers in favor of a Keynesian belief in a society of propagators, expanders and spenders.

One of the clearest statements of the new gospel came from Leslie J. Reese, director of the western division of the Pennsylvania Economy League and a key figure in Pittsburgh's postwar surge of rebuilding. In a 1957 speech to the Cleveland Citizens League, Reese said:

> Corporation executives have become community conscious. They also want markets and customers. They want more people in America and they want those people to be made financially capable of buying eight million cars a year and financing a million and a half housing starts. . . . The population of America will increase 20 percent in the next ten years. Our expanding and shifting population, our rising living standards, the community services which are essential to industrial production, all mean that we have to revise old ideas of what is true economy in government. . . .
>
> True economy in government today is not only a matter of nursing nickels. It is a matter of assisting and guiding the participation of public bodies in the great sweep of change that is upon us. The failure of a community to modernize itself in terms of our immediate future may save it pennies now, but will cost its people untold millions in the future.
>
> True economy in government today calls for the rescue and reconstruction of our central cities . . . for the planned and guided development of our suburban areas . . . the construction of schools, water supply, the transportation network, the sewage treatment system, the land-use pattern that alone will prevent them from becoming our problem areas of tomorrow. . . .
>
> Economy in government lies in the public improvements that are necessary to economic expansion—notably the assurance of water for industrial use, protection against floods, navigation on the inland waterways, airports, and a highway system that will not be obsolescent as its units are being dedicated. . . .
>
> Certainly we want to keep the lid on unnecessary public spending. But equally we must agree to and encourage necessary public spending.[10]

Some mugwumps understood what Reese was talking about. Others nodded agreeably but heard it only as so many words.

Most of those who understood lived in the older metropolises already paying the price of decay.

With the new gospel calling for action to save the core sections of American cities, to save both their physique and their spirit, it became clear that this was no job that could be handled alone by a $14,000-a-year bureau director or Chamber of Commerce secretary, aided by the collection of assistant vice presidents, young lawyers, insurance men and securities sellers who had become the business leaders' stand-ins in civic affairs.

And so the Number Ones themselves took over.

THE TOP-BRASS COMMITTEES

Pittsburgh had been in a condition of governmental stalemate for as long as anyone could remember. The steel town was really no more paralyzed than many other cities, but the results were more obvious, with thousands of smokestacks dumping their grimy burden on the old red brick buildings, the narrow streets and the ugly little houses. Everybody knew Pittsburgh was a mess, including the inhabitants. But nobody seemed to feel anything could be done about it. That was the situation in 1943.

One version credits Mrs. Richard K. Mellon with starting the revolution, or the Renaissance, as they began calling it in Pittsburgh. She reportedly told her husband, principal owner of the Mellon Bank, Gulf Oil, Alcoa and other huge corporations, that she could not stand living in Pittsburgh as it was any longer. If true, this may not have sounded like an empty threat to Mellon. Back in 1909 his uncle, Andrew Mellon, had received a similar ultimatum from his wife, who thereafter returned to her native Ireland; they were divorced three years later.

Other sources in Pittsburgh give much credit for starting the Renaissance to the late Dr. Robert Doherty, the 120-pound dynamo who was president of Carnegie Institute of Technology, and to Wallace Richards, who, after helping New Dealer Rex Tugwell establish the "Green Belt" towns in Maryland, went to work for the Pittsburgh Regional Planning Association and became civic-affairs assistant to Mellon.

In any event, Mellon threw his influence behind the formation of a committee known as the Allegheny Conference on Community Development. The forty key members or "sponsors" included Mellon, H. J. Heinz II of the canning company, the president of United States Steel, several executives from different Mellon corporations, the mayors of Pittsburgh and three suburban cities, the three Allegheny County commissioners, and the presidents of the University of Pittsburgh, Duquesne and Carnegie Institute of Technology.

In appearance the Pittsburgh group resembled the top-brass committee that had been formed in Texas in 1937, the Dallas Citizens Council of a hundred leading citizens. But Dallas faced no such problems as Pittsburgh, and the Mellon group was soon attracting national attention as it began hacking away at the challenge. It used a double-bitted ax. One edge was Mellon money and influence in the business world; the other was the political power of the Democratic boss, Mayor David Lawrence.

This partnership of Lawrence and the wealthy Republicans pushed the "Pittsburgh package" of enabling bills through the legislature at Harrisburg in 1945 and 1947, permitting the mayor and city council to create an urban redevelopment authority, a public parking authority, a public auditorium authority, and the Allegheny County Sanitary Authority.

With these tools, the Lawrence-Conference coalition undertook the Pittsburgh face lifting. The job began at the oldest part of town, the tip of land where the Allegheny and Monongahela rivers flow together to form the headwaters of the Ohio. On this peninsula stood Fort Pitt during the French and Indian wars, and from here the city grew back along the wedge of land between the rivers. The area eventually became Pittsburgh's downtown, known as the Golden Triangle. By World War II the point of the triangle near the river had become a tarnished commercial slum of railroad sidings, warehouses and loft buildings.

As the war ended, the Allegheny Conference got two breaks. One, in 1945, was a promise by the state government to build a 36-acre park on the tip of the peninsula, restoring Fort Pitt. The second break, which came in 1946, was a major fire that destroyed the sprawling terminal of the Pittsburgh and West Virginia Railroad, the largest property owner on the point.

After that, things happened fast. Conference members got

in touch with the Equitable Life Assurance Society and interested them in building four office skyscrapers on the twenty-three acres adjoining the new state park. This was to be known as Gateway Center.

The conference persuaded Mayor Lawrence, who had taken office in January, 1946, to appoint an urban redevelopment authority, as permitted by the law passed the year before. With the added urging of the Chamber of Commerce, Lawrence consented to name himself chairman of the authority, provided that three prominent Republicans would serve with him—Arthur B. Van Buskirk, Mellon's right-hand man for civic matters; Lester Perry, president of Carnegie Illinois Steel; and department-store owner Edgar J. Kaufman.

The authority agreed with Equitable Life that it would condemn the land for Gateway Center, clear it and sell it to Equitable for a reduced price. The conference also helped Equitable sign up nine large corporations as long-term tenants even before the building plans were drawn or the property acquired. Later, when two of the tenants withdrew and the project faced possible collapse, Mellon helped find two others to replace them.

The year 1946 also ushered in a change few people had ever expected to see in Pittsburgh: the elimination of smoke. Members of the conference assured Mayor Lawrence that they and the newspapers would support him fully if he would enforce the anti-smoke ordinance that had been on the books since 1941. Lawrence did, cracking down first on industry and railroads, and a year later on home owners. The board of county commissioners followed suit in the early 1950s. By 1955, Pittsburgh claimed to have reduced the smoke in its air by 90 percent.

To many this was the most dramatic change of the whole Renaissance. But there were others.

The parking authority, created in 1947 over the opposition of private parking operators, began erecting six garages to increase by half the downtown parking space.

In 1949 the Mellon family, acting through the conference, gave the city $4.4 million for acquiring a blighted block which was squarely in the center of downtown and transforming it into a park. Beneath the new expanse of shrubs, fountains and tiled walkways went a six-level underground garage with parking for

1,000 cars. The parking authority handled the leasing of it to private operators.

In 1950 the conference bit off another chunk. It prodded the city planning commission into designating a new area for redevelopment, ninety-five acres of slums sloping up the hill east of the downtown Golden Triangle. The redevelopment authority approved a conference plan whereby Lower Hill, as it was known, would be covered with new apartments, business houses, boulevards, and a huge auditorium with a sliding metal roof that could be opened or closed like a fan, depending upon the weather. The city-county public auditorium authority was set up in 1954 to build and operate the auditorium. The authority received contributions of several million dollars from the city, the county and wealthy Pittsburghers, floated revenue bonds for the remainder, and opened the $20-million structure in 1961.

The conference also had a hand in creating a $100-million sewage disposal system to clean up the polluted rivers, and in promoting educational television station WQED, new highway projects, the children's zoo, the purchase of $17 million worth of land for city and county parks, and many other programs. In the 1960s, the conference has turned its attention to providing middle- and low-income housing for Pittsburgh, especially for families uprooted by redevelopment projects.

While Mayor Lawrence and Mellon, along with other wealthy citizens, provided the high-level push behind this sweeping program during the 1940s and '50s, the burden of planning and legal work fell upon a small group of professionals behind the scenes. Planning engineer Park H. Martin assembled a staff of fourteen in the Allegheny Conference office, and from there worked closely with the Pittsburgh Regional Planning Association technicians in an adjoining suite, and with legal and financial analysts at the Pennsylvania Economy League a few blocks away. Among them they put together the ideas, the blueprints and the legislation that were needed to make the Renaissance a reality.

Word of the miracle of Pittsburgh spread across the nation and across the seas. Delegations of activists and mugwumps from dozens of cities made the pilgrimage to western Pennsylvania, seeking the magic formula. Some came away shaking their heads, saying it could only happen in Pittsburgh. As one Cincinnati official reported when he got back home: "This is purely a relocation problem. All we've got to do is relocate the Mellons in Cincinnati."

Several cities moved to imitate Pittsburgh. In Philadelphia two different groups of big businessmen began holding luncheons, each group discussing the low state of civic affairs in their town. One man determined on action was Harry Batten, president of the N. W. Ayer advertising agency. He had been fighting mad ever since Detroit automobile makers turned down his suggestion that they move some of their facilities to Philadelphia, basing their refusal partly on the city's bad water supply and bad government. Batten helped get the two luncheon groups together, and after a period of pulling and hauling, the Greater Philadelphia Movement was born.

The following year in Cincinnati, a group intended to be an Allegheny Conference-type organization was started—the Citizens Development Committee.

In Milwaukee a group calling itself The 1948 Corporation, which had been started to promote a relatively modest program of civic betterment by 1948, reorganized as the Greater Milwaukee Committee.

Following an intra–business community fight, another high-level committee, the Milwaukee Development Group, appeared in August, 1959.

In 1953, the mayor of St. Louis—next to Pittsburgh and Boston probably the most run-down city in America—stirred a score of leading businessmen into establishing Civic Progress, Incorporated.

The year after that, a top-brass committee that Cleveland's Mayor Thomas Burke had named to expedite slum clearance became the Cleveland Development Foundation. About the same time Mayor Albert Cobo revived the Detroit Tomorrow Committee of a hundred eminent citizens who had stimulated the city's 250th anniversary celebration in 1951.

Mayor John B. Hynes called Boston business leaders to a meeting in historic Faneuil Hall in the spring of 1957. There they heard Mayor Lawrence of Pittsburgh and Mayor Raymond Tucker of St. Louis describe their Allegheny Conference and Civic Progress groups. Boston had made two attempts previously at a top-brass committee, but both had disintegrated after the public relations man who in each case was running the committee as largely a one-man show dropped from the scene. Following the Faneuil Hall meeting, Mayor Hynes named a new Committee of One Hundred.

San Francisco joined the parade in 1957 with the Blyth-Zellerbach Committee.

On the surface, all these groups seemed replicas of the one in Pittsburgh. Yet they did not get the same results.

In some cases it was because they had no Mellons who would risk or give away large chunks of money to make sure a project went through. In some cases it was lack of a Mayor Lawrence who could crack the political whip. In a few cases it was the absence of able technicians behind the scene.

And in all cases it was lack of the Pittsburgh state of mind, a kind of civic intoxication that only a city so sunk in grime and apathy could know as it discovered it had a chance, like Cinderella, to become beautiful and sought after. As Park Martin said, "I guess you've got to feel way down before you can feel way up."

Not that other top-brass committees showed no accomplishments. The Greater Philadelphia Movement played an important role in supporting that city's new charter; and it was almost solely responsible for the $100-million produce distribution center that rose on reclaimed swamps south of the main business area.

In St. Louis, Civic Progress raised $60,000 to rescue the symphony orchestra and won campaigns to preserve the city income tax, to lift the $10,000-a-year ceiling on the salary of the mayor and other top officials, and to obtain voters' approval of $150 million in bonds for new streets, parks, hospitals and slum clearance. Civic Progress, however, also suffered crushing political defeats in 1957, when St. Louis voters decisively turned down its new city charter, and again in 1959 when a plan for metropolitan government sank under another avalanche of "no" ballots.

The Cleveland Development Foundation, moving quietly along in typical Cleveland fashion, concentrated on clearing slums and replacing them with middle-income housing projects. The foundation lent money from its $2-million revolving fund to expedite financing for private builders. The group also prepared plans for a huge Mall Center along Lake Erie.

The Blyth-Zellerbach Committee in San Francisco raised $55,-000 for the planning studies that got the $60-million Golden Gateway development of apartment towers and office buildings under way north of Market Street. And the committee lent moral and political support to the city's two other major renewal undertakings in Western Addition and Diamond Heights.

Looking at the top-brass committees in general, it is clear they have been mostly concerned with getting someone to tear down old buildings and replace them with new ones, with obtaining new expressways and other physical improvements. True, the Greater Philadelphia group studied the local juvenile court and the plight of the derelicts on skid road; and the Dallas Citizens Council issued a report demanding something be done for the poor folks living miserably in West Dallas. But such sociological forays have been rare.

Politically, the top-brass committees have made three great contributions. They have created a place where influential men can reach quick decisions. They have provided a way to avoid bickering politicians who can abort any major project in its prenatal stage; being private agencies, the top-brass committees can finance studies and planning without waiting for approval by councilmen and county supervisors. And they have cracked down on the old American habit of passing the buck.

When Dallas banker Bob Thornton called his fellow civic leaders together in 1937 to form the Dallas Citizens Council, he laid down the principle that only top men should belong, men who as presidents or owners of their firms need not check back with anyone before committing themselves. Thornton was quoted as saying at the first meeting: "If you're here and you cain't say yes and you cain't say no, you ain't here at all."

This Dallas principle has been followed on most top-brass committees elsewhere. It is understood, too, that nobody is to send substitutes, a practice that has reduced many a Chamber of Commerce to futility. Civic Progress in St. Louis even has a written rule that anyone who misses three meetings without satisfactory excuses is to be dropped from the group.

Unlike the research bureaus and citizens leagues, most of the top-brass committees expect their members to do the major work personally instead of relying on a paid staff. Committee members themselves originate and thresh out policy decisions, rather than merely rubber-stamping the proposals of a director. And instead of leaving the direct contact chores to a staff man, the member himself gets on the telephone to city hall, the state capitol or Washington.

As a result, the staff for most top-brass committees is small, frequently only a director and a woman secretary. Civic Progress in St. Louis and the Dallas Citizens Council have no staff at all in the usual sense—only an employe from a public relations agency who acts as committee secretary. The agency handles the committee as just another account, like a soap company or an automobile dealer. Whenever heavy research is necessary, the committee may call on the local governmental research bureau or planning association, or it may retain a commercial research firm.

Most top-brass committees keep their meetings deliberately informal with no reporters, no audience, and often no records or minutes kept. The atmosphere is more that of a "bull session" than a business meeting. One group that does retain minutes is Civic Progress, and these give a picture of a typical meeting. Nineteen St. Louis business leaders and Mayor Tucker gathered at the Racquet Club one September evening for their monthly session. Excerpts from the minutes of that meeting follow:

> Mr. C—— reported on favorable results in elections on city charter amendments raising the mayor's salary from $10,000 a year to $25,000 and eliminating the $10,000 ceiling on city salaries, and on two sewer bond issues for St. Louis County areas that were backed by Civic Progress . . .
>
> The members agreed that it would not be appropriate for Civic Progress to endorse or support the fund drive of the Bach Society . . .
>
> The members voted to authorize Mr. C—— to appoint a special committee to undertake whatever action may be feasible to oppose Constitutional Amendment No. 4 that would allow municipalities to provide plants to be leased to industries, and authorizing the issuance of general obligation bonds to finance such plants by municipalities. . . . Mr. M—— [a banker] said

he was very much opposed to authorizing any community to issue general obligation bonds as a means of financing plant facilities to be used by new industry. Mr. McD—— said the state of Arkansas uses tax-exempt revenue bonds supported by the lease rather than general obligation bonds for this purpose . . .

The West End Community Conference, the St. Louis Council on Human Relations, and the Urban League of St. Louis have asked for Civic Progress assistance in persuading the two daily newspapers to abandon their practice of using the heading "Real Estate Available for Colored" in their classified ad listings . . . and discouraging real estate dealers who engage in so-called "block busting". . . . Mr. M—— said Civic Progress is regarded by many persons as a big-business organization. The public reputation of Civic Progress would benefit, he said, if it gave very serious consideration to this problem. Mayor Tucker suggested a special committee could assemble more facts to determine if there is anything Civic Progress can do . . .

All top-brass committees, of course, have impressive fronts. Behind these, however, some have been inert. Others have seemed energetic but confused about their objectives. Still others have been hobbled by factionalism. Thus a committee's real influence can range from considerable, as in Pittsburgh, to near impotence in certain other cities.

Physically, the eight major top-brass committees in the country looked like this in 1961:

PITTSBURGH The Allegheny Conference on Community Development, with a suite of offices in the Civic Building and a staff including executive director Edward J. Magee, an assistant director, a planner, legal counsel, and two clerical workers. Annual budget is $130,000. Governed by an executive committee of twenty, with one hundred and twenty-five sponsors.

PHILADELPHIA The Greater Philadelphia Movement, a four-room office in Western Savings Fund Building. Director William H. Wilcox with an assistant and four clerical workers. Annual budget, $50,000 plus $30,000 for research contracts. Thirty-five directors.

CLEVELAND The Cleveland Development Foundation, a small office in the Midland Building. President Upshur Evans, with one assistant and one clerical employe. Annual budget $100,-000 for the office plus funds for engineering, architectural and legal services. Thirty-six trustees.

ST. LOUIS Civic Progress, Incorporated. No office. Harry B. Wilson of Fleishman-Hillard public relations firm acts as committee secretary. Expenses of $7,500 a year plus special assessments ranging from nothing up to $35,000 a year. Twenty-six members.

MILWAUKEE The Milwaukee Development Group, managed by Edmund Fitzgerald, retired chief executive of Northwestern Mutual Life insurance company, from his office at 626 East Wisconsin Street. Budget $20,000 to $30,000 a year. Twenty-one members.

The Greater Milwaukee Committee, office at 110 East Wisconsin Street. Director Rudolph A. Schoenecker, with a consultant and one clerical employe. Budget $40,000 to $50,000 a year. One hundred and fifty members.

CINCINNATI The Citizens Development Committee, a two-room office in the Union Central Building. Executive secretary George C. Hayward and one clerical employe. Budget of $30,000 a year plus up to $25,000 for special studies and services. Seventy-five trustees.

DALLAS The Dallas Citizens Council. No office. Mrs. Lillian McDonald of Watson Associates advertising agency acts as secretary. Budget of $12,000 a year. Two hundred and thirty members.

Although the top-brass committees have enjoyed considerable adulation in the local press and in national magazines, not all observers take them seriously. Some regard them as a businessman's postwar fad that will fade as the novelty wears off and the committees suffer a few political beatings, as in St. Louis. Said one committee secretary of his employers: "I don't know whether these boys have the constitution for politics. They may have glass jaws."

Yet the top-brass committees represent nothing basically new. They are merely a revised version of what has always existed in city life—a gathering of wealthy men to agree on what is good for the city. The Allegheny Conference, for example, looks not too different from groups found in West European cities nearly a millennium ago. The historian Henri Pirenne described them thus:

> It was necessary, in the midst of a population so heterogeneous as that of the *portus*, for a group of men to take control of the mass and to have enough power and prestige to give it direction. The merchants, in the first half of the eleventh century, assumed this role. Not only did they constitute the wealthiest element in each town, the most active and desirous of change, but they had in addition the strength that union gives. The needs of commerce early impelled them . . . to organize in gilds or hanses —autonomous corporations independent of all authority, in which their will alone made the law . . .
>
> At regular intervals the colleagues assembled to drink and deliberate over their interests; a treasury supported by their contributions provided for the needs of society. . . . At St. Omer the gild devoted a part of its revenues to the construction of defense works and to the maintenance of the streets. . . . At Bruges the contributions of the brothers of the hanse supported the municipal treasury up until its disappearance at the time of the democratic revolution of the fourteenth century.[11]

In modern American cities, men of substance have spoken of civic matters as they met in their Union League, Duquesne Club, Fifty Club, Rainier Club or whatever the name of the local plutocratic bistro might be. But these sessions have tended to degenerate into a goddamming of Socialists, Democrats, labor unions, public power—political discussions little more productive than those heard in most other barrooms.

The significance of the top-brass committees, as they have emerged in the past decade, seems to be that they have taken on an organized form with enunciated principles and objectives, rudimentary as these may still be; thus they are able to begin acting as instruments for cooperation between wealthy nonpoliticians like themselves and the mayors, city councils, planning commissions, county governments, governors, legislators, members of Congress and even the White House.

These men of wealth are moving into a partnership with the politicians because they have become aware of several things: that they have a great stake in the central cities, both in terms of money and in terms of pride; that the central cities need help, and in an automobile age with adequate rapid transit for goods and people yet undeveloped, it is entirely conceivable that city centers could become permanent slums; that most city hall politicians and administrators trying to cope with these problems are neither crooks nor fools; that private enterprise is not going to save the central cities by itself; that it is possible to spend other people's money—tax money—to save the decaying areas; and that only government has the legal power to seize large areas of run-down properties despite the owners' protests, clear the areas and offer them at cut prices to private investors—and this is the only method that appears to offer hope of obtaining major reconstruction of cities, unless government itself becomes the builder.

The top-brass committees, as we have admitted, are not yet interested in much besides real estate. Still, real estate can become a pretty broad concept. Architecture and esthetics, transportation and parking are obviously involved. When it comes to slum clearance, however, a good many more factors enter. Slums consist not only of old buildings but of people who can pay only thirty or forty dollars a month rent. When their homes are torn down, it is necessary to find them other places in the city to live. This means either moving them off to other slums or doing something about low-rent housing, public or private. And since many of the displaced slum dwellers are Negroes, the whole problem of segregation and restricted neighborhoods is opened up—with the threat in the background that if the problem is not solved, the central areas of many cities may become solid Negro ghettos.

As the full implications of these and similar matters of poverty and prejudice begin to unfold, it is possible that we may hear leading businessmen starting to advocate policies that will make the New Dealers of the 1930s sound as tame as William McKinley.

But all that lies in the future. For the moment, the important point is that business leaders in cities, with or without formally organized top-brass committees, have set up new lines of communication with city hall. Increasingly they and public officials are becoming allies in promoting the new gospel of condemn, clean out, spend and build.

This postwar change of signals has caught some mugwumps by surprise. Many conservatives, confused, are balking. Others, especially in the western and midwestern cities, where crowding and decay are less advanced, are unaware of any pressing need for change. Their motto for city government continues to be: keep it clean—and cheap.

This call for economy, once a powerful chorus, can still be heard. But like the thunder of buffalo hooves in another day, it is growing ever more faint.

7

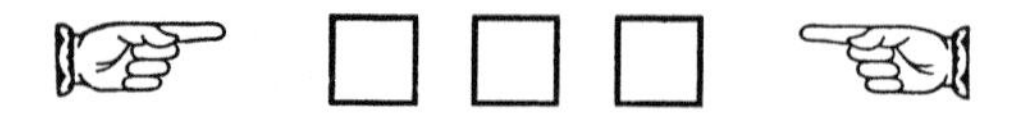

The Second Revolution

How long the top-brass committees will continue, as such, is anybody's guess. They may be a permanent addition to the mugwump arsenal of organizations. Or they could fade into disuse after serving their purpose, much like the Committees of Correspondence in the 1770s. What seems most likely is that the top-brass committees will retain their present form until a broader type of political organization develops in American cities to accomplish the same purpose.

That purpose is to overthrow the ancient accumulation of laws, attitudes and inertia that holds the big cities in bondage.

This will be the shape of the second revolution.

The first revolution in municipal government was essentially an anti-Jacksonian effort to throw out the old personalized cracker-barrel ways of running big-city government and to replace them with dehumanized, mechanized, formalized modes of administration, studded with the same type of automatic controls that simultaneously were becoming a part of big, private industry. It was basically an anti-political revolution.

Now, in the second half of the century, leading mugwumps are fomenting a different kind of revolution—a political one. It will be fought both within the cities and without.

Internally, the first objective will be to harness the political forces already existing in the major cities, but existing in a raw state—confused, uncatalyzed, inarticulate. Much of the time these forces lie idle. Even when stirred to action, they often clash and cancel each other, stopping all forward motion. The problem is to devise a container, a cylinder, within which these several forces can push unitedly in the same direction.

Just as the first revolution sought to bring a new level of professionalism to municipal administration, so the second revolution will seek to bring a new level of professionalism to municipal politics.

Most working politicians probably think of themselves as already accomplished professionals, just as the 1880 fireman who could drive a belching Gould boiler and six horses careening through the streets undoubtedly regarded himself as quite a professional—which, for his time, he was.

But politics in a modern metropolis must involve more than politicians. An instrument for hitching together the leaders of retail business, finance, industry, labor and other power elements needs to be forged. And then a means must be created for allying these local power groupings with similar power groupings in other major cities so that they can act effectively at state capitols and the national capitol. They must form a metropolitan bloc.

As to their program, we can make a fair guess by observing the little brush fires of revolt that have already sprung up.

One brush fire consists of city planners, academic writers and mugwumps agitating against the patent absurdity of having solid metropolitan areas that look to the naked eye like a single city, yet are chopped up idiotically into a dozen or a hundred independent pieces of government with independent water systems, transportation systems, street departments, planning departments, rubbish disposal, fire departments, and myriad other side-by-side services. The people distressed by this fragmentation form committees and study plans for taking different functions away from the geographically limited city governments and giving them either to the county government or to a new form of "metro" government covering the whole area. Universities, the Ford Foundation and other foundations have been responsible for most of these studies.

Another rebel faction, composed largely of city officials, cries out for relief of the cities' financial plight. The cost of services demanded of cities increases, they point out, but the federal and state governments have monopolized the big sources of tax revenue and are giving little of it back. Delegations of city officials and mugwumps troop to every session of the state legislature, asking that cities be granted a larger share of the gasoline tax, the sales tax, or any tax; and they constantly demand more "home rule" so that lobbies of firemen, policemen, teachers and others cannot use the legislature to extract more money from city budgets. The U. S. Conference of Mayors calls on Congress for $6 billion for a ten-year slum clearance program. The American Municipal Association talks of $3 billion a year in federal aid for slum clearance, airports, hospitals, mass transit, sewage disposal plants, bomb shelters and training public health workers. In Washington State, the Association of Washington Cities threatens to put on the ballot a state initiative to give municipalities a $25-million-a-year subsidy from the state treasury. Mayors Daley of Chicago, Dilworth of Philadelphia, Wagner of New York and Tucker of St. Louis travel to Los Angeles to plead with the 1960 Democratic platform committee to include a plank on federal assistance to cities. And from all sides come proposals for a Secretary of Urban Affairs in the President's cabinet.

Loudest of all rises a new voice, a frightened and angry chorus from those whose civic pride and economic interests are threatened by the decay of the central cities. These property owners, retailers, suppliers, bankers, lawyers and others whose careers are based on a flourishing central district watch in dismay as the number of people coming downtown drops year by year. They watch the value of downtown property falling, downtown newspapers folding. Meanwhile, new buildings, new newspapers, new values appear in the suburbs—small as yet compared with the huge investment downtown, but growing.

By the 1950s, it had become plain that to save the heart of the city from becoming a drab and half-used pile of concrete and wood, to avoid its decline into a crummy farrago of aging stores, warehouses, slum dwellings and fractured streets, somebody had to act. Somebody had to tear out old structures and put up new. Somebody had to improve transportation for people and goods, and tackle a dozen other problems as well. And for all this, somebody had to pay the bill.

Most governors and legislatures proved to be of little help. And so, from the big cities began a stream of mayors, leading citizens, telegrams and pleas to Washington. Billions were needed to subsidize urban renewal. But Washington said no, or maybe some day, or reluctantly handed out a few dollars.

At first it is difficult to understand how state and federal officials could afford to shrug off the major cities' calls for help. After all, these cities are the nation's centers of economic power; men there make the key decisions for industry and organized labor. Men there write most of the news, the editorials, the speeches, the books and reports upon which the country's opinions and actions are based. From these cities come most of the big campaign contributions. How could any legislator or congressman or political appointee ignore their voice?

The answer is, of course, that the big cities have had no voice, no clear voice. And they still have none. If they did, it would be deafening. But cities have been heard, when they did speak, as only a part of a babble. The occasional mayor or city attorney or prominent citizen venturing into a state or federal capitol to ask something for the citizens of Baltimore or Milwaukee or St. Louis has been drowned out by the spokesmen for railroads, oil, weapons plants, banks, AFL-CIO, the Farm Bureau, and a hundred other economic interest groups.

The cities have never developed a voice for the obvious reason that few persons of importance ever have felt they needed one. It has always seemed more pressing to look after the interests of one's own industry or profession.

This attitude is changing. The cities are in trouble, and what happens to them has suddenly come to mean a great deal to many important people. From Philadelphia, Pittsburgh and elsewhere, teams of local politicians and businessmen have begun to go arm in arm to the capitols asking for money and legislation for their home towns. Sometimes a labor representative goes along, too.

This is undoubtedly only the beginning. But before the movement can go anywhere, before it can attain significant proportions, somebody must step in and pull together the diverse discontents, worries and ambitions of the urban renewers and the home rulers and the "metro" advocates and the grumbling city dwellers in general—pull them together into an integrated set of objectives, a program.

This task will probably fall to the mugwump. No one else,

over the past century, has shown his talent as a theologian for political change in big-city government.

This time, however, the mugwump will have to broaden and lengthen his sights. Big-city reform heretofore has been largely an intramural project. The crooks, the hacks were in city hall; the campaigns to eject them have taken place, for the most part, within the city limits. The new undertaking can only begin inside the city; to finish it will require operations much farther afield.

In this assignment the mugwump will have to juggle several factors. They include money, laws, political power, and a dream.

The dream is the first essential. This will be the vision, the myth, creating the picture of what everyone is working toward. Without it (or them, because each person will have in his mind a slightly different picture) the movement cannot get started. It cannot gain support or momentum.

This dream, like other political myths, will undoubtedly combine elements tangible and intangible. Tangibly, it may conjure up a Sunday-supplement kind of city, free of smoke, fumes, garbage cans, skid road, tenements, traffic jams, overhead wires, junkyards, creeping transit and grim concrete canyons. Instead it will portray happy citizens moving about the city in fast monorail cars or subways, riding on moving sidewalks through spacious shopping plazas, working in fluted aluminum-glass shells, parking in automatic pigeonhole garages, driving radar-controlled autos on uncrowded pastel freeways, living in tree-shaded mechanized low-taxed homes near a public nursery, supervised playground and new schools staffed with good teachers. For dad on his four days off a week there will be a golf course, bowling green, ball park and boating marina. For grandma, a senior citizens' card room and recreation center. And so on.

To make even a part of this dream come true will cost huge sums of money, several hundred billion dollars.[1] Some of the physical redevelopment—the actual cost of the new commercial buildings themselves—may come from private investors, but the buying and clearing of downtown land, the installing of streets and utilities, the parking spaces and rapid transit will have to be subsidized by the public treasury. Without these public gifts, private owners will apparently remain satisfied to collect rents for their old buildings rather than destroy them to make room for new high-cost structures; and as a result the central cities will continue to wear out faster than private enterprise is able or willing to rebuild them.

The needed billions in subsidies can come from just one source —the pocket of the general taxpayer. The only question is which branch of government shall collect it from him—the federal, state or municipal?

None wants to. City officials declare they cannot. The state, they contend, has fenced them in with limitations on cities' taxing powers. And the federal government has even colluded with private business to defraud local governments of tax income by such devices as placing defense plants and their inventories technically under federal ownership, thus exempting them from local taxes.

Municipal officials also argue that the federal government in the past two decades has assessed such heavy income and excise levies that the sheer weight of federal taxation makes much increase in local taxes impossible. The economy, they say, could not stand it.

Whether this argument holds water in an economic sense is debatable. Canadians, Britishers and others have carried heavier tax burdens and survived. Politically, however, the argument may be valid. Even though the economy itself might stand more taxes, local voters might not. To tell the hometown citizen that he should pay an extra $100 or so a year in taxes, to be used for giving the Bon Marche a cut-rate site for a new downtown store, or to persuade Metropolitan Life that it can profitably erect a new cluster of office towers, or to provide another public links for the golf players, or to enlarge the sewers to accommodate a new Dow Chemical plant—this might be hard to sell locally. If, however, the subsidy comes from the far-off federal government, that is something else.

Whatever the rationalization, it is certain that the cities' drive for funds will be made against the federal treasury and to a lesser degree against the states' treasuries. The proposition will no doubt be advanced that the proper role for federal and state governments should be that of tax collectors because of their broader jurisdiction, while the proper role for municipal governments should be that of tax spenders because they are closer to the people and their needs.

Federal and state officials may not relish this division of labor. Yet it is already to some degree a fact. Of every tax dollar collected during a recent typical year, the federal government took in close to 75 cents, state governments about 13 cents, local governments 12 cents. But when it came to spending, Uncle Sam disposed of less than 70 cents, the states slightly over 10 cents, and local bodies—thanks to state and federal grants—about 20 cents.[2] The goal of big-city forces during the coming years may well be to increase these grants until cities are spending some 30 cents of every tax dollar.

To accomplish anything like this will require, needless to say, tremendous political effort. Every extra penny the cities gain will embroil them in a tug of war with the present beneficiaries of tax dollars. The competition will almost certainly involve the recipients of farm subsidies, foreign aid and defense contracts. There are others. All will fight like demons to prevent any diversion of their funds.

To overcome such opposition, the mugwumps will need every friend they can find. The question is—can they find enough?

8

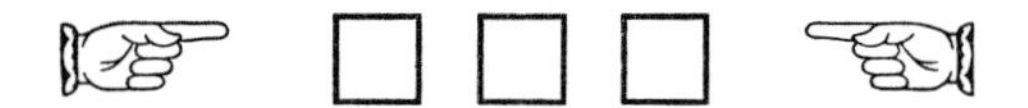

Friends and Foes

The mugwump, politically, has few lifelong companions. He has many temporary bedfellows.

This state of affairs is inevitable for the mugwump. He has chosen the role of spokesman for the General Citizen, and since there is no such animal, at least in the organized sense, the mugwump stands essentially alone.

He is surrounded by promoter groups. These speak not for the general citizenry but for special interests—for business, for labor, for minority groups, for schools, for welfare services, for property owners, for libraries, for a hundred other things and causes.

Each promoter group, acting as if it wore blinders, moves straight ahead toward its own interest. The Chamber of Commerce demands more downtown parking space, the Friends of the Library demand more books and a stack annex, the homebuilders association demands free sewers for tract developments, the welfare council demands more children's clinics, the Better Schools Committee demands more teachers and classrooms, the labor council demands higher pay for municipal grave-diggers—each group pushes its claims regardless of the others and regardless of the effect on the general welfare.

This behavior is normal enough, since it is the reason the promoter group was created in the first place. Yet somebody must weigh demand against demand, and against the resources of the public treasury. Officially, this job falls upon the mayor, the councilmen and others elected to protect the public interest.

But the mugwump, as self-appointed guardian of the citizen, also decides what demands are reasonable, what are not, and exerts his influence accordingly. This means that sooner or later the mugwump must bump heads with almost every promoter group.

With some, these collisions are rare and relatively gentle. Such groups remain political allies of the mugwumps most of the time.

In other cases, collisions are frequent and hard. Here a reservoir of ill will and suspicion has built up that the mugwumps will have a difficult time removing. Yet some reconciliation is necessary if the mugwumps are to help weld a political front strong enough to win the second revolution.

The alignment of mugwump friends and foes varies, naturally, from city to city. In a few places the friends include organized labor, Negroes, and Americans for Democratic Action. More often the list includes the Chamber of Commerce, the real estate board, the League of Women Voters.

And nearly everywhere, the mugwump has another ally—the one that is most important of all: the press.

THE PRESS—KEEPER OR KEPT?

A long time ago, Chicago *Times* editor Wilbur F. Storey declared: "It is a newspaper's duty to print the news, and raise hell."

There is some argument about how well newspapers have handled the first part of their obligation, but nobody denies that the press can and does raise hell when it wants to. Ever since the New York *Times* took on Boss Tweed there has been little doubt that a major newspaper could knock over almost any politician it caught in wrongdoing. This threat of exposure has been the most powerful single weapon that the press has wielded in big-city politics. Fortunately for the mugwumps, this weapon has nearly always been in the hands of friends.

There is no mystery about why the newspapers have usually been part of the mugwump coalition. Most newspapermen are a breed of mugwump themselves. They feel the urge to influence government without actually becoming a part of it; and also, like other mugwumps, they regard themselves as spokesmen for the general citizen, not promoters of special interests. Furthermore, especially in the higher echelons, most of the newspaperman's friends and business associates are either mugwumps or mugwump sympathizers.

An exception has been Cincinnati. There the long battle between the mugwumps and the regular Republican organization found the two largest papers, the *Enquirer* and the *Times-Star*, along with the leading businessmen, siding with the GOP regulars. In other cities, certain papers such as the Houston *Chronicle* and the Cleveland *Press* still make little attempt to mesh their political efforts with those of local mugwumps. But these situations are not common. In most cities the leading papers have been the indispensable right arm of the mugwump forces.

It has become difficult in some places to distinguish which is the right arm of which. Some observers, including former Mayor Elmer Robinson of San Francisco, contend that the decline of the old-style political machines and the corresponding rise in political importance of the big dailies, has progressed to a point where the newspapers have become the new bosses of American cities. In certain cities that appears to be close to the truth. The "boss papers," if it is fair to call them that, exist mostly where mugwump elements are comparatively weak and the newspaper is run by a strong-willed editor deeply interested in local politics.

Direct participation in politics, of course, is nothing new for editors. Horace Greeley, Carl Schurz and other newsmen were prominent in the mugwumps' Liberal Republican movement after the Civil War. A handful of newspapermen spearheaded the California Progressives, who overthrew the Southern Pacific Railroad's political machine in that state before World War I. In 1948, editor Edward J. Meeman of the Memphis *Press-Scimitar* led the mugwump revolt against Boss Crump. There have been many others.

A more common pattern, however, has been for the newspaper executive to avoid top billing and instead merge himself among the mugwump cast. The publisher or his proxy, the political editor, may sit in at the small luncheons and dinners where the mugwump party line and candidates are decided upon. Or if he does not attend the meetings himself, someone calls on him soon afterward to outline the plans and obtain his nod of agreement.

Inevitably, perhaps, with growing power, most big-city newspapers have seemed to drift further and further from the principle of print the news and raise hell. Instead of following the early city-room credo that the story's the thing, just print the facts and let the chips fall where they may, major papers have displayed an increasing paternalism—a trend possibly accelerated by the conservative revival after World War II. In their political coverage, editors have come to concentrate not so much on what will make a good story as on what they believe is good for the city.

The political editor of a Pacific Northwest paper, for instance, discovered that certain school officials were spending above the legal limit on cost-per-square-foot for new school buildings. Twenty years before, when he was a young reporter, he would have written the story and his paper would have splashed it across page one. Now he called the school officials, said he realized how much new classrooms were needed and what damage bad publicity would do to future school bond issues at the polls, and told the officials if they would observe the legal limit from now on, he would not print the story. The school officials, of course, agreed.

This habit of deciding what is good for society has filtered down to the humble ranks of reporters. It is not uncommon to find them sitting around a city-hall press room debating, like a caucus of baggy-pantsed senators, how the city government should dispose of a current problem, then proceeding to fashion their stories in this direction. This game-playing is sometimes carried to the extent of letting officials know the press-room decision. Such lobbying now and then involves a small pay-off to a reporter by a backer or an opponent of a proposal. More often the reporters do it just because of a mugwumpish urge to throw their weight around a little.

Another symptom of paternalism has been the growing number of newspaper "slates." These layouts usually appear in the Sunday edition before election day—lists of recommended candidates for whom readers should vote. This practice would have a slightly less patriarchal air if the newspapers also printed the information on which they base their conclusions; this at least would be a nice gesture toward the democratic theory that the people should be provided the facts and permitted to form their own judgments.

Many editors no doubt believe they are already providing such information. It might jolt them if they would go through their own newspapers for, say, the three months preceding any recent municipal election and note just how many facts they have given, or not given, the voters about the men running for office. The author conducted such an experiment in certain West Coast cities, checking the information printed about the two leading candidates for mayor, the most important office on the ticket. The search was for personal data about the man or his views, the kind of thing one would want to know in deciding whether to vote for him.

It developed that in the ninety days preceding the election, the readers of the leading newspaper in one city, San Francisco, would have learned this much about one of the candidates for mayor:

(a) he was governor of the Loyal Order of Moose,

(b) he was a member of the state board of equalization,

(c) he had a wife named Kathryn and four children.

As for the other candidate, who, incidentally, won in a landslide, the readers would have learned only:

(a) he was a member of the city-county board of supervisors.

The second-largest paper in San Francisco did slightly better. Eight weeks before the election it advised its readers that the Democratic candidate, who lost, was born of Irish immigrant parents, reared in the city, the father of four, grandfather of six, became election commissioner in 1930, was appointed city-county supervisor, was elected to the state board of equalization in 1938 and re-elected four times since.

All this appeared in a single statement on September 21. After that, until the November election, there was no further information about the man's experience, qualifications or views.

The same paper carried somewhat more about his Republican opponent, at least in the early days of the campaign. On August 2, fourteen weeks before the election, an article outlined his views on city problems. Thereafter these bits of description appeared:

August 3, "supervisor"; August 19, "his own dairy business"; August 23, "businessman"; September 9, "supervisor, president of the board and businessman"; September 19, "president of the board of supervisors"; September 20, a statement by the candidate describing himself as "son of an immigrant . . . this city has been my home since I was two. The death of my father when I was fourteen left our family on its resources and forced me to leave school. . . . Working by day, studying and attending classes by night, I acquired a degree in accounting. This city has given me business success through the dairy company that bears my name. Since 1945 . . . a member of the board of supervisors."

This sketch appeared eight weeks before the election. After that the paper carried nothing more on the man's personal background or views until the week before the election, when it mentioned again that he was a "businessman . . . elected to the board of supervisors . . . was president of the board twice."

These cases are not extraordinary. Most United States publishers seem to expect the public to cast intelligent ballots for candidates about whom it has less information than the publisher himself would insist on having about someone he was considering for the job of copyboy.

Things have begun to improve in recent years. Some papers are making serious efforts to step up their pre-election coverage. The Seattle *Times*, for one, began devoting several pages a few days before election to brief biographies and campaign statements from dozens of local candidates. The conscientious citizen who actually wanted to know something about the men he would vote for had at least a fighting chance if he would study the *Times* layout.

Most papers, while weak on describing candidates, do better at explaining the initiatives, bond issues and other ballot propositions. The San Antonio *Express and News*, for instance, prepares a special section with clearly written copy in large ten-point type, illustrated with pictures, cartoons and maps. Like many other papers, however, the *Express and News* slants its explanations either to favor or to oppose the ballot proposals, so that the reader must proceed with care.

Pre-election coverage, of course, is only a minor part of a newspaper's civic obligation. What counts far more in the long run is how well a paper covers the day-to-day operations of municipal government. Here it is hard to know whether to rejoice that some newspapers do as well as they do—like the New York *Times* and the Milwaukee *Journal*—or to deplore the fact that most newspapers, even the best, are doing a much poorer job than they realize.

One could pick flaws by pointing to stories that are inaccurate because a green or not-bright reporter misinterpreted statistics or was ignorant of municipal law or just plain did not comprehend what was happening under his nose.

But there is not much point in blaming the shortcomings of individual reporters. The principal fault lies higher up, with the publishers and editors. They have failed to create an adequate system for covering local governmental affairs. Most of the good work that is done comes from the solo efforts of a few gifted reporters—Paul Crowell of the New York *Times*, Ross Cunningham and "Stub" Nelson in Seattle, and a few dozen others. These men, however, cannot handle the bulk of daily stories that have to do with local government. Those must come from the city hall reporters, the courthouse reporters and others on the regular beats, who transmit their stories directly to the city editor or his assistant on the city desk in the newspaper office. This beat-reporter-to-city-desk system may once have been satisfactory in small cities. But the government of a modern metropolitan city cannot be covered by run-of-the-mill reporters turned loose to roam a beat without supervision, picking up stories at random and transmitting them to a harried city desk man who knows even less about municipal affairs than the reporter.

Years ago newspaper publishers learned that they could best cover the field of sports by creating a special department, headed by a seasoned editor who knew sports thoroughly and could make sure none of his younger writers had Babe Ruth hitting sixty-one home runs in 1927 instead of sixty. In addition to catching boners, the sports editor could develop the talented members of his staff, weed out the unfit, and see that his men covered the local sports scene with such thoroughness and imagination that they sold more papers than the opposition.

For some reason it never occurred to publishers that municipal government is a specialized field, too, requiring just as careful handling as sports.

One newspaper made a tentative move in this direction. The Detroit *News* in July, 1955, created a city-county bureau under veteran newsman John M. Carlisle and gave him a staff of six young reporters to cover the city, county and state offices in Detroit, along with the courts. From its spacious press room in Detroit's new city hall, the bureau sent copy by teletype to the *News* office uptown. Its stories, however, were not departmentalized but were scattered with general news throughout the paper. Even this preliminary attempt at better local government coverage broke down as an economy wave hit the *News* in 1959 and the city-county bureau was discontinued.

One can hopefully predict that some day the *News* and other large dailies will give municipal government and politics the same facilities long since given to football, baseball and pole vaulting—namely, a specialized staff and a section of the paper where they can do justice to their subject.

When this takes place, the newspapers' already leading role in big-city politics will grow even larger. And the presence of more numerous and better-trained, better-paid reporters will tend to overshadow the position of the activists in the mugwump research agencies, who now often enjoy almost oracular prestige because they are the only ones in town who take time to delve thoroughly into municipal problems.

Stronger newspaper coverage, when it develops, will play a key part in the second revolution. Politically, the press already looms as a giant—admittedly a rather confused giant who is still a little slow to figure out for himself just what is going on in big-city government, and so has to accept pretty much what other people tell him. But once the big fellow develops a sharper nervous system, he will possess political influence of almost frightening proportions. (Whether this proves in the long term a good or bad thing for the American system is another question.) The speed with which this development of the press takes place will determine, to a great extent, the pace of the second revolution.

A FINE BUNCH OF WOMEN

Not all mugwumps wear trousers. There are lady mugwumps, too. The gentlemen, however, do not seem entirely aware of their existence.

An incident in Philadelphia is typical. The conversation with the quiet-voiced young man who often manages reform campaigns in the city had ranged over the ADA, the Republican and Democratic organizations, labor unions, the Committee of Seventy, the Greater Philadelphia Movement and other elements that figure in the city's politics. Finally there was the question: "What about the League of Women Voters?"

His reaction was a blank look. Then: "Oh, they're fine. Mostly a study group. They don't get much involved in local affairs."

It was as if one had asked about the garden club or Christian Endeavor.

Nationally, the League of Women Voters has chapters in nearly every major city and a thousand smaller ones. It claims 127,000 members, making it by far the largest nonpartisan political organization in the country. Yet nearly always one encounters this blank reaction whenever he brings up the league, as if he had introduced something irrelevant into an otherwise serious political discussion. Replies from prominent mugwumps, newspapermen and politicians run like this:

(Boston) "The League of Women Voters? They're interested mainly in schools . . . essentially a self-education group . . . they're trying to do more."

(Cleveland) "You're glad to have them on your side, but they're not too effective."

(Cincinnati) "Pretty weak, although they have been better in the past few years."

(Milwaukee) "They used to be more active. They supported public low-rent housing after the war. Now they concentrate mostly on getting out the vote."

(Kansas City) ". . . not too active."

(Memphis) ". . . not too many members. They haven't made much of a dent. But they've done a good job of training poll watchers and election officials."

(Houston) ". . . fine people, fine bunch of women, but they have never meant much here . . . purely a study group . . . they quiz candidates but they don't get down to cases."

(St. Louis) ". . . very busy, but they don't get far in some of their campaigns . . . never accept defeat, can't be insulted . . . lots of the Don Quixote type."

(Seattle) ". . . a fine bunch of gals, but they always seem to be studying something nebulous."

These remarks came, of course, from men. As such they must be discounted. For the gap between the sexes, when it comes to politics, is wide. Men do not encourage women to join in their political councils—except as one may be brought in, like a Negro or a minister, for window dressing. And women do little to force their way into the inner circle.

Among mugwumps, the alliance between men's and women's groups appears actually to have been stronger in days gone by. Back when militancy was in flower, with crusades against strong-arm politicians, red-light districts, saloons and sin in general—an era that lasted until the twin victories of prohibition and the woman-suffrage amendment—the male and female reformers often battled side by side. The women proved excellent foot soldiers. They could not only wreck saloons, but on occasion (as in the Terre Haute, Indiana, election of 1915) they fought hand to hand with the machine's bully boys to prevent fraud in the polling places. In 1917, East St. Louis women headed the campaign that installed a new commission form of government, replacing the old regime that had permitted the grisly three-hour race riot in which thirty-seven Negroes were hanged, clubbed and burned to death.

But militancy passed from fashion. Male mugwumps, even before World War I, had begun to discard slam-bang reform fights in favor of municipal research and lobbying. And by 1920, with the saloon outlawed and their vote secured, women reformers had put away their hatchets, chains and padlocks. The thirty-year-old National American Woman Suffrage Association became the League of Women Voters. Thereafter, the gentlemen and lady mugwumps tended to walk separate ways.

The men became ever more practical, spending less time on reform philosophy and more on specific questions of the moment

—should a new library be built, should a hundred more policemen be hired, should the city float $10 million in water bonds?

Meanwhile, the League of Women Voters turned its attention to broad issues like outlawing child labor, conserving natural resources, disarmament, promoting civil service, studying tax systems and discussing the forms of local, state and national government.

In theory, league members are not supposed to do anything about these matters except to become informed about them, and if they can agree on a point of view they may adopt a "consensus," which is merely an expression of opinion. Yet now and then league members in a given city erupt into action, sometimes in the name of the league, sometimes not. At such times the old-style alliance of men and women mugwumps reappears, with the men raising most of the money and making the policy decisions, the women doing most of the door-to-door work in the precincts and licking envelopes at campaign headquarters.

Women played an important part in the 1940 overthrow of Pendergast in Kansas City. They helped vigorously when San Antonio mugwumps pushed through their city-manager charter in 1951. Women have always provided the rank and file for the Cincinnati Charter Committee. And housewives in Cleveland, in the early 1920s, not only helped make it the first major United States city to adopt a council-manager government with proportional representation voting, but later, when most male mugwumps had lost interest in defending Cleveland's charter from constant assault by professional Republicans and Democrats, the League of Women Voters single-handedly fought a rear-guard action until 1931, when the manager charter finally succumbed.

League chapters have always been among the most unwavering defenders of city-manager government. Permanent voter registration is another gimmick that has often had league backing—as long ago as 1929, when the Michigan State League of Women Voters aided the Detroit Citizens League in shoving the needed bill through the legislature; more recently in 1954, when the New York league, with the Citizens Union, buttonholed enough legislators at Albany to obtain, at long last, passage of a permanent personal registration measure.

Today the New York City league is the nation's largest with 3,300 members. As in most leagues, only a small fraction of these are active. They raise an annual budget of better than $60,000. Of this, approximately a third goes to the state and national offices, and $40,000 remains to operate the local office at 461 Park Avenue South with its five women employes. The paid staff is outnumbered, however, by the bevy of women volunteers who bustle around the league office in a constant state of excitement. Unlike most male-run mugwump organizations, in which the staff strongly influences all decisions, the League of Women Voters uses paid help largely as clerks and stenographers. If there is any deciding to be done, the members do it. The same holds true for whatever research a league may undertake. The ladies themselves handle it.

The New York league spends considerable time taking a voting machine into different sections of the city and demonstrating its use. This started in 1954 after someone discovered that 88,000 New Yorkers evidently had gone into the voting booth, pulled down the levers of their choice, then pushed the levers up again before pulling back the curtain, thus leaving no impression on the machine and no vote.

The New York league is best known, however, as an information center. The telephone jingles steadily with inquiries from radio, television and newspaper writers, and from citizens wondering who is their councilman or their assemblyman. The league also publishes and sells booklets, such as *They Represent You,* in which any New Yorker can find the name of his senator, congressman, state legislator or city councilman, and the well-written *Big City, Big Government,* which describes the mechanics of New York City government.

Leagues in other cities issue similar publications. The Minneapolis league's fact-stuffed *ABC's of City Government* is one of the most ambitious (forty-four pages, fifteen thousand copies). The league has had little difficulty distributing them at 25 cents each among the Minneapolis schools and business concerns.

Most League of Women Voters publications are written straight, although now and again some mugwump propaganda shows through. The New York booklet, for instance, plumps for giving the city administrator control of the city budget, the city planning commission and the city personnel office—all moves favored by mugwump elements in New York.

The New York league, like others across the country, draws its members from the same socio-economic groups as the male mugwump organizations—largely from the upper middle class who live in the better neighborhoods and, in most cases, have a college diploma stuck away in a drawer. The New Yorkers declare they wish they could recruit more wives of blue-collar workers but "we just don't seem able to do it."

The Chicago league experimented with an unusual answer to this problem. In a moment of self-appraisal, the women noted that almost all 1,300 of them lived either around the University of Chicago or in the respectable North Shore, North Side and Southwest neighborhoods. Great sections of the city had no contact with the league at all. So in 1953 the league formed a separate nonprofit corporation, the Citizens Information Service, acquired a $44,000-a-year budget, employed a staff of four social workers, and launched three pilot projects on Chicago's South Side. Working with neighborhood leaders, they organized a Between-the-Tracks Council to help a Negro area cope with the problems of a new expressway routed through its midst; another committee was formed in Parkside, which was having housing pains as it changed from a white to a Negro neighborhood; and a third committee undertook to teach Puerto Rican residents how to register and vote, in hopes that this might end certain politicians' practice of buying Puerto Rican votes for two dollars each.

Election time sends most League of Women Voters offices into a buzz of "voter education" events. These generally include two or three radio and television shows (the time is donated by the stations) on which candidates are introduced and speak for a few minutes each, and a panel show or two explaining the ballot propositions. Some leagues present similar fare at street meetings or in auditoriums. These are not always a box-office smash. When the San Francisco league and the Junior Chamber of Commerce staged a noontime get-out-the-vote rally in Union Square, the San Francisco *Chronicle* reported an audience of "thirty-five pigeons, forty voters and one hundred and twenty-five habitual loungers."

Most leagues prepare brief explanations of the ballot measures and distribute 5,000 to 25,000 copies. These digests are usually well done and impartial; in some cities, newspapers reprint them. For those who prefer to get the information by word of mouth, most leagues provide speakers. Their steadiest customers are other women's clubs.

When it comes to candidates, the League of Women Voters is wary. Its bylaws prohibit endorsing anyone. Most leagues send a questionnaire to each candidate asking for biographical information and perhaps his stand on a half-dozen issues. The answers are usually collected into a mimeographed sheaf to be read by league members, but seldom by anyone else. Minneapolis is an exception. There before each election the League of Women Voters releases jointly with the Citizens League a report on candidates that is printed in a special section of the Minneapolis *Tribune*, thus blanketing the city.

Minneapolis, incidentally, is one city where the League of Women Voters is *not* regarded as an innocuous ladies' club. With a membership of 1,150, they are the third largest league in the nation, behind New York and Chicago. They have played a real, although indirect, role in the post–World War II uprising of Minneapolis mugwumps against the long political domination of the Central Labor Union. Many of the women's husbands are active in the fight; indeed, the league finds itself plagued repeatedly with vacancies on its governing board as someone's husband files for office and his wife has to resign.

Several leagues make it a practice to send observers to meetings of the city council and school board. Often this becomes merely a boring duty, with the league observer sitting mousily in the back row taking no part in the proceedings. The Minneapolis women, however, not only follow the meetings closely but dig for additional facts and figures, and distribute them in a monthly newsletter *Once Over Lightly*. This roundup of city-hall developments, when seen for the first time, opens the eyes of those males who may have doubted the feminine capacity for hard-fact governmental research.

The Minneapolis women have also devised an ingenious method of raising money. On election night, they take over the big Donaldson's department store telephone switchboard and there receive calls from league members stationed at 262 precincts in the city and suburbs. As the vote count progresses during the evening, the members report the tallies to the central switchboard, and the league passes on the totals to the Minneapolis *Tribune* and six local radio and television stations. These pay the league a cost-plus fee for the service.

Another group that plunged into the political arena after World War II was the Seattle League of Women Voters. Formerly a rather bookish lot, the Seattle group and twelve other leagues in the state, goaded by Seattle newspaperman Ross Cunningham, seized one of the prickliest issues around—reapportionment of the state legislature. Berating Washington lawmakers for ignoring their constitutional duty to redesign the legislative districts every ten years to conform with changing population, the women in 1956 forced action by getting 80,000 voters to sign initiative petitions. When the measure appeared on the November ballot (despite court fights by certain legislators to keep it off), it carried comfortably, 448,000 to 406,000. Washington law, however, permits the legislature to amend initiative measures, and the 1957 legislature proceeded to amend the initiative right out of existence. The league vainly fought the matter up to the state supreme court, claiming the initiative had been butchered rather than amended. The high court sided with the legislature, five to four.

The Seattle league pitched in again in 1958 to help win voter approval of a "metropolitan council" to handle sewage disposal in most of King County. The women provided more than half the campaign work force of four hundred volunteers; they arranged speeches, obtained endorsements from clubs, mailed 150,000 postcards and trudged from door to door talking with voters.

In 1960, the St. Louis League of Women Voters shared credit with male mugwumps in winning popular approval of a charter amendment placing five hundred jobs in the patronage-ridden St. Louis county government under civil service. That same year the Michigan League of Women Voters and the state Junior Chamber of Commerce circulated thousands of initiative petitions across the state to place an amendment on the ballot requiring a state convention to revise the Michigan constitution. Voters passed the amendment in November, 1960.

Probably no group of women has proved more formidable,

politically speaking, than those in New Orleans. Their leaders possess both money and determination. Avowed enemies of the Long faction, the women organized a "broom squad" in the 1946 campaign and marched through the streets, brooms over their shoulders, showing they intended to sweep the city clean of Mayor Robert S. Maestri, a Long man. That they did. And after their candidate, handsome young deLesseps Story Morrison, took office, the women remained active in politics.

One task they set themselves was to police the voter rolls. A small group of affluent women headed by Mrs. Edgar B. Stern, Sr. (then the wife, now the widow, of one of America's wealthiest men, and daughter of Sears Roebuck founder Julius Rosenwald), organized a Voters Registration League. By court action they forced the registrar of voters to permit them to photostat his registration books. The photostats showed certain peculiarities.

For instance, a remarkable number of voters seemed to be physically disabled or illiterate; as such, someone could accompany them into the voting booth to help them mark their ballots. One photostat revealed thirty-one persons registered in one day in one precinct by one deputy, and all but two of them were listed "physically disabled." After more than nine thousand such listings came to light, a wholesale purge of the registration books began, and several deputy registrars were indicted.

In 1952, hoping to nail down their voting reforms, the women helped get eleven bills through the Louisiana legislature, including permanent registration, voting machines, fixed hours for opening and closing polls, and the placing of numbers beside each candidate's name so that illiterates could vote without assistance.

Today the operation of the Voters Service, as it has been renamed, has become routine. It is virtually a part of the city government. Two women employes, hired by Mrs. Stern and her friends, occupy a large room in the basement of the new city hall, along with an IBM keypunch machine, an IBM tabulator and rows of filing cases. The files contain thousands of cards, one for each voter, giving his name, address, ward and precinct, birth date, color, sex, political party, whether a property owner or tenant or boarder, and whether disabled or illiterate. The women keep the files up to date by adding the names of new voters as they register (a simple procedure if a friendly governor has appointed a cooperative registrar of voters for Orleans parish, not so simple if an anti-Morrison governor has made the appointment).

This system gives the Voters Service a continuing check on the registration rolls. In addition, the service sells copies of its lists to ward leaders and precinct captains at campaign time; they may buy either cards bearing full personal information about each voter, or gummed labels with the voter's name and address only. At five dollars per thousand names, business is brisk, with income during a presidential election year exceeding $20,000. This is not quite enough to meet all expenses. Operating the Voters Service costs about $25,000 a year. The annual deficits of $5,000 to $10,000 are met by Mrs. Stern and the eleven other women on the committee.

Aside from these groups in New Orleans, Minneapolis, Seattle, St. Louis and a few other cities, women continue to be regarded largely as political dilettantes. The League of Women Voters' emphasis on study programs, its ponderous "consensus" machinery under which the members take six months to two years to make up their minds on an issue, the atmosphere of feminine groupiness about the whole operation—all this has led male mugwumps to dismiss them as unreliable political allies. A veteran New York City councilman said: "They're active on one or two things they pick at the beginning of the year, but they're not very good at pitching in on emergencies."

There is another side to the picture.

League of Women Voters members probably do more reading and discussing of the general political theory of state and local government than any but a handful of male scholars and government administrators. The leagues' practice of taking one current issue after another, studying it and reaching conclusions about it slowly but steadily is building a body of political beliefs, a dogma, that some day should make them an intellectually well-armed force.

The league leaders include many tough-minded, intelligent women. Not only have they shown political imagination, but in a fight they often display more reckless courage than their husbands. They are less frightened of economic reprisals. And once aroused, they work harder at ringing doorbells, telephoning, mailing pamphlets and harassing public officials.

One thing has been lacking. In most cities, the women seem out of touch with the day-to-day actualities of politics around them. This, however, is something easily remedied by getting out of the office and the library, and down to the battle line at city hall and the state capitol.

When and if the women begin doing this, they should develop into some of the most effective shock troops in the second revolution.

CHAMBERS OF COMMERCE

Mugwumps and men of property have been such firm allies in recent decades that it is difficult to remember they were not always so. Yet to mugwumps around the turn of the century, the great enemy of good government was the favor-seeking businessman and his companion in corruption, the professional politician.

The man of property might sympathize occasionally with the mugwumps and even abstractly agree with their high principles, but as a practical matter he had to deal with the forces in power, honest or otherwise. What was more, the mugwumps' righteousness sometimes became irritating. They just did not seem to understand. As railroader Collis P. Huntington explained about bribery: "If you have to pay money to have the right thing done, it is only just and fair to do it." [1]

Such misunderstandings sometimes led to open breaks. In San Francisco when the mugwumps' famous graft trials in 1908 began to implicate leading businessmen, the business community turned on Hiram Johnson, Francis J. Heney and the other mugwumps to defeat their ticket at the next city election. Similarly, in the 1920s, Cincinnati's men of property, after briefly helping the mugwumps overturn Republican boss Hynicka, swung back to the GOP machine. To this day the breach has not healed. As a result, Cincinnati remains an interesting case of arrested development—probably the only major city in the United States where one can study the type of bitter antagonism that so often existed between mugwumps and men of property back in the days of Teddy Roosevelt.

Elsewhere nearly all remnants of such conflict evaporated during the 1930s. In that depression period, Republicans lost and Democrats gained control of many municipal offices. The mugwump organizations, in their customary role of critics, sank barbs into the Democratic officeholders just as they had into the Republicans. This, of course, pleased pro-Republican business elements, and they moved into closer support of mugwump groups.

Besides this, the mugwump agencies had always preached economy in government—a theme that the men of property found agreeable but not particularly exciting in the roaring twenties. They were too busy making money to worry about saving a few dollars in property taxes. After the 1929 crash, however, this nonchalance turned to concern, then to panic as income from property fell while taxes and assessed valuations remained high, and even climbed as local governments scraped for funds to keep the unemployed from starving in the streets.

As some owners of marginal properties stopped paying taxes altogether, the squeeze on the remaining taxpayers increased. Threatened with wholesale tax foreclosures, many property owners had no time for the deliberate pace of the mugwump research bureaus and citizens leagues. Instead, almost overnight, they formed scores of taxpayer organizations and advanced on city halls, courthouses and legislatures, demanding that government fold up almost everything but the police and fire departments in order to cut taxes. Other property owners worked within mugwump agencies, urging stiffer stands against government spending. The end result was that most citizen agencies became consistent advocates of rigid economy.

The rapprochement of the men of property and the mugwumps was hastened, also, by the depth of feeling against That Man Roosevelt in the White House. Numerous mugwumps supported Roosevelt; some even entered government service under the New Deal. But many devout Republicans, excluded from any other voice in government, joined mugwump organizations and sublimated their spleen against the New Deal by working for good-government-in-general. Whether they would have been equally diligent reformers in a Republican era is hard to say.

In any event, the infusion of business elements into the political reform movement proceeded rapidly during the 1930s. The same men whose contributions financed the chambers of commerce and other business groups also contributed to mugwump organizations. The solidarity established then still endures with few signs of cracking.

There have been, to be sure, occasional tiffs between a mugwump organization and a Chamber of Commerce, but most of these have sprung merely from staff jealousies in one group or another, and the contributors usually see that they never grow to serious proportions.

From the mugwump viewpoint, organized business, as a fighting ally, has left something to be desired. The typical Chamber of Commerce handles itself in the political arena less like an agile gladiator than a heavy-footed pachyderm.

This must be expected. Chambers of commerce are sprawling, loose-knit organizations set up primarily not for political purposes but to advance the numerous and sometimes competing business interests of a large membership. Consequently, when a chamber tries to intervene in local government, it often looks inept.

The Seattle Chamber of Commerce, for instance, sent spokesmen for two different committees to a city council meeting. Within a few minutes of each other, one urged repeal of the city business tax, which would have cut off a major source of city income, and the other recommended a city construction program costing $37 million. The councilmen spent an enjoyable quarter-hour needling the chamber representatives as to which of the two proposals they preferred—since they plainly could not have both.

Such bumbling symptomatized the general debility that by the forties had crept through many chambers of commerce. Toward local government the average chamber's attitude had become a mixture of pinch-penny economy (a product of the thirties), relieved by occasional flashes of boosterism (a relic of the twenties), and lethargy. Empty slogans became a substitute for action.

It was a common complaint, even among members, that the chamber "never does anything."

As a result, when Pittsburgh's leaders launched their postwar boom in physical redevelopment and leaders in other cities tried to follow suit, they did not utilize the chambers of commerce. They created totally new top-brass committees. Tracing what led to this situation, the executive of a large Midwest Chamber of Commerce explained:

> Some chambers of commerce went downhill when the leading members began sending their Number Two and Number Three men to meetings. Communication among the leading men broke down. United action became impossible. The business community, like some county governments we like to criticize, became headless. And so the business leaders, instead of renovating their Chamber of Commerce when the postwar urge for big-scale action came, started new organizations.

This story of frustration has not been universal. In Chicago, for instance, the Association of Commerce and Industry made its influence felt for many years under the guidance of the late Leverett Lyon, formerly of the Brookings Institution. Houston's chamber vigorously pushes public works, planning and metropolitan government, publicizing its efforts with a handsome hundred-page monthly magazine (ten thousand copies); its committees provide an important outlet for Houston mugwumps wishing to have a voice in local affairs. San Antonio's post–World War II reform movement incubated in the Chamber of Commerce there. The Greater Detroit Board of Commerce remains close to city and county government in the automobile capital. In Los Angeles, municipal bond attorney James Beebe for years has made his Chamber of Commerce committee on state and local government one of the chief mugwump spokesmen in that politically confused city.

It is conceivable that a series of shake-ups in the chambers of commerce could transform most of them into politically "hip" organizations capable of originating and pushing through creative programs. But this appears unlikely. As far as the mugwumps are concerned, a sufficient victory will be achieved if the chambers can be kept up to date on what is happening in the second revolution so that they can serve as intelligent allies in a time of change, rather than becoming well-intentioned obstructionists.

THE ADA

While their right flank is bolstered by the chambers of commerce and other business groups, the mugwumps have on their left flank a smaller force, the Americans for Democratic Action.

The ADA, formed as a refuge for homeless New Dealers and other liberals in the late 1940s, has paid relatively little attention to municipal matters. Its mind has been on doings in Washington and the larger state capitols. In only a handful of super mets and major mets—New York, Philadelphia, Boston, Chicago—has ADA been even visible in local affairs. And in only one, Philadelphia, has it played a leading role.

There the ADA chapter provided a volunteer army of young socialites, lawyers, businessmen and housewives who, as one observer put it, "went out and worked like fools" in the 1951 campaign that overturned the ancient, corrupt Republican machine. Two former chairmen of the ADA chapter, wealthy Joseph S. Clark and Richardson Dilworth, were elected mayor and district attorney.

From then on ADA served as the core of the reform Democrats' campaign organization. The usual technique was to establish an independent campaign committee, rent a headquarters on Chestnut Street, and submerge ADA efforts and funds within the front committee. These committees included the Volunteers for Stevenson in 1952 and 1956 that delivered to the Democratic presidential nominee majorities of 160,000 and 125,000 in Philadelphia while he was losing elsewhere in the country; the Volunteers for Leader in 1954 that helped elect George Leader governor; the Citizens Charter committees in 1954 and 1956 that prevented emasculation of the new city charter by the Democratic regulars; an Independent Committee for Dilworth and Blanc that managed their successful campaigns in 1955 for mayor and district attorney; and the Clark for Senator Committee in

1956 that sent the former mayor to Washington. The committee to re-elect Mayor Dilworth won a sweeping victory in 1959.

The ADA office on South Fifteenth Street, near city hall, houses an executive director, a part-time researcher, a part-time assistant director and three clerical employes. Approximately one thousand members contribute a budget of $32,000 a year.

ADA in the Boston area has more members, less money, and a wealth of brain power from the Harvard faculty across the river in Cambridge. The Cambridge chapter is the largest, with smaller ones in Boston and the suburbs of Newton and Brookline—a total of around 2,500 members.

Like everyone else in Boston, ADA has slight hope of doing much about improving the city government. It devotes most of its attention to state legislation and to the voting records of those running for the legislature and Congress. In 1960, the organization wrote speeches and collected campaign funds for the Democratic candidate for United States senator (he lost) and for a half-dozen ADA-ers running for the legislature; each received $50 to $1,100 for campaign expenses.

ADA in New York is essentially an anti-Tammany Democratic group, part of the city's large bloc of welfare-minded reform organizations. It shows special concern over middle- and low-income housing, and racial integration in the city's schools. (An ADA officer wryly observes that thirtyish female members show an equal concern over the organization's supply of eligible men.)

The three ADA chapters in Manhattan—on the West Side, East Side and in Greenwhich Village—have about a thousand members, with nearly as many scattered among six chapters in Brooklyn, Queens, and Nassau and Westchester counties.

ADA's affiliate in Chicago, the Independent Voters of Illinois (IVI), is one of the few organizations openly bucking the city's powerful Democratic machine. IVI's gains so far have been microscopic. An IVI former chairman, attorney Leon M. Despres, in 1955 and 1959 won election to the city council, where he serves surrounded by some four dozen machine aldermen.

The group has a young executive director, a three-room office in a downtown office building, and a membership and budget that fluctuate widely—1,000 to 3,000 members and $20,000 to $50,000 a year. The members live largely in the middle-class wards around the University of Chicago and along the north lake shore, and do most of their campaigning in these thirteen of Chicago's fifty wards.

Like most ADA groups, Chicago's Independent Voters believes that its main function is to distinguish between good guys and bad guys running for office. It has little time or money for analyzing the day-to-day problems that confront the city government.

In addition, the IVI and other ADA chapters try, as does the League of Women Voters, to encompass the whole political cosmos—local, state, national and international affairs. Inevitably they can only dabble in each.

In New York's ADA, some members are beginning to wonder whether this concern with candidates and all levels of political policy should not be modified. They suggest that maybe ADA, with its limited resources but varied intellectual and academic talent, should take a leaf from the mugwump research bureaus and concentrate more on analysis of close-to-home metropolitan problems.

Some such step, these New Yorkers argue, is necessary. ADA membership in many areas has been falling as the members seek a political outlet more direct than the passage of resolutions and more far-reaching than helping a nice guy get elected to the legislature.

The ADA's penchant for liberal candidates and liberal-sounding resolutions has made it a whipping boy in state and national elections. Conservative office seekers, as every newspaper reader knows, like to imply that ADA is some kind of radical underground, usually having a baleful hold over the office seeker's opponent.

If ADA is indeed a menace at the federal and state level, it is a declining one. Its effect at those levels is not our concern here, but it is interesting to note that in those few cities where ADA members have bent themselves to municipal politics, they have shown much in common with traditional mugwumpism. Their avowed opposition to the Chicago, New York and Philadelphia machines, their impatience with businessmen who accept the machines, are reminiscent of the pre–World War I mugwumps of the Progressive era.

Like the mugwumps of that generation and this, these ADA members come from the middle class, they are generally well educated, and they apply to big-city politics a yardstick of morality. They ask the same old uncompromising questions: is it right, or is it wrong? is it just, or is it unjust?

ADA as an organization may not survive, but the people who ask such questions will. And the questions themselves will be heard many times during the second revolution as the fight goes on for the redistribution of political power, and the use of governmental money and authority to rebuild America's cities.

NEGROES

It must seem ironic to many a mugwump, if he stops to think of it, that his grandfather or great-grandfather may well have been among those who campaigned tirelessly, even fanatically, to give Negroes their freedom and the vote at a time when Tammany Democrats were marching the streets shouting "Down with the Nagurs!"; yet a century later the Negro vote has become one of the most reliable weapons of the big-city Democratic machines, a weapon often turned against the mugwumps.

Just as nineteenth-century mugwumps made little effort toward political alliances with the early Irish and Italian immigrants, so twentieth-century mugwumps have made few gestures toward the cities' inflowing Negroes and Puerto Ricans.

Until recently there has been slight basis for working together. Like the early Irish and Italians, the Negro has felt no concern for the mugwump abstractions about "good government." He wants paternal government. He wants somebody on his side, to listen sympathetically to his needs for housing, jobs, welfare, leniency in court. The big-city Negro, in general, does not care two hoots about efficient government, impartial government. He wants friendly government.

To a degree, of course, every group in society wants a friendly government, but the Negro needs a friend more than most. And the mugwump, along with others, has been slow to extend his hand.

Like the European newcomers, the Negro has learned that

nobody is going to give him anything on a platter, except a few minor positions. For real political recognition, he must struggle.

This the big-city Negro is doing. Successfully.

The author visited more than twenty major cities in 1957 and returned to the same cities in 1960. The change in only three years was startling. Few basic movements in politics occur quickly, but the growing strength of Negroes in nearly every city, both North and South, was unmistakable.

Memphis mugwumps in the mid-fifties were avoiding an alliance with the Negroes, even though they made up 30 percent of the registered voters, because the mugwumps feared it would be political suicide. So in August, 1959, the Negroes for the first time entered a Negro slate in the city and school-board elections. The Negro candidates lost. A heavy turnout of white voters saw to that. But a young Harvard-educated Negro attorney, R. B. Sugarmon, Jr., finished second in a city-commissioner race, ahead of three white candidates, and it was clear from the returns that he had received a considerable number of white votes. The following year, in 1960, an anti-mugwump group of Shelby County politicians approached the Negro leaders and made a deal with them as equals—something unheard of in Memphis—and the coalition defeated the mugwumps for control of the county government. After this lesson, Memphis mugwumps decided to seek support among the city's Negroes.

In Houston, Negro influence is being felt more and more on election day. Despite the Texas $1.75 poll tax, Negroes now vote heavily. They combined with liberals in 1958 to elect the first Negro, housewife Hattie Mae White, to the conservative-dominated Houston school board.

In northern cities, Negroes show increasing strength by placing more members on city councils. During the late 1950s, Pittsburgh and Detroit elected their first Negro councilman, and Milwaukee chose a Negro councilwoman—Mrs. Vel R. Phillips, later Wisconsin's Democratic national committeewoman. Philadelphia elected two Negroes to its seventeen-member council. In cities that already had Negro councilmen, the number grew—to six each in St. Louis and Cleveland, and to five in Chicago. These cities also had the heaviest concentrations of Negro population in the North.

It appears that Negroes can seldom expect representation on a city council until they make up at least 15 to 20 percent of the population (Milwaukee is an exception). Even after they pass this point, their share of the council seats lags well behind their percentage of the population. In 1961, this was the situation in major northern cities:

	Size of City Council	Number Negroes	Percent Negroes	Percent of population Negro
St. Louis	29	6	21%	29%
Cleveland	33	6	18	29
Philadelphia	17	2	12	26
Detroit	9	1	11	29
Pittsburgh	9	1	11	17
Chicago	50	5	10	23
Milwaukee	20	1	5	8
New York	33 *	1	3	14

* Includes 25 councilmen plus eight members of board of estimate

The proportion of Negro population and therefore political power in these major cities moves steadily upward. This might not be the case if the cities had not become geographical mummies. Were cities natural organisms instead of political ones, their skins—that is, their boundaries—would expand to accommodate their growth. But this is impossible for several reasons. Many people who move outside the city do not want to be reabsorbed into it (except each day to make a living). Politicians who sprout in the satellite communities do not want to lose their big-frog status. And short-sighted legislatures write laws pandering to this provincialism. For these and allied reasons, most attempts at annexation fail, and city boundaries remain rigid. Within these artificial limits, the proportion of low-income workers, pensioners, Negroes and others who cannot afford suburban living (or, like the Negro, are barred from it) grows ever greater. So does their political importance.

This situation does not always make Negroes unhappy. Indeed, the big-city Negro in some places is developing a provincialism of his own. He does not want his city to grow. For instance, when a plan for a Cleveland-and-suburbs metropolitan government lost at the polls in 1959, nearly two-thirds of the within-Cleveland majority against it came from six heavily Negro wards. The accepted explanation was that the Negro political leaders feared their influence would be diluted if the city and the all-white suburbs joined in a "metro" government.

Mugwumps in St. Louis are finding Negroes difficult to sell on political reform. Votes from the Negro wards helped defeat a new city charter in 1957 and a metropolitan-government proposal in 1959.

Chicago mugwumps have been too weak to place any reforms on the ballot in recent years. But if they should, the opposition from the powerful South Side Negro bloc could be taken almost for granted. This organization has been built over the years by Congressman William L. Dawson, sometimes called the most influential Negro politician in the country. In 1955, the last time that mugwump forces, led by Councilman Robert E. Merriam, tried to fight the Democratic machine, they made Dawson chief target of their attack. It failed utterly.

In contrast, Cincinnati Negroes joined forces with the mugwumps. After voting with the old Republican regulars for decades, the Negroes switched in the depression years of the 1930s to the City Charter coalition of liberal Republican reformers and Democrats. Under the reformer-backed system of proportional-representation voting, the Negroes saw one of their number, attorney Theodore M. Berry, elected and re-elected to the city council. He was finally ousted in 1957 after the GOP regulars succeeded in removing P.R. voting from the city charter.

In Philadelphia, too, Negroes have felt kindly toward the Clark and Dilworth reform administrations, because they cleaned up the civil service system and enabled many Negroes to obtain city jobs. Several Negro churches have organized classes for would-be city employes, where they can study some five thousand questions they may be asked in civil service tests.

Cincinnati and Philadelphia, however, have been unusual. In most cities the Negro community has provided a bloc of opposition votes to mugwumps and mugwump programs. This distresses some good-government men. They have been trying to discover a way toward better relations, perhaps by having a Negro or two on their boards of trustees.

"But," complains a research bureau director in New York, "we can't find anybody to talk to. The Negroes and Puerto Ricans so far haven't developed any leaders we can deal with."

Possibly such minority leaders do not exist. Or possibly the mugwumps just have trouble recognizing and communicating with them. Certain so-called leaders among the minorities leave much to be desired. A few Negro ministers seem able to make much better sermons on political topics after a healthy contribution to the church. A few "leaders" from other professions have their own methods of accepting tokens of esteem. Yet these tokens, it should be remembered, are usually handed out eagerly by white politicians wanting to invest something in the Negro community, hoping for election-day results. Such shenanigans have always been present among politically emerging groups in this country and probably always will be. Eventually, however, a solid, responsible leadership arises as the group develops a strong middle class; this process is well under way among the big-city Negroes.

For the moment, the gap between the mugwump and the Negro seems a deep one. To bridge it will be a vital step in the second revolution. And the mugwump must make the overtures. He must demand that the huge slum-clearance programs of the future include better housing for the Negro, instead of leaving him a homeless victim. And the mugwump must make clear to the Negro that rapid transit, better schools, clean air, unpolluted water, better public recreation and more beautiful cities are for him, too. Indeed, the urban Negro should be among the first to benefit.

On this basis a political alliance seems eminently feasible. The immediate need is for someone to start stitching it together.

9

☞ □□□ ☜

The Old Pros' Last Stand

New York • Philadelphia • Chicago

Like a tough old tiger, the machine politician has grudgingly retreated before the gongs and bushbeating of good-government forces in American cities. He has finally holed up in three strongholds—New York, Philadelphia and Chicago.

Other cities, of course, still have some hack politicians around, but these relics are for the most part small operators. They work as isolated little clans. In New York, Philadelphia and Chicago, the hacks are organized into more or less disciplined machines, much as they were two or three generations ago. Now, as then, they seek patronage and hand it out, ask favors and grant them, fish for city contracts and award them, solicit cash contributions and get them, round up votes and deliver them.

The three big machines vary in strength. The Cook County Democratic organization dominates Chicago with hardly token opposition. Philadelphia's old regulars, bounced out by reformers in the early 1950s, have regrouped and counterattacked in hopes of bouncing the reformers in turn. In New York a scarred Tammany Hall finds itself beset by two groups of reformers—one on the outside trying to destroy it, one on the inside trying to capture it.

In Chicago, the machine dominant; in Philadelphia, the machine resurgent; in New York, the machine defendant. In all three, the machine surviving a while longer as the men of property put off the day of deciding, irrevocably, that it must go.

NEW YORK—THE SLOW AWAKENING

Tammany Hall, in the mythology of nineteenth-century American reformers, served as the symbol of political Hades, complete with Irish-Catholic Democratic devils tending their bubbling brews and hatching their wicked plots. The Tammany of today, with some Italian devils added to the scene, still fills the same murky role.

Early mugwump drives against this iniquitous crew, as we have already seen, brought mixed results—the crusading Reverend Mr. Parkhurst's exposures of sin and graft that defeated Tammany in 1895 and put businessman William L. Strong into the mayor's chair for one term; another two years of reform, 1901 to 1903, under the Citizens Union candidate, Seth Low; the quick triumphs of the first municipal research bureau before World War I; and the election of yet another single-term reform mayor, John Purroy Mitchel, in 1914.

Then came the long Tammany rule, with quipster Mayor Jimmy Walker providing a dapper front through the latter twenties. Like a good party gone on too long, Walker's romp ended in 1932 after the Republican-dominated legislature moved in with an investigating committee, retained former Appeals Judge Samuel Seabury as special counsel, and the Judge, with relentless dignity, drew from witnesses a story of bribes, influence, and large sums of money stashed away in tin boxes. Walker resigned under pressure from Governor Franklin D. Roosevelt.

The furor over the Seabury findings might have cost Tammany merely the usual one term of standing in the corner, had the sachems sensed the tide of the times. But Tammany committed the gross political blunder of sticking with its by now unhappy warrior, Al Smith, and opposing Roosevelt for president and Herbert Lehman for governor.

This gave the mugwumps and other anti-Tammany elements their chance for Fusion.

Among New York reformers, Fusion is the symbol for good, just as Tammany is the symbol for evil. It connotes hope, and light breaking through the darkness, and the hosts of righteousness marching against the legions of the damned. Fusion is what happens when everybody gets mad enough at Tammany to unite behind a reform ticket and boot the old tiger out of city hall.

Fusion came to pass in 1933. A coalition of mugwumps, Republicans, New Deal Democrats, assorted liberals, Socialists and labor formed behind Congressman Fiorello La Guardia, with the blessing of Judge Seabury, and installed him as mayor. The Fusionists also won control of the board of estimate, the city's major legislative body. Moving to secure themselves against a Tammany comeback, the Fusionists promoted a new city charter providing for a city council chosen by proportional representation elections.

The Little Flower and his reform regime lasted twelve years. Then, in 1945, as the reform coalition splintered, Tammany rolled back in with William O'Dwyer as mayor. Four years later a patched-together group of Fusionists, Republicans and Liberal party members again entered one of the 1945 losers, Republican Newbold Morris, but O'Dwyer squeezed through with a small plurality over Morris and the American Labor Party candidate, Vito Marcantonio.

Things soon got even more confused. With police and gambling scandals piling up, O'Dwyer resigned (President Truman named him ambassador to Mexico), city council president Vincent Impellitteri took over as acting mayor until the November election, at which time he beat both the mugwump and the Tammany candidates—beat them running as head of the Experience party, an entity that the *New Yorker* magazine described as "without any previous existence, let alone experience."

The few years of experience the Impellitteri regime thereafter did acquire failed to impress anyone, and the way was open for Tammany's new leader, Carmine De Sapio, to step forward with the mayoral entry he had been carefully grooming—Robert F. Wagner, Jr., Manhattan borough president and son of the New Deal senator.

Against Wagner, the conservatives backed Republican Harold Riegelman, temperance worker and counsel of the Citizens Budget Commission; the Liberal party supported independent city-council president Rudolph Halley, still basking in stardom from his days as counsel for the Kefauver crime hearings a couple of years before. Wagner received almost as many votes as both of them combined.

Wagner, the man of Tammany, surprised the mugwumps. On his first day in office in 1953, he named a veteran reform activist, Dr. Luther Gulick, to the new post of city administrator. The job, like comparable ones in Los Angeles, New Orleans and elsewhere, carried little direct administrative authority over city departments, but it did offer a chance to exert advisory influence over the mayor and the board of estimate.

The mayor also made it a point to consult with eminent mugwumps and men of property, even though he did not always follow their advice. He appointed some leading figures to committees, such as telephone company president Keith McHugh, whose Citizens Committee to Keep New York City Clean waged a reasonably successful war against the big town's notoriously littered streets.

Wagner made more friends among mugwumps by his espousal of a favorite mugwump gimmick, metropolitan area government, and by his cautious, discriminating appointments to top administrative positions. Respected attorney Francis W. H. Adams was named police commissioner, and he started housecleaning the graft-ridden department. Adams was succeeded by roughhewn but honest career-cop Stephen R. Kennedy, whose blunt ways finally led to his replacement in 1961 by another clean-record officer, Chief Inspector Michael J. Murphy.

After scandals hit the city bureau of real estate and the city's slum-clearance program, Wagner brought in well-known mugwump J. Clarence Davies, Jr. (former Citizens Union treasurer, former president of the Citizens Planning and Housing Council), to sanitize both operations. And La Guardia's one-time deputy mayor, William Reid, became chairman of the reorganized City Housing Authority.

The mayor sought technical advice from mugwump organizations and their staffs on writing a stricter city code for multiple dwellings. Wagner also formed the habit of asking Citizens Union secretary George Hallett to drop by Gracie Mansion for breakfast on Thursday mornings and then ride downtown for a back-seat discussion of city problems.

Under Wagner, the list of temporary or provisional civil service jobs—the reservoir for patronage among the clubhouse boys—was cut to some 12,000 (out of more than 200,000 municipal employes). This was the lowest point in decades.

Shortly before Wagner took office, *Life* magazine lamented: "What New York has been suffering from for the past half-dozen years is government by slob!"

By the 1960s, mugwumps generally agreed that, under Wagner, the process of downgrading the slobs had begun. The fact made them feel more kindly toward the mayor. But it did not impel them to call off their war against Wagner's early sponsor, Tammany Hall. That conflict continues as bitter as ever.

Ranged against Tammany is a heterogeneous assortment of good-government forces that could happen only in New York.

First are the traditional mugwumps, the intellectual and in some cases blood descendants of the upper-middle-class reformers who created the old City Reform Club (1882), the City Club (1892), the Citizens Union (1897) and the first municipal research bureau (1906). Today this group centers in the Citizens Union, flanked by the League of Women Voters, the Women's City Club and, less important, the Men's City Club.

The signal-caller for this group, the Citizens Union, relies largely on the time-tested techniques of municipal research agencies—observing actions of the city administration, offering criticism, proposing new procedures, urging changes needed in the city charter or in state law to make the new procedures possible.

Frequently allied with the Citizens Union entourage are a large number of organizations one might lump together as the ideological liberals. They are more or less willing to let the Citizens Union keep day-to-day watch on city administrative matters. They worry little about procedures or efficiency. What they do care about is attitudes on social issues—the attitudes of government, officeholders and candidates.

Largest of these groups is the Liberal party, chiefly supported by David Dubinsky's big International Lady Garment Workers Union (ILGWU) and Alex Rose's milliners union.

The leaders of the merged AFL-CIO council also participate by expressing objections or approval to city hall; their influence, however, over their one and a half million rank and file members is undeveloped compared with the ILGWU.

This ideological wing includes several anti-discrimination organizations—the American Jewish Congress, the American Jewish Committee, the Anti-Defamation League of B'Nai B'Rith, American Civil Liberties Union, National Association for the Advancement of Colored People, Urban League, and the State Committee on Discrimination in Housing.

Another ideological group, Americans for Democratic Action, concentrates on the discrimination issue and on helping anti-Tammany candidates in campaigns.

A third category of allies is the promoter groups such as the Public Education Association, United Parents Associations, Citizens Committee for Children, Community Service Society, Regional Plan Association, Citizens Housing and Planning Council, and the United Neighborhood Houses representing some forty settlement houses. These organizations have staked out special areas of interest—schools, health, slum clearance, relief work, area planning—and they try to make sure that city and state officials give these matters adequate attention and money.

Other large cities possess organizations roughly comparable to these. In New York, however, they have attained a high degree of political intercommunication. From their varied emotional-intellectual heritages—Marxian Socialism of mid-nineteenth-century Europe, middle-class Progressivism, hatred of racial discrimination, Protestant righteousness, New Dealism—these New Yorkers have arrived at a common philosophical ground. They believe that government should act as an instrument for rendering justice and service, even kindness, to the general run of citizens.

So agreed, these groups have developed confidence in each other. They have become an informal "egghead" bloc. When one member formulates a program, the others tend to swing support behind it. The result is a joint list of objectives that all keep advocating at every opportunity.

In 1961, for instance, the Citizens Union was urging such varied proposals as adoption of a municipal "performance" budget, long-range fiscal planning for the city, an expanded city welfare staff to provide family counselors for the needy, more day-care centers for children of working mothers, a bigger city planning budget, and re-adoption of the P.R. voting system abandoned in 1947. Other members of the egghead bloc endorsed the same proposals.

The bloc's envoy within the city council for many years has been its lone Republican member, elderly attorney Stanley Isaacs, who introduces most of the bloc's measures. Isaacs says of his role: "I regard myself as more a representative of these social service and civic groups than I do as a representative of the Republican Party."

New York, of course, contains good-government elements outside the egghead bloc. The Citizens Budget Commission takes the lead in speaking for the business and conservative element. Heeled with a $150,000 yearly budget and a ten-member staff, the Budget Commission frequently aligns itself with the Chamber of Commerce, the Commerce and Industry Association, and the real estate board in opposing municipal spending. This earns the Budget Commission little love from some members of the egghead bloc. Said one: "The commission always wants to reduce the number of city employes. They're always urging the mayor to set up a unit-cost system showing how much it costs to clean each square yard of street and how long it takes a secretary to type a letter and a public health doctor to examine a child."

Observed a labor official: "They're competent, but they represent big business. We place little credence in their recommendations. They believe in meat-ax economy."

The Budget Commission, however, often finds itself on the same side of the fence as the Citizens Union, the League of Women Voters, the Women's City Club and similar organizations. All support the idea of performance budgets, fiscal planning, a city career and salary plan, changing the state constitution to give New York City greater home rule, and decentralizing the city administration.

The idea of decentralization would have sounded strange to New York mugwumps of a generation or two ago, who strove for ever more centralization and ever tighter controls. Today's reformers propose to free city department heads from close supervision by the mayor, the comptroller and the budget director, and to give them lump-sum budgets so that they can run their departments as semi-independent city managers. The reformers also advocate a system of "little city halls" for branch operations of the police, health, fire, welfare, and complaint-and-inquiry departments, as well as the city schools.

The same groups lobby to permit city department heads to hire employes without having to obtain approval of the city budget director (yet it was these same groups that originally campaigned to have the budget director given this authority, so that department heads could not secretly juggle jobs on their staffs).

In the early 1950s, the mugwumps worked hard for the creation of the post of city administrator. When it developed in practice that the administrator was little more than a research man for the mayor, the mugwumps began to demand that his power be increased by giving him control of the budget and the personnel system.

Among the ideological liberals mentioned a moment ago, one should include another group, the reform Democrats. This movement, which started to gain significant strength in the late 1950s, contains two elements: would-be Democratic political leaders who find themselves excluded by the present Tammany bosses; and a mugwump element who believe the way to good government in New York lies through gaining control of the Democratic organization (just as a half-century ago Charles Evans Hughes, Elihu Root, Henry Stimson and others believed a cleaned-up Republican party could be used as an instrument of reform).[1]

Although the first reform group, the Lexington Democratic Club, appeared in 1949 and others emerged from Stevenson-for-president committees in 1952 and 1956, the insurgents did not really gain momentum until after the uproarious 1958 Democratic state convention at Buffalo. There Tammany leader De Sapio, controlling the majority of delegates, crammed his choice for the U. S. senate nomination—District Attorney Frank S. Hogan —down the throats of the liberal wing, who favored former Air Force Secretary Thomas K. Finletter, one-time head of the pro-Stevenson forces in New York.

After Hogan lost in November to Republican Kenneth Keating, the liberals grimly set out to unseat De Sapio. Led by former Senator and Governor Lehman, Mrs. Franklin D. Roosevelt and Finletter, they formed the New York Committee for Democratic Voters and raised enough money for a full-time office and staff.

By 1961 the insurgents had formed thirty clubs in state assembly districts, mostly in Manhattan, and had dug seriously into Tammany's strength on the island. The elected state assembly district leader is the unit of political strength in New York, and the insurgents had wrested one-fourth of these positions from Tammany in Manhattan.[2]

Some New Yorkers thought the insurgents had a good chance to win more district elections. The insurgents themselves predicted that they soon would gain control of half the leaderships, and De Sapio's reign would end.

Others said that even were the insurgents to dethrone De Sapio, they would merely take over his functions, and the new Tammany would quickly become indistinguishable from the old.

While the intellectual liberals take their active part in New York's struggle for good government, there is another sector of the reform ranks that has a yawning gap. That is the place where the city's businessmen and property owners should be standing. Like the traditional man of property in most cities decades ago, New York's man of property today just cannot be bothered.

In some cases this is understandable. The man of property has a comfortable, if slightly corrupt, understanding with the inspectors or other city officials who regulate his business activities. Or perhaps the man of property does not even live in New York; he may live in London, Athens, Mexico City, Hong Kong or Houston. And he does not own anything in New York; he just owns a part of something. He belongs to a syndicate that has pooled funds to buy or construct a Manhattan commercial building or hotel; his main interest is in selling his share (as a capital gain, of course) for a quick profit. The days when big property holders were members of prominent families with roots in the city have gone. Of the eminent names, few besides the Rockefellers remain.

In other cases, the man of property discharges his civic obligation by endorsing United States policy on Pakistan or sending a check to the Committee for Economic Development. It befits his station to show some concern about such cosmic affairs, but not to grub around with problems of local government.

Businessmen and conservatives have been content to let the Republican party and a few organizations like the Citizens Budget

Commission, the Commerce and Industry Association and the Chamber of Commerce take care of their municipal interests.

The Republican party has been a poor shattered thing, rent by liberal and conservative factions blaming each other for continuous defeat. The party unwittingly cut off its own nose in 1947 when it joined the Tammany-led movement to repeal P.R. voting. Before P.R. was adopted in the mid-thirties, Tammany regularly won around 90 percent of the seats on the city council, or board of aldermen, as it was then called. But under P.R., the Democrats got seats in relation to their share of the vote, ranging from 50 to 67 percent. The Republicans and other minority parties divided up the remaining 33 to 50 percent of the council positions.

In 1945, however, when the Russians and Americans were wartime buddies, the Communist party entered a council slate, received 9 percent of the vote and elected two men (9 percent) to the council. When Russo–United States buddiness gave way to the cold war in 1946, Tammany seized upon the presence of two Communists in the city council as proof that P.R. was unsavory, un-American and unworkable. Most Republicans and the press went along. P.R. was repealed the following year, and since then the Republicans have reverted to their former insignificance on the council—one or two members among the twenty-five. On the more powerful board of estimate, they now have no representation. All eight members are Democrats, and have been for many years.

New York's business community, then, has developed no effective means of intervening in city affairs. It has not chosen to use the Republican party, the Citizens Budget Commission or the Commerce and Industry Association except in a desultory fashion.

The leading citizens had a chance to establish a civic instrument in the mid-fifties when Wagner appointed the Mayor's Advisory Council, with 130 gilt-edged names like Straus, Gimbel, Rockefeller, Finletter, Odlum, Lasker, Lilienthal and others. The council started off with a rush of publicity, then lapsed into oblivion.

There have been other flickerings of life, such as McHugh's Citizens Committee to Keep New York City Clean. Again, certain businessmen lobbied among Republican legislators at Albany to help the Wagner administration obtain passage of a bill making permanent the city's 3 percent sales tax, along with another measure increasing the city's limit on real property taxes to 2½ percent. Wealthy Robert W. Dowling, president of the Citizens Budget Commission, headed a committee that urged the legislature to approve one of Mayor Wagner's favorite money-raising ideas—legalized off-track horsebetting with a city agency handling the wagers.

These stirrings may indicate that some day New York's financial and industrial figures will decide they should get around to organizing themselves into a responsible part of the city's politics and government, rather than leaving the job to Tammany and its critics. At the moment, however, their condition can only be described as dormant. The awakening promises to be a slow one.

PHILADELPHIA—THE RETURN OF THE HACKS

It was perhaps too much to expect Philadelphia to change its character overnight.

Since the gaslight era it had been governed, or misgoverned, by a Republican machine whose reputation for corruption stood second to none. The reek from city hall never bothered the city's business leaders seriously until after World War II. Then, with the arrival of suburbs and suburban shopping centers, and with the new cities of the West and South casting their fresh allure as sites for industry, the leading citizens suddenly saw that staid old Philadelphia was getting older, retail business was dropping, and downtown property falling in value. A feeling of panic began to grow among men whose real estate and professional fortunes were tied to downtown Philadelphia.

The old Republican machine seemed unaware of its danger. It continued operations as usual, which meant controlling the elections, giving jobs to the boys, making a bit on the side, and doing as little as possible about the foul water supply, the sinking property values and the city's widespread reputation for bad government.

About this time well-to-do attorney Richardson Dilworth took it into his head to run for mayor. He had dabbled in politics years before as a Democratic committeeman and as a candidate for the state senate, but dabbling was about all a Democrat could do in Philadelphia in those days. When Dilworth, a youthful-looking forty-eight, returned from war service with the Marines, he found he was not the only one who had come back feeling somebody should clean up the old home town.

Aided by a pick-up organization of liberals and mugwumps led by fellow socialite Joseph Clark, Dilworth campaigned in 1947, charging the old pros with assorted graft. He named names, times, places and amounts of money. Dilworth lost, but he upset many of the good citizens and ate into the usual Republican majority.

Oddly enough, it was the victor, Mayor Bernard Samuel, who set off the downfall of the machine. He was being plagued by city employes for pay raises. Since raises would mean higher taxes, the mayor fell back on a customary device for blunting public disapproval; he named a committee of fifteen leading citizens to study the problem and recommend what should be done.

The fifteen, nearly all Republicans, did not behave according to the book. Instead of handing in a bland report regretfully conceding that the employes deserved more pay and property taxes would have to go up, the committee retained the Philadelphia Bureau of Municipal Research director, Robert K. Sawyer, to study whether the city could not raise pay with money it was now wasting. The thirty-eight-year-old Sawyer and his aides began moving through the musty city hall like a scourge. They went from department to department, scrutinizing records, uncovering evidence of larceny and graft.

The public shock began when quiet-spoken William Foss, head of the city amusement tax office, hanged himself, leaving a note identifying six fellow workers who had helped him embezzle $200,000. Soon after, the city water superintendent was found dead behind the shrubs in Fairmount Park, his wrists slashed. The chief of the police vice squad parked beside a country road and put a bullet through his head. A city plumbing inspector killed himself leaping from a bridge over Wissahickon Creek. The city purchasing director was indicted on more than forty charges and convicted.

In the meantime, Philadelphia's top business figures had begun to stir things up in less violent fashion. Egged on by the silk-stocking Citizens Council on Planning, the businessmen raised $400,000 and staged a "city exhibition" in 1947 covering a full floor in Gimbel's department store. The chief attraction was a $100,000 scale model showing the city planners' dreams of how downtown Philadelphia could look if dozens of decrepit structures were razed and replaced with broad plazas and gleaming office towers. Some of the dreams were later to come true in the Penn Center development.

A delegation of business leaders made the pilgrimage to Pittsburgh to learn the secret of its renaissance; they came home determined to create their own version of the Allegheny Conference. They first thought to establish a tight group of nine eminent men who would raise several hundred thousand dollars and start the Philadelphia face-lift. The "nine big men" plan was ditched, however, after acrimonious debate, in favor of a twenty-five-man group that would include a labor official, a Negro and a Democrat or two. Thus, on December 16, 1948, the Greater Philadelphia Movement began.

Its policy statement declared GPM's interest in "good health and better living conditions, in the growth of business, industry and employment, and in all legislation which affects the future of the area—whether it is local, state or national. . . . As a bipartisan group, it will take a keen interest in the form of local government . . . It will insist on good government . . . characterized by competence, honesty and a high degree of performance." The statement closed with a clear slap at the Chamber of Commerce: "The Greater Philadelphia Movement will work to organize the civic-minded leadership that the metropolitan area has long needed."

GPM was as good as its word regarding legislation. Those of its members who were big Republican campaign contributors sent word to GOP legislators at Harrisburg in 1949 to support the "Philadelphia package." This group of bills, drawn largely by the mugwump bureau men, included measures permitting Philadelphia to write a new home-rule charter, permitting consolidation of Philadelphia city and county, and relaxing the city's debt limit. The package passed.

A strong reform coalition by this time was taking shape. It included the prominent Republican businessmen of GPM and the Bureau of Municipal Research, liberal Democrats like Clark and Dilworth who were building a vigorous chapter of Americans for Democratic Action (ADA), and AFL-CIO elements who had never received much help from the old Republican machine.

Opposing the coalition was the Republican machine consisting of a large fraction of the city's 24,000 employes and a handful of kept Democratic politicians who had cooperated with the GOP professionals for years.

Since there was no mayoralty race in 1949, Dilworth and Clark kept up the reform pressure by filing for city comptroller and city treasurer, respectively. Both won by 100,000-vote margins. The most startling event of the campaign took place twelve days before the election. The staunchly Republican Philadelphia *Inquirer* came out for the Democratic slate. Less than a week later the Philadelphia *Bulletin*, which had supported only one Democratic ticket in its one hundred and three years, followed suit.

The next year Dilworth ran as the Democratic nominee for governor; he lost in the state but carried Philadelphia by eighty thousand. That night he announced, over protests from the regular Democrats, that he intended to support Joe Clark for mayor in 1951, and he would run for district attorney.

A group of anti-machine Republicans tried to prevent Clark and Dilworth from dominating the reform movement. They entered manufacturer Walter Miller, a former chairman of the venerable Committee of Seventy, as candidate for mayor in 1951. The Republican machine, however, put up the noted Baptist minister and editor, the Reverend Daniel A. Poling, and he defeated Miller in the GOP primary by 130,000 votes. The machine regulars did not have long to enjoy their victory. The November finals proved a Democratic landslide. Clark was named mayor, the first Democratic one since 1887; Dilworth became district attorney; and Democrats captured fourteen of the seventeen seats on the council, plus every other city-wide office.

Mayor Clark, taking office in January, 1952, chose nearly a score of his ADA colleagues for key spots in his administration, while pointedly ignoring the regular Democrats. For two of the most important posts Clark turned to mugwump organizations.

His managing director (a kind of city manager created by the 1951 city charter) was Robert Sawyer, the young Republican who had left the Bureau of Municipal Research to head the Committee of Fifteen, and afterward had become first director of the Greater Philadelphia Movement. For city finance director, the mayor appointed Lennox Moak, who had been director of the New Orleans Bureau of Governmental Research before replacing Sawyer at the Philadelphia bureau in 1949. Clark also selected nonpolitical career men to manage the street, water and police departments, appointed well-fixed Philadelphians as fire and recreation commissioners, imported a thirty-four-year-old health commissioner from Denver and a thirty-seven-year-old personnel director from Sacramento.

These appointments understandably infuriated the regular Democrats. As if this were not enough, the mayor ordered strict adherence to the civil service provisions of the new city charter. It had been an old Philadelphia tradition that nobody passed a civil service examination unless he had an endorsement from his Republican ward leader. It seemed to the Democratic regulars most unfortunate to upset this tradition just when they had returned to power for the first time in sixty-seven years.

It soon became clear that while the Clark-Dilworth reform Democrats might control the executive departments, the old pro Democrats controlled the city council. Their council majority began pushing more than a score of charter amendments to remove this category and that category of city positions from civil service. They also attempted to prohibit hiring anyone who had not been a long-time resident of Philadelphia.

The mugwumps and men of property in GPM and the research bureau (who had largely financed and engineered the new charter through its successive stages—getting the permissive bill through the 1949 legislature, persuading Mayor Samuel to select an able charter-writing commission instead of a roomful of hacks, and finally fueling the campaign that obtained voter approval of the charter in a 1951 special election) joined with the Clark-Dilworth battalions in repelling the old regulars' attack on the charter in 1954.

By this time it was becoming difficult to tell who were Republicans and who were Democrats among the regulars. Many who had made their living as Republican ward leaders and committeemen were turning in their GOP suits and becoming Democrats. Apparently, like professionals in any line, they could play as well for one team as the other. Election returns began to show that many a committeeman was swinging approximately the same number of votes to the Democrats as in former days he had swung to the Republicans. These converts, needless to say, were fully as hostile to the reform administration as the Democratic regulars.

Today, Philadelphia's reform coalition includes mugwumps, men of property, independent Republicans, independent Democrats, labor, some Negroes, and the major newspapers. Lines of communication among this unusual set of allies are good. Staff men move from jobs with the research bureau to GPM to the city administration. All coalition members seek similar goals—to rebuild the downtown district, solve the transportation tangle, obtain more industry and more industrial sites, get rid of Philadelphia's archaic system of having the common-pleas court judges appoint the school board, the park commission and the tax assessment board (generally from names suggested by the local Republican and Democratic organizations). Above all, the reform coalition wants to prevent the old regulars from regaining their grip on city hall.

Whether they will succeed is uncertain. Since the mid-fifties, the regular Democrats have built an effective organization headed by Congressman William J. Green, Jr., and wealthy trucker James P. Clark. Green is chairman of the Democratic city committee, Clark the strong behind-the-scenes manager who handles the funds.

Their sources of strength are three: control of the city council, control since 1955 of the state's non-civil service patronage in Philadelphia (Green says this runs to seven hundred jobs, others say the figure is closer to seven thousand), and control of the election machinery.

This voting machinery has long been under attack as susceptible to manipulation. The city is divided into 1,600 districts or precincts, each with an elected board of three election judges. Customarily the judges' names are entered on the primary ballot by each party's district committeeman, and the names tend to be those of a committeeman's relative, or a friend who will appreciate the judge's stipend of twenty-five dollars, or perhaps a fictitious person who does not exist at all except on election day when he materializes to oversee the voting.

A federal grand jury sitting in 1956 estimated that some 100,000 fraudulent ballots are cast in Philadelphia at each election, a heavy proportion of them in the so-called "controlled" wards covering a strip forty-eight blocks wide running from river to river in the central part of the city. The most common offense was said to be permitting a loyal party member to go into the booth with the voter to help him mark his ballot. Other methods were described in the University of Pennsylvania *Law Review:*

> The voter is often expected to permit another to do the actual voting for him after he signs the voter's certificate. This, of course, requires the connivance of the district election board. So also does the practice of removing voter certificates from the district register and taking them to the residences of voters in order to obtain their signatures so that votes may subsequently be cast on their behalf. In the controlled wards the nicety of obtaining the proper signature is sometimes ignored, and people who no longer live in the district, or who are dead or in prison on election day, are voted.
>
> In sections of the city where outright bribery is deemed improper, "workers" are hired. . . . Since there is no legal maximum to the number of workers a party can hire, the employment of a large number of people from large families can accomplish the same results as bribery.[3]

The Committee of Seventy has been trying since 1904 to police this sprawling election system. After each election it hands over evidence of fraud to the district attorney, and sometimes institutes civil suits. But with a crew of only fifty or so lawyers and law students to watch the 1,600 polling places on election day, the committee has little more chance than a dog trying to watch a hundred gopher holes.

Philadelphia mugwumps realize they must act if they are to prevent the city's government from sliding back into the control of a political machine—a Democratic one this time.

One proposal is to modernize the election machinery, eliminating the local elected judges and appointing balloting supervisors from a central elections office.

A second proposal is to amputate the Democratic machine's patronage strength by bringing state jobs under civil service.

To regain control of the city council, some mugwumps talk of organizing a reform political party, like Cincinnati's Charter Committee or Kansas City's Citizens Association. The reform party would enter a slate of candidates for the council and other municipal offices, hoping to defeat the machine's incumbents.

This proposal to broaden the base of the reform movement comes late, although perhaps not too late. In Pittsburgh, Mayor Lawrence headed a strong top-to-bottom Democratic organization which he allied with the big businessmen of the Allegheny Conference. In New Orleans, reform Mayor Chep Morrison captured the political organization of the old regulars. But in Philadelphia, Clark and Dilworth, entering politics in middle life as relative amateurs, built almost no ward-level organization after coming to power. This left a vacuum that the old regulars wasted no time in occupying.

As Philadelphia moves into the 1960s, the reformers still hold the city government's administrative offices. They have kept the civil service system free of the patronage-hungry regulars. The able administrators installed by Clark and Dilworth remain at their posts (and some not so able have been removed in the wake of 1961 scandals involving transit repair contracts). But the city charter forbids a mayor more than two successive terms. Dilworth thus became ineligible to run for reelection after finishing his second term in January, 1964.

The reformers have had to cast around for a new general to lead their troops. And, tardily, they realize he needs more troops to lead.

CHICAGO—AUGEAS WITH NO HERCULES

It is not that Chicago mugwumps never tried to clean up the place. They did try. And for some twenty years before World War

I, they succeeded rather well. But then the city got away from them; it grew too big and boisterous and liquored up, and the reformers found nobody was listening to them any more. Just sometimes, after an unusually loud blast of bomb or gunfire or scandal, the voice of the mugwumps could be heard in the shocked silence. But they had to talk fast while the city was yet stunned. This period never lasted long. Chicago always had great powers of recuperation.

The mugwumps were stimulated to action early. They were shaken by the riots in Haymarket Square in 1886. And they were more aroused a few years later by Britisher William Stead's book, *If Christ Came to Chicago*. An eminent group headed by Marshall Field, Mrs. Potter Palmer, Jane Addams and Cyrus McCormick, Jr., called a meeting of their peers in 1894 and voted to establish "a Federation of all good citizens in a vigorous movement for relief of the poor, industrial conciliation, to battle against the vicious elements of society and slum conditions, and for improvement in the quality of local government." The resulting Civic Federation did not spend much time on relief of the poor and industrial conciliation, but it endured to become one of the nation's large municipal research bureaus.

Two years after starting their Civic Federation, the mugwumps established a Municipal Voters League. Its job was to remove the city council from under the thumb of street railway magnate Charles T. Yerkes and other favor-seeking businessmen. This the Voters League accomplished with admirable simplicity. Consisting only of a committee of nine and a director, the league possessed two weapons—publicity, and a host of citizens who accepted its word about candidates. Brandishing these twin clubs, the league forced some crooked aldermen to retire upon threat of exposure; from others it extracted promises of good behavior. In this way the Voters League maintained influence over a majority of the seventy aldermen for almost two decades.

Another source of strength lay in a coterie of respectable citizens, mostly young men, who were willing to run for the city council. Their leader was Professor Charles E. Merriam, University of Chicago political scientist, who was only thirty-four when he first took his seat on the council in 1911.

Among this group for a brief time was a large, athletic fellow who had made some money in Wyoming cattle and inherited a great deal more from his father. William Hale "Big Bill" Thompson served one term on the council at the urging of reform Councilman William Kent, a founder of the Voters League.

When Big Bill reappeared on the political scene some years later in 1915, it was to run for mayor. He had matured into a sombrero-wearing rootin' tootin' campaigner who could outdo Merriam and the other Progressives at blasting the Privilege-seeking Interests and the Forces of Predatory Wealth. He took on the traction company, the gas company and every utility in sight. Later he added the League of Nations and King George V to his list of menaces. Behind Thompson was a clique of clever, hungry politicians led by Fred "the Fox" Lundin.

The election victory of Big Bill and Lundin in 1915 marked the end of a mugwump era. Moving like wolves among sheep, the newcomers seized control of the city civil service system, turning it into a patronage machine. Next came the school board and the city council. Aided by the Hearst press, Thompson forced Merriam and other mugwumps into retirement. Within five years fifty faces had disappeared among the seventy aldermen.

Big Bill in his first two terms (1915–23) got Chicago well started down the road to probably the worst government it will ever know. Mugwumps frothed at the very mention of his name, just as they did at that of Boston's James Curley. They felt brief jubilation in 1923 when Judge William Dever took office as a reform mayor (Big Bill, momentarily embarrassed by scandals, had discreetly decided not to run), but Dever proved unable to cope with Chicago, and Thompson returned to beat him easily for re-election in 1927.

Big Bill's machine, however, was about to blow itself to smithereens. The unintended suicide took place at the April, 1928, Republican primary.

The mugwumps, never knowing when they were licked, had put up a good-government slate. Their campaign leader was veteran reformer Charles S. Deneen, and the most important position at stake was Deneen's old job, that of state's attorney (prosecuting attorney) of Cook County. For eight years it had been in the hands of Robert E. Crowe. The mugwumps hoped to defeat Crowe for renomination with Circuit Judge John A. Swanson.

Their chances appeared remote as usual. The opposition included Crowe, Mayor Thompson and Governor Leonard Small (whose trial for mishandling state funds a few years before had broken down in a confusion of technicalities, missing evidence and vanishing witnesses). The powerful Small-Thompson-Crowe combination apparently had the primary in the bag. Then two weeks before the election, a good-government campaign worker was found on the West Side with fifty-eight slugs in his back. Five days later the homes of Senator Deneen and Judge Swanson were bombed. Both men escaped. Threats of more bombings were received, causing the reformers to cancel several meetings.

The better people of Chicago had been able to accept gang killings, averaging better than one a week, philosophically. But when the boys moved into election campaigns with their pineapples and gats, that was too much. Businessmen raised a fund to hire hundreds of men deputies to watch the polls on April 10 in the tough river wards and on the South Side. Hundreds of mugwumps volunteered to police the less dangerous polling places. On election day a good-government precinct captain was murdered, but the vote count that night revealed an almost total sweep for the good-government ticket. In the big race for state's attorney, Swanson defeated Crowe by 190,000 votes.

The next year, 1929, was a bad one, too, for Mayor Thompson and his Republican organization. The machine-gun massacre of seven men lined against a garage wall on St. Valentine's Day threw the public into a civic rage. One or two mobsters quietly dumped into a ditch at night wasn't so bad. But this! And at ten-thirty in the morning!

The hubbub over the massacre probably would have faded before the next city election two years away, but a second blow—the stock market crash and depression—insured that neither Big Bill nor any other Republican had a chance in the 1931 race. Merriam and the mugwumps had the pleasure of helping administer the coup de grâce to Big Bill. They supported his winning Democratic opponent, Anton Cermak.

The mugwumps liked Cermak not only because he was not Big

Bill but because, as chairman of the Cook County Board of Commissioners, he had shown some interest in better government. He had even sent a message to the National Municipal League convention in 1929 approving the county-manager plan. It is interesting to speculate what course Chicago local politics might have taken if Cermak had not gone to Miami in February, 1933, and received an assassin's bullet as he rode beside President-elect Roosevelt.

But Cermak's death left the newly powerful Democratic machine in the hands of Pat Nash and Edward J. Kelly. Nash, the Democratic county chairman succeeding Cermak, was getting along in years and soon was to withdraw from the scene. Kelly, chief engineer of the metropolitan sanitary district, had a powerful friend in the *Tribune's* Colonel Robert McCormick, who was president of the sanitary district board that had named Kelly its chief engineer. Observers thought they saw the Colonel's hand as Nash and the city council selected Kelly as successor to the dead mayor.

The mugwumps found Kelly during his thirteen-year reign an even tougher opponent than Thompson. Big Bill had been a flamboyant demagogue but an erratic politician. Kelly was less dramatic but he was a political craftsman. Under him the Democratic organization in the wards reached a high degree of effectiveness. The mugwumps cut into this effectiveness somewhat in 1940 by mobilizing an army of eight thousand men and women to serve as poll watchers and to work with the board of election commissioners in detecting fraud. They uncovered 181,000 faked registrations which, by coincidence, was almost exactly the margin by which Kelly had beaten the mugwump candidate for mayor the previous year. (The mugwump candidate had been a personable young anti-New Dealer, Dwight Green, who as assistant United States attorney had helped send Al Capone to Alcatraz for income tax evasion. Green later was to win election to the governor's office, where, in accord with the Chicago mugwumps' customary bad luck in their choice of candidates, his administration rolled up a highly undistinguished record.)

The mugwumps never did beat Kelly. They outlasted him. By 1946, the old boss had lost his touch, the school system was again in a mess, and the smell of reform (to say nothing of a nation-wide Republican sweep) wafted through the postwar air. Attorney Jacob Arvey, the Democrats' new county chairman, persuaded Kelly to step aside so that Arvey could run respectable trucker-warehouseman Martin Kennelly for mayor in 1947.[4] In the same election, fifteen liberal Republicans and four "egghead" Democrats gained seats on the city council; there they soon formed a so-called economy bloc.

Although the bloc held less than twenty of the fifty seats, mugwumps hoped a new era was in sight. With the newspapers on their side, a reform-minded mayor controlling the administration and a strong, vocal minority in the council, the good citizens glimpsed a chance to overthrow the ward-based Democratic organization. The hope flowered as Kennelly and his appointees cleaned up the civil service system, filled holes in the streets, got the garbage collected, and brought in a nonpolitical superintendent to raise the low reputation of Chicago's school system.

But Kennelly the conscientious administrator was also Kennelly the amateur politician. He created no personal organization. He angered the regular Democrats in many ways—notably by reducing the "temporary appointment" list of civil service workers, a handy haven for party hacks, from 18,000 jobs to 3,000. He ignored the wishes of Congressman William Dawson, who controlled the all-important South Side Negro vote. He broke with his natural allies, the economy bloc in the council. He dismayed potential supporters by his lack of decisiveness. *Commonweal* magazine described him as "a tall, white-thatched, vacillating bachelor of sixty-seven, who has done good things in developing a civil service system for the city, in making honest and efficient the city's purchasing department, but who has not won wide popular support."

The machine Democrats reluctantly marched out in 1951 and re-elected Kennelly. Soon, however, they redeployed behind their county chairman, County Clerk Richard Daley, and when the 1955 mayoralty arrived, Daley knocked out Kennelly for the Democratic nomination by 103,000 votes. That took care of one mugwump opponent. Daley still had to dispose of another in the April finals—Councilman Robert E. Merriam, son of the professor.

Young Merriam, aspiring to become Chicago's La Guardia,

filed on the Republican ticket (he had been a Democrat) and organized a fusion of mugwumps, ADA-ers, intellectual liberals, clubwomen, orthodox and liberal Republicans. Aided by the press, he continued Kennelly's campaign of Good versus Evil with Congressman Dawson cast as chief devil. But Chicago was not New York, and Merriam was not La Guardia. As his father had twice before him, young Merriam lost his bid for the mayor's chair. The vote was 708,000 to 582,000; and nearly half of Daley's edge came from Dawson's five South Side wards.

When Daley took office, mugwumps groaned and settled down for another siege of mediocre government, or worse, under the Democratic organization. Daley, however, chose another course. He showed little eagerness to return to the good old days of Kelly and Thompson. Like Wagner in New York, another mayor produced by the regular organization, Daley seemed to be searching for a workable compromise between the traditional demands and pressures of the party hacks, along with the business and criminal elements for whom they spoke, and the newer demand placed on every big-city administration by conditions of the latter twentieth century: govern effectively or go under.

Daley faced a task of almost incredible difficulty.

Every city has its underworld. Generally it is a remote, shadowy casbah that the bulk of citizens never enter. The average person can spend his whole life in a city and never be aware of its underworld except for an occasional paragraph in the newspaper. But Chicago's underworld has not remained in the shadows. It has come out and walked the streets and entered the places of business and government, and with it has come an infection.

Chicago mugwumps have long been resisting the disease. They formed the nation's first crime commission back in the relatively innocent days of 1919 after two men were shot down in the city's first daylight payroll robbery. More than two dozen other cities soon established crime commissions, too, but few of them survived the 1920s. And none became the smooth, hard-hitting operation that the Chicago Crime Commission did.

Its director, former FBI man Virgil W. Peterson, heads a staff of twenty-five court observers, investigators, statisticians and office help. Some 150 respectable citizens make up the commission; nearly 2,000 others contribute toward its annual budget of

$165,000. The commission staff follows some 3,500 criminal cases through the courts each year, observing the conduct of judges, prosecutors, defense attorneys, police and defendants, and adding the information to the commission's cross-indexed file of a million-and-a-half cards and dossiers. Its investigators, mostly former FBI and military intelligence agents, spot bookie joints and gambling houses seemingly invisible to the police. It offers protection against intimidation to grand jurors and trial witnesses. Hundreds of ordinary citizens come during the year to its spacious offices on West Monroe Street to ask help or to report what appears a miscarriage of justice.

The crime commission has gained respect. But it has not succeeded in civilizing Chicago. Through the years it has remained active and financially well supported for one obvious reason—in a city where the upper world and the underworld are at times indistinguishable, it is needed.

The commission conducts a running war against certain members of the state legislature from Chicago's West Side. This unusual group of lawmakers, representing eight of the city's fifty wards, were described by Carey McWilliams in 1952 thus:

> The mobsters who really elect these legislators are seldom interested in more than a dozen bills out of perhaps 2,000 that may be introduced. . . . The candidates of the West Side bloc seldom face opposition in either the primary or the election. . . . Occasionally some naïve person has the temerity to oppose a bloc representative, but such upstarts usually withdraw at the last minute citing "ill health" as the reason. . . . Sometimes they admit they have been chased from the field by threats or actual violence.[5]

The West Side bloc concerns itself with sidetracking bills backed by the crime commission, the bar association and others trying to strengthen law enforcement. Sometimes the bloc succeeds, sometimes it loses. It also attempts to slip through bills of its own. One that the crime commission caught would have made it mandatory to destroy all police records, including photographs and fingerprints, of every ex-convict who had not paid a fine or been in prison during the past ten years. Since this would have included most of the major rackets men, the crime commission raised enough hue and cry to stop the measure.

The West Side also has been a favored locale for political shootings. Chicago had what were apparently six such murders from 1950 to 1952. The sixth one involved Charles Gross, a horse-betting bookmaker and Republican committeeman for the thirty-first ward. He was shot down in the street, gangster fashion. Despite the victim's lack of social eminence, the killing caused a wave of indignation. Councilman Merriam and his economy bloc forced an ordinance through the city council creating an investigating committee, which retained former FBI man Aaron Kohn to hold a series of hearings. And the crime commission, the Chicago Bar Association and Junior Chamber of Commerce launched a new organization, the Citizens of Greater Chicago, which was supposed to bring decency to the city. After raising $125,000 in its first "dollars for decency" drive in 1953, and hiring a dozen staff workers, it dwindled within a year to a director and a part-time secretary.[6]

In 1959 and 1960 the city was pricked awake again by a series of police and court scandals. A Chicago police lieutenant was found touring Europe with gang leader Tony Accardo. Soon after, it was revealed that the municipal court had "forgiven" certain favored bondsmen from paying an estimated $250,000 in forfeited bail money. Then somebody discovered that hundreds of thousands of dollars in traffic fines had disappeared before reaching the city treasury. A ring of policemen was identified as burglars, working partly on their own time, partly on the city's.

These exposures led the Democratic organization to put up and elect a new candidate for municipal court chief justice in 1960—Augustine Bowe, the distinguished former president of the Chicago Bar Association; and Mayor Daley appointed the University of California's dean of criminology, Professor Orlando W. Wilson, as new police commissioner to clean up the department.

Such moves were designed, of course, to placate the press and public. Yet just how much placation they required was open to speculation. There has long been something faintly spurious about Chicago's recurrent seizures of righteous indignation. They come and go so quickly. Councilman Leon M. Despres says:

"Most Chicago scandals last only three weeks." There is a similar hollow ring as the better citizens protest that the outside world maligns Chicago, talking about its mobsters and the syndicate and thuggery. "We suffer the worst damn public relations in the world!" cried the director of one civic agency, as if in physical pain. The mayor's public relations chief, when interviewed, was spitting mad over an article that had appeared in the *Saturday Evening Post*, John Bartlow Martin's "To Chicago, with Love."

Still, the outsider gets the feeling that Chicago does not really want to drive out its mobsters and political racketeers, any more than Los Angeles wants to eliminate its Hollywood characters. While they may be bums, they are glamorous bums, high-living bums, celebrated bums. A. J. Liebling observed: "It is typical of well-off Chicagoans to be passionately interested in good government. . . . People you meet at a party devote a great deal more time than people elsewhere to talking about it, but they usually wind up the evening boasting about the high quality of crooks they have known." [7]

This attachment for Chicago's seamy side extends apparently to the city's press. In the same issue of the Chicago *Daily News* that carried the headline "Magazine Does City Dirt: Daley," these other headlines and items appeared:

> "HOW DEMO CHIEFS KEEP HEAVY HAND ON ELECTION BOARD—PRECINCT CAPTAINS' INFLUENCE UNCOVERED BY DAILY NEWS"
> "OPPOSES CLEMENCY FOR SLAYER COP"
> "NEW JUDGE ASKED IN COP TRIAL HERE"
> (A column, lead item) "Same argument comes up every election year at County jail. Who's gonna stay and watch the store on Election Day? Practically every guard in the huge calaboose is a precinct captain. And you know where they've gotta be."
> "RADIO CALL PILE-UPS SLOW COPS"
> "2 S. SUBURB COPS SEIZED IN ASSAULT"
> "CHICAGO'S IMAGE OVERSEAS GETS PAINTED BLACKER"
> "COPS AREN'T SO CIVIL IN SERVICE" [8]

The man chiefly responsible for uncovering the 1959–60 police and court scandals was Cook County State's Attorney Benjamin

S. Adamowski, a Republican foe of Mayor Daley. The voters turned him out of office within the year and elected Daley's choice, DePaul University dean of law Daniel Ward.

At the same November, 1960, election the Democratic machine captured all other county offices on the ballot, and a Daley man, former Judge Otto Kerner, was elected governor of Illinois. The scandals that a few months before were supposedly rocking the Democratic machine to its foundations evidently had no effect whatever at the polls.

After the 1960 results were in, the *Daily News* commented that in Chicago "Republicans are almost extinct."

While perhaps not extinct, Republicans in Chicago are certainly lying low. And almost no other organized opposition to the Democratic machine can be found. Only the ADA-affiliated Independent Voters of Illinois openly opposes the machine and operates a precinct organization (effective in thirteen of the city's fifty wards). Its bastion is the fifth ward, long a source of trouble for both Republican and Democratic machines. The area, which surrounds the University of Chicago, has produced councilmen like political scientist Merriam, 1911–17; economist and later United States Senator Paul H. Douglas, 1939–42; the younger Merriam, 1947–55; and attorney Leon Despres, the former Independent Voters chairman, who was elected to the council in 1955, succeeding Merriam, and was re-elected in 1959.

Despres today is the chief anti-machine gadfly, writing and speaking against it at every chance. He encourages constituents who find used "policy" gambling tickets to bring them to his fifth-ward headquarters, where he posts them in the window. His prize display so far is ninety-nine tickets brought in by a small girl who picked them up in front of the Meadville Theological School.

Another open foe has been Stephen Mitchell, Democratic national chairman in the Adlai Stevenson era, who attempted to break the Cook County machine's hold by starting the Democratic Federation of Illinois. It was to be a state-wide network of clubs similar to the California Democratic Council begun a few years before. Daley's regulars infiltrated Mitchell's clubs and neutralized them.

In addition to Mitchell, Despres and the Independent Voters, a handful among the Protestant clergy, League of Women Voters, Chicago City Club and other smaller groups have made clear their distaste for the organization. But the opposition of this egghead wing of mugwumps seems to have slowed the machine no more than a boy throwing rocks at a passing freight.

Downtown mugwumps in the Loop have adopted a different tack. These business and professional men, operating mainly through the Civic Federation, the crime commission and the Association of Commerce and Industry, have accepted the Democratic machine as a fact of life. They hope to bring better government to Chicago despite the machine. Their tactic has been to work directly with the city's mayors—first with Kennelly, since 1955 with Daley.

In 1952, Kennelly appointed a Little Hoover Commission. The Civic Federation's executive secretary, Harland Stockwell, was its staff director. This led the next year to creation of the Chicago Home Rule Commission, headed by Leverett Lyon, chief executive of the Association of Commerce and Industry. These groups submitted a list of reforms. Most of them the professional politicians ignored, such as the proposal that Chicago, with the largest city council in the United States—fifty aldermen from fifty wards—be redivided into twenty-five aldermanic districts, with ten more aldermen elected at large.

The reformers also urged that the aldermen stop selling permits for driveways, loading platforms, illuminated signs, water lines, and railroad switching tracks. The time-honored practice had been for each alderman to introduce the ordinance granting the permits in his district, an action usually preceded by a campaign contribution to the alderman ranging from fifty dollars for a private driveway to many times that for a commercial installation. At one meeting, the council approved 293 permits for driveways alone. Following the Home Rule Commission's recommendation, Despres and twenty-seven Republicans and Daley followers formed a momentary coalition against a score of fellow aldermen from the West Side, Southwest Side and Negro South Side; the coalition pushed through an ordinance removing the permit-granting power from the council and giving it to the city department of streets and sanitation.

Mayor Daley, after taking office in 1955, made other efforts to cooperate with the Loop mugwumps. He kept the school system free of politics, as it had been under Kennelly. He put into effect an executive budget, prepared in his office instead of by the council, and presented in "performance budget" style. He named a recognized municipal finance expert, Carl H. Chatters, as city comptroller. The mayor and his law partner, Democratic legislative leader William Lynch, teamed with the mugwumps to persuade the 1957 legislature to consolidate the city's park system with the independent Chicago Park District and to merge the park district police force with that of the city. The mayor also supported an improved classification system for city jobs in the civil service department.

Where jobs were involved, however, the mayor ran up against a fact of life, too. He could change administrative methods, if he wanted to. He could adopt new kinds of financial reports, and otherwise try to convince the mugwumps and men of property that he stood for good government. But jobs are the lifeblood of the machine, insuring the organization at least one to five men to handle the political chores in each precinct—and the machine has somebody in almost every one of Chicago's three thousand precincts. So the civil service system cannot be permitted to get in the way of patronage. The patronage secretary, working in the mayor's office, must have something to pass out to the parade of ward committeemen who come to his desk day after day.

The mayor is free to juggle forms. But he must move slowly, if at all, when it comes to matters of substance. Thus, politically, Chicago backs and fills, going nowhere in particular.

Daley himself enjoys a reputation for personal honesty and integrity, but as mayor he is a product of the machine and is tied to it. He professes to believe he can build a superstructure of good government, while yet using the machine as the foundation. "This is not the last of the old machines," the phrase goes, "this is the first of the new machines."

The downtown mugwumps and men of property hold no illusions about the machine, but they do not seem terribly worried about it. They have placed their chips on Daley to keep things from getting too bad. The ideological liberal mugwumps have declared unending war on the machine. They want to clean it out completely. But they are too few and too obscure to pose an immediate threat.

Only the downtown mugwumps and men of property can get this situation off dead center. They will have to throw their support behind a campaign to fumigate the parasites from city hall so that Chicago can play the part it should in the second revolution.

What can stir these Loop leaders to action? Plainly, police scandals and goggle-eyed stories of the syndicate will not. These have become old-hat. Perhaps Chicago's men of property will have to feel the pangs of economic fear, as their Philadelphia counterparts did when they discovered in the late 1940s that incompetent machine government was threatening them in the pocketbook. Perhaps the Loop is to be goaded by a different kind of fear, one that can be detected in private conversations. This is the fear that Negroes, aided by Puerto Ricans, will gain ascendancy in the Democratic machine and will subsequently assume a major voice in control of Chicago's government. The Negro and Puerto Rican population increased rapidly from 1950 to 1960 while Chicago's population as a whole dropped 2½ percent. With the businessman's customary fear of the unknown, the downtowners wonder among themselves how they would get along with Negro political bosses and what the effect would be on the Loop's future.

While this is hardly an admirable reason for undertaking a political crusade, it could prove a decisive one in making Chicago's men of property decide to join with the mugwumps in sending the old ward-based machine to the junkyard.

One possibility mentioned is that of enlarging the city and merging it with the white middle-class suburbs, either through the annexation procedure or by creating a powerful metropolitan-area government that would overshadow the present city hall.

Another possible crusade would be to set about systematically wiping the ward-based machine out of existence. In practical terms, this calls for starving the ward organization to death. And to accomplish this will probably require the aid of a third ally—the good-government elements within the machine itself. With the help of these leaders, the starvation process could proceed, cutting off the ward committeemen's patronage by a genuine civil service system, and severing their threads of influence into administrative offices and the courts. The archaic council of fifty ward-chosen aldermen could be replaced by a smaller body elected partially or wholly at large. The city's leading politicians would shift their base of support from the ward hacks to the support pattern prevalent in other cities—a base composed of mugwumps, men of property, and the press.

All this would be a large order for Chicago.

And something else will be required. Seventy years ago, injured pride led the town to unite for a while behind "a Federation of all good citizens in a vigorous movement . . . against the vicious elements of society and slum conditions, and for improvement in the quality of local government." From somewhere, Chicago will have to revive this spirit, and this capacity for injured pride.

10

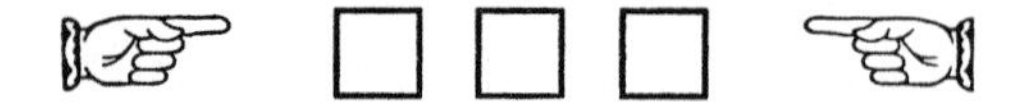

The "Good" Machines

Cincinnati • Dallas • Kansas City

San Antonio • Memphis • New Orleans

Mugwumps in every city have faced the choice: Shall we campaign for issues, or shall we campaign for men? Shall we operate an organization primarily to study specific problems, methods and procedures in local government? Or shall we concentrate on getting good men into office and let them worry about the problems, methods and procedures?

Mugwumps who choose the first path establish a municipal research bureau or a citizens league. Those who choose the second organize a municipal party.

In a half-dozen cities mugwumps have chosen to create such reform parties, their own varieties of "good" machines.

CINCINNATI—THE CITY DIVIDED

Upon first impression, Cincinnati seems a gentle old calm-paced music-loving beer-drinking city where the affairs of government, if any, are probably left to a jovial burgomaster and his faithful aides. In fact, Cincinnati is a city torn by dissension, as enmeshed in political feuds and enmity as a Borgian palace.

The lines of conflict run back to the 1920s. At that time mugwumps in many other cities had already managed to throw out the worst of their political hacks during the Progressive upsurge. Not so in Cincinnati.

The reason was a formidable object named George Barnsdale Cox. The former bootblack and saloon owner had fastened on Cincinnati a Republican political machine so well contrived and so closely allied with business interests and the GOP national party organization that only a breakdown in health finally dislodged him. Cox's heir as party leader, John Holmes, died suddenly. And so, after a brief reform administration under Democrat Henry T. Hunt in 1911–12, another heir, Rudolph Hynicka, took over the Republican organization and regained power.[1]

The mugwumps disdained Cox because he was blunt and rough-mannered and ran the city from his Mecca Saloon. Hynicka, although more suave, also offended the mugwumps' civic pride; he operated a burlesque theater in Cincinnati which he soon expanded into a chain; thereafter he managed the city long-distance from his burlesque house in New York.

One of his telegrams fell into the unfriendly hands of the Cincinnati *Post* in 1921 and ended up on page one. It directed the Republican majority on the city council to assist "our friends" at the Cincinnati Gas & Electric Company in their campaign for a higher gas rate. This outraged not only householders but many businessmen who opposed the increase.

Meanwhile, a group of young mugwumps had returned from the war brimming with ideals about democracy. They discovered that a most unusual brand of democracy existed in their home town. It went under the name of "party responsibility." The Republican leaders of the county worked through the Republican Executive and Advisory Committee, consisting of themselves and a number of leading citizens they had invited to join them. This group made all important decisions in governing Hamilton County and Cincinnati. It passed upon appointments, financial matters, taxes and all other major policies. Republican officeholders automatically accepted its decisions. There was nothing clandestine about the committee; everybody knew of its existence, and its actions were reported fully in the press.

The Democrats had no similar committee because there were

hardly enough Democrats and Democratic officeholders in Cincinnati to make one worth while.

Unhindered by the minority of Democrats, and protected by state laws that barred independent candidates from the ballot and prohibited nomination by petition, the machine under Cox and later Hynicka needed only to control the Republican primary to retain power. This it did by exerting iron discipline over the 6,000 city and county employes. With an estimated 25,000 votes thus in its pocket, the machine merely had to let other candidates split any opposition vote, while the machine concentrated its bundle of 25,000 on its chosen man. This nearly always assured him a plurality, all that was required for nomination. The system worked with few setbacks for nearly forty years.

The public, however, grew restive in the early 1920s. Not only was it irritating to have one's gas rates increased upon word from a New York burlesque house, but the city government was slipping into a hopeless fiscal situation. It was spending above its income and was borrowing money to pay day-to-day expenses. Forty percent of the city's taxes were going for debt charges, yet the debt still mounted—and the city had hit the upper limit of the taxing powers allowed it by the legislature.

News of the city's difficulties began to reach the people through the Cincinnatus Association, a discussion group of two dozen young lawyers and businessmen who met on Tuesday evenings to hear each other read papers on civic matters. Newspapers sent reporters to cover the meetings, and stories about Cincinnati's woes started appearing in print. (Among the discussion group was young Charles P. Taft, who, after finishing law school and coaching football briefly at Yale, had come home in 1921—the same year that his older brother Bob opened his political career by going to the legislature backed by Hynicka's Republican organization.)

As public criticism increased, the Republican Executive and Advisory Committee, assuming its customary "party responsibility," appointed a citizens commission to make an independent report on the city and county governments. This commission retained Lent D. Upson, who took six months' leave from the Detroit Bureau of Governmental Research to head an investigating staff of eighteen specialists. Their combined reports issued in June, 1924, were not complimentary to the Republican administration.

Using the Upson report as a club, the mugwumps set out to overturn Hynicka's regime. They organized a City Charter Committee, raised $10,000 and circulated petitions to place on the November ballot a charter amendment creating a city-manager government with a nonpartisan nine-man council elected by proportional representation (the existing council consisted of thirty-one Republicans and one independent).

Leading spirits in the Charter Committee were attorneys Henry Bentley, Murray Seasongood and a handful of young Republican lawyers and insurance men, but they had powerful support from several sources—businessmen who were disturbed by the city's financial condition, Democrats who had everything to gain from Hynicka's downfall, and prominent citizens of German and Jewish extraction whose families had brought a heritage of political liberalism when they fled Europe after the abortive revolutions of 1848.

Other Charter strength came from the Women's City Club and the League of Women Voters, who provided hundreds of volunteers; the ladies had long been furious with the regular Republicans, anyway, for opposing woman suffrage and excluding women from running for the school board.

Perhaps a decisive factor in the machine's defeat was the La Follette Progressive movement. Cincinnati, like Cleveland, had many insurgent Republicans in that year, 1924, who gave added push to the anti-regular forces.

When the votes were counted on election night, the mugwumps found their manager–P.R. charter amendment had carried by an overwhelming 92,500 to 41,000.

At their victory dinner, the Charter Committee decided it would not disband but would form a permanent municipal party and run men for office. It recruited a slate of nine to file for the city council. Six of them were elected the next fall (1925), to only three for the Republican regulars. The six Charterites chose one of their number, Seasongood, as mayor and sent to Washington, D.C., for Lieutenant-Colonel C. O. Sherrill of the U. S. Engineers to become the first city manager.[2]

Cincinnati had unbroken good luck in obtaining able city

managers. Sherrill was succeeded by Clarence A. Dykstra of Los Angeles, who had been director of the Cleveland Citizens League in 1918–20 and later was to head the University of Wisconsin and then the University of California at Los Angeles. After him came local businessman Wilbur R. Kellogg, who finally retired in 1953, to be replaced by C. A. Harrell, former city manager at Norfolk and at San Antonio.

But while the mugwumps had relatively little trouble with city managers, they had plenty of trouble with the Republican regulars.

For the first few years the reformers enjoyed a honeymoon, as the voters gave them six-to-three council majorities in 1925, 1927 and 1929. In 1931, the Charterites margin slipped to five to four. Then came the depression and the New Deal, and a major shift in the make-up of the Charter coalition.

The Charter Committee's chief source of leaders and financial support had been the upper-middle-class Hilltop residents. This support had included almost none of the highly conservative big businessmen, who continued to back the regular Republicans. In those pre-depression days the workers and Negroes who lived in the low-lying Basin wards voted with the Republican machine.

When the Roosevelt era came, it might have been expected, as it did in most cities, to drive the liberal and conservative Republicans together in united opposition to That Man. Cincinnati conservatives, however, were always of a peculiarly deep-dyed breed; they would not hear of any rapprochement with Charles Taft and his wild-eyed comrades who had actually had dealings with the Democrats.

With loyalty to the Republican party the main issue, much of the Charter group's Hilltop support fell away. The then two leading newspapers, the *Enquirer* and the *Times-Star*, followed suit, leaving only the third-ranking Cincinnati *Post* as a Charter friend. These losses were only partially replaced by votes from the Basin wards, which began to swing against the GOP after 1932. From 1935 to 1947, the Charter Committee could elect no more than a minority of four to the nine-man council. Then came a postwar revival led by Taft and Councilman Albert D. Cash, a liberal Democrat, aided by liberal Negro attorney Theodore M. Berry, the AFL building trades unions, and Jack Kroll of the CIO.

With their help, the Charter Committee regained a bare council majority in 1947 and 1949, lost it in 1951, won it back in 1953 and 1955.

Meanwhile the regular Republicans centered their attack on another front, that of trying to repeal the P.R. voting system. The Charter Committee, convinced that P.R. was essential to keep the regulars from returning to power, fought back with everything it had. The GOP circulated petitions and placed the repeal proposal on the ballot five separate times. The first four times the Charterites and P.R. won—by a narrow 831 votes in 1936, by 742 in 1939, by 7,602 in 1947 and by 672 in 1954. But the tireless regulars moved in again in 1957 and this time, after a campaign heavily flavored with anti-Negro propaganda, P.R. went under. Despite the efforts of more than a thousand volunteers and a $25,000 war chest, the Charter forces saw their beloved P.R. rejected by a convincing margin of 65,600 to 54,100.

Many Charter supporters, wearied by years of fighting, thought this was the end. Yet disaster, if it was to be that, did not come immediately. In the first election after P.R.'s repeal, the Charterites lost only one council seat, reducing them to a minority of four. The casualty was Theodore Berry, who had been Charter floor leader in the council and the special object of the regulars' campaign.

A harder blow fell upon the Charter Committee a year later in January, 1959. The city's twenty-six Democratic ward captains voted to withdraw from the Charter coalition and enter their own Democratic ticket in future municipal elections.

This setback was not unexpected. The old-regular Democrats, mostly a no-necktie and battered-hat crew, had never felt at home with the upper-middle-class Charterites. They had grumbled about their minority representation on the Charter Committee board, and the fact that liberal Republicans, who made up the board majority, framed the platform and picked out the Charter slate for each election, giving the Democratic organization only a veto power over which three Democrats should be on the slate. The Charter nine-man slate usually included three Democrats, three Republicans, and a Negro, a Jew and a labor unionist who might be either Republicans or Democrats.

Back in 1934 the Democratic regulars had almost bolted the

coalition. The mugwumps, after winning control of city hall in 1925, had created a Citizens Movement to run candidates for Hamilton County offices as well; the Movement, like the Charter Committee, was a coalition of independent Republicans and Democrats. The first few elections went well. By 1932, the reformers had a majority on the county board of commissioners, and they installed a civil service system for the departments under their control. The Democratic county clerk, however, who was independent of the commissioners, fired most of his eighty-man staff, replacing them with Democratic cronies. When the 1934 election rolled around, the Citizens Movement reformers declined to endorse the county clerk for re-election, and the Democrats withdrew from the Movement, causing its collapse. It was said that the Democrats might have withdrawn from the Charter Committee, too, had they not lost almost every county office at the polls a few months later.

The election of liberal Democrat Albert Cash as mayor after World War II solidified the coalition. But Cash was drowned in 1952 when a sudden squall caught his fishing boat in Torch Lake, Michigan. Some Cincinnati observers believe that, had he lived, Cash might have been able to cope with the next development—a revolt within the Democratic organization that saw the long, easygoing leadership of insurance man William J. Leonard replaced by a younger, more militant element. The new leaders wanted no more of the junior partnership. In the mid-1950s they began to build their own precinct organization in Cincinnati, paralleling in many districts the Charter precinct organization. From then on it was clear that a final split was only a matter of time.

The break was no doubt hastened by Charles Taft's continued participation in Republican state and national politics. He had been a close adviser of presidential nominee Alfred M. Landon in 1936. In 1952 he sought and won the GOP nomination for governor. And in 1958 he permitted his name to be entered as a "standby" candidate in the event that Republican Governor O'Neill, who had had a serious heart attack, was unable to campaign. When O'Neill remained in the race and won the nomination, Taft supported him against Democrat Michael V. DiSalle, the eventual winner.

That same November, in the Democrats' state-wide sweep, the Cincinnati organization elected three Democrats to the legislature. While still outnumbered as usual by the Republican delegation, this was the Democratic organization's best showing since 1948, and is believed responsible for its decision a few weeks later to cut loose from the Charter Committee.

So it was that Cincinnati voters faced three tickets in the 1959 city council election—Democratic, Republican and Charter. When the vote was in and the smoke cleared, it was hard to tell who had gained and who had lost. In 1957, Charter candidates Taft, Vincent Beckman, John Gilligan and Dorothy Dolbey had finished first, second, third and ninth in the voting. In 1959 they finished second, fifth, sixth and eighth, but this time Beckman and Gilligan ran as Democrats. The Republicans still held a five-to-four edge on the council, as they had before. The GOP ticket had received 41 percent of the vote, the Charter Committee ticket 29 percent, the Democrats 26 percent.

Some thought the third-running Democrats would change their minds and move back into the Charter coalition. But the Democratic leaders themselves declared that time was on their side, and their percentage of vote would creep up as the proportion of workers and Negroes within the city increased.

Some Republicans began hinting to Taft and Mrs. Dolbey that they should give up the Charter ship and accept places on the next ballot as Republicans.

A number of Charter adherents agreed with the Republicans that the days of their reform organization, after nearly forty years, were numbered. Other Charterites refused to concede any such thing.

The Charter Committee still had plenty to fight with. A standing army of 1,200 volunteers (three-fourths of them women) could be counted on to ring doorbells in any campaign. Another 700, half of them men, would serve as poll watchers. The $30,000 or so required to meet each campaign's expenses came in without too much difficulty, just as it always had.

Yet while the Charterites still had plenty to fight with, there was an important element in Cincinnati that wished they would stop fighting, at least for a while—they and their Republican opponents, too. The battle had been going on for nearly four decades. It had come to dominate nearly every public question. Neither the Charter coalitionists nor the Republican regulars seemed able to view any issue except in terms of—will it help us or will it help them at the next election? The political rivalry had gone on so long, year after year without compromise or accommodation, that, like the Martins and the Coys, few on either side could remember when things had been any different. The feud had inflicted upon the city a partial paralysis.[3]

One group attempting to shake off this paralysis was the Citizens Development Committee. This postwar group of seventy-five prominent citizens included representatives from both the Charter and conservative Republican camps. But the leading figures were middle-of-the-roaders, Democrat and Republican. Among them were Charles Sawyer, who had been secretary of commerce in the Truman cabinet; Neil McElroy, president of Procter and Gamble soap company, who became President Eisenhower's secretary of defense; Howard Morgens, who took over at Procter and Gamble during McElroy's absence; John J. Emery, the town's major property owner and former president of the Charter Committee; Fred Lazarus, Jr., head of the nation's top retail chain, Federated Department Stores; Frederick V. Geier, president of the world's largest machine tool plant, the Cincinnati Milling Machine Company; and Joseph B. Hall, president of the Kroger chain of 1,500 food markets.

Impatient with the city council's habit of delaying improvement projects while councilmen quibbled over which side, Charter or GOP, should get the credit, the Citizens Development Committee called for action. Stepping out as individuals, they collected money and led campaigns that obtained voter approval of $41 million in bonds in 1944, another $38 million in 1950, $45 million more in 1956, and $17 million in 1960. The bulk of the funds were earmarked for new expressways; and when this program bogged down, department store tycoon Lazarus, at the invitation of Mayor Taft, held night meetings with councilmen and other officials in Cincinnati and suburban cities until he obtained everyone's agreement on a route for the Millcreek expressway.

On another occasion a freeway project was held up because city officials could not get Kentucky state officials to settle on a location for the big Cincinnati-to-Covington bridge across the Ohio river. City officials asked Sawyer for help. He telephoned a fellow Democrat, Governor Albert B. "Happy" Chandler of Kentucky, on a Monday. The following Friday morning state officials of Kentucky and Ohio met in the Cincinnati city hall, and by 11:00 A.M. they had agreed on where the bridge should go.

CDC members disposed of lesser obstacles, too. When a property owner in nearby St. Bernard protested that a freeway would wipe out the two hundred tomato plants he had just put in, the CDC spokesman stopped the meeting long enough to buy the tomato plants on the spot for his own back yard.

The Citizens Development Committee, while it has scored some accomplishments, has been no Allegheny Conference. It has done comparatively little about rooting out Cincinnati slums, which are among the nation's worst. And although the city has a relatively low density of population (about 6,800 per square mile), it has great difficulty finding room for new industries. When it comes to tearing down old structures and erecting new ones, private initiative has been spectacularly lacking. As one Cincinnati newsman put it: "The high brass on the CDC have not gone so far as the high brass in Pittsburgh. They don't spend their own money for redevelopment. But they tell the city where it should spend *its* money."

Working quietly behind the scenes is another mugwump organization, the Bureau of Governmental Research. It was established at Upson's suggestion, in 1925, about the same time as the Charter Committee was born.[4] Today, housed in an ancient building near Cincinnati's medieval city hall, the bureau staff of four makes financial and population studies upon request of city, county and school officials.

Moderating forces like CDC and the Bureau of Governmental Research are still secondary figures in Cincinnati, overshadowed in public attention by the long mugwump-versus-regulars feud. But a current of compromise is detectable below the surface. A growing number of the city's leaders admit they have grown bored with the feud and wish that the hundred-percent Republicans who think of the party first, last and always, and the most doctrinaire Charter reformers who can vizualize good government only on their own terms would both sink into the background.

As if to demonstrate that there may be more than one road to reform, Councilman Beckman—the Charterite turned Democrat—won election in November, 1960, to the three-member board of Hamilton County commissioners, giving the Democrats their first majority on the board since 1936; and Beckman promptly announced that he would move to establish a classified civil service system based on competitive examinations for the 2,700 county employes, thus removing them from the age-old spoils system maintained by the GOP regulars. In an important gesture of conciliation, Beckman promised there would be no wholesale firing of Republican workers before granting the protection of civil service.

A few more such gestures, made in good faith, and Cincinnati might be on its way to attaining its vital objective—a political community capable of united action in the metropolitan age.

DALLAS, KANSAS CITY—AND THE OLD BULLS

No mugwumps ever had a city better organized than those in Dallas.

They started in 1931 with the Citizens Charter Association, pushing through a new city charter that ousted the commission government and replaced it with a council-manager form. At the same time the association elected a city council of nine leading businessmen. Then the depression slowed them for a time. Those were rough days for businessmen in politics, and in 1935 the association lost all nine council seats back to the old pros of the Catfish Club (so called because they allegedly met in secret like catfish hiding in the mud). The Charter Association regained four seats in 1937, took all nine in 1939, and thereafter held almost every council position and total control of Dallas city government.

The core of the association was twenty-two presidents of banks, insurance companies, utilities, newspapers, big retail stores, oil companies, and a theater chain. They decided in 1937 that perhaps they should get together oftener than every two years before elections, so they created the Dallas Citizens Council and invited eighty of their fellows to join. Holding closed meetings and abstaining from open political activity, the council set the pattern later followed by the Allegheny Conference in Pittsburgh, Civic Progress in St. Louis and other top-brass committees.

The Citizens Council with its monthly meetings proved an effective way for the town's leaders to reach quiet agreement on civic matters. But it had a drawback. It lacked a full-time staff for keeping tab on technical developments in municipal government; and so in 1946, they supported the formation of a research bureau, the Greater Dallas Planning Council.

Then, although the city had no organized crime to speak of, the leading citizens decided to play safe and have a crime commission like Chicago's. They established one and employed a staff.

Thus fully equipped—some observers thought even over-equipped—the mugwumps operated the city with a minimum of fuss and publicity. Each Monday noon the mayor and city councilmen lunched with the city manager in a private room at the Statler-Hilton for a briefing on what was coming up at the weekly council meeting that afternoon. If there were any questions, any controversy, they were threshed out behind closed doors. Then, as one newsman put it, "they'd go over to city hall for the public meeting at two-o'clock and pass everything."

Candidates for mayor and councilmen were chosen with equal dispatch. Twenty or so Dallas leaders usually gathered on a December evening in a hotel conference room and discussed who should run in the spring election. Thereafter the Citizens Charter Association held its biennial "organizational" luncheon. Anyone who wished to pay two dollars for a ticket might attend; several hundred usually showed up. After speeches, the meeting would elect the association president and empower him to appoint the committee to nominate the association ticket for mayor and council.

The perennial president of the association after 1947 was Laurence R. Melton, former national commander of the Disabled American Veterans. Stocky, heavy-jawed, with graying hair worn long around the ears like a southern senator, Melton was interviewed in his office at the printing plant he and his brother own at 2930 Commerce Street.

Q. How do you select your candidates?

A. Anyone who asks for a place on the council is never considered. It's entirely a draft proposition. We want to get unselfish people who will think of the good of all Dallas. So far we have been able to get men of statue [*sic*] and with good business judgment.

Q. Do you have trouble finding candidates?

A. Oh, yes, especially since we have six councilmen elected from districts as well as three at large including the mayor. Sometimes it's difficult to find a resident in each of the six districts. . . . When we call on a man and find he's reluctant to run, we say—Dallas has been good to you, now it's time for you to repay Dallas.

Q. Do you ever run any Negroes or Mexican-Americans on your slate?

A. We have never made any particular play to the minority groups. We run advertising in the Negro and Latin-American papers. But no Negro candidates.

Q. How do you run your campaigns?

A. We don't hire a campaign manager. I generally handle the campaign myself. We hire someone to take care of publicity. . . . The candidates are not allowed to contribute funds to their own campaign, and they may not spend any money except that of the association. A man either runs as a member of the slate or not. . . . Women volunteers give us a lot of help. Without these women in campaigns we would be sunk.

Q. Do you ever choose a woman for a candidate?

A. We got one woman on the council and it wasn't an easy job. She was the only one who had to face a run-off election.

Q. How large is your budget for a campaign?

A. (after a hard stare): I don't think I would want to tell you that. . . . Well, it's thirty-five thousand dollars. Or thirty thousand.

Q. Do you have any problem with contributors after your men take office?

A. In all my years as president I have never had a contributor ask a favor. The city councilmen who are elected don't know who has made contributions. . . . The chief of police has absolutely free rein. Even though I am president of the Charter Association, I don't know ten men in the police department.

Q. You must get a certain satisfaction from this job as president if you have stayed in it since 1947.

A. Just one thing makes me mad. I hate political bosses passionately. And they call me Boss Melton.

Melton and the Citizens Association rolled up such large majorities during the 1940s and 1950s that organized opposition in elections almost disappeared. Margins of two to one and greater discouraged any substantial citizen from filing against the association slate.

The mugwump position, however, was not quite so rock solid as it seemed. Better than 87 percent of the association vote in the 1957 election came from the northern half of the city whose white-collar residents paid the $1.75 state poll tax and voted in large numbers. In the southern portion, however, where the cornbread-and-blackeyed-peas folk lived, the association had little support. A tally of the April, 1957, ballots showed:

PRECINCTS CARRIED	by Charter Association	by the Opposition	Even
Northwest Dallas (Walnut Hill, Preston Hollow)	42	2	2
Northeast Dallas (Lakewood, White Rock)	16	14	2
Southeast Dallas (Pleasant Grove, South Dallas)	2	18	1
Southwest Dallas (Oak Cliff)	6	20	5
Total	66	54	10

These figures foretold trouble for Dallas mugwumps of the Citizens Association group. Elections were becoming closer and time was not on their side. Labor unions and Negroes were not yet politically organized, but they were gaining strength and their members were increasing.

There was another and more immediate factor to contend with. The men of the Charter Association and the Citizens Council had been managing Dallas for nearly thirty years. In that time they had built up resentments. They became known behind their backs as "the fat cats on Main Street" and "the Main Street gang." What was more, they were getting old. The rugged individualists who in the 1930s had formed the association and the Citizens Council were tough, but they were not indestructible. Yet, like the old bulls in any herd, they resisted giving way to the young.

The young ones rebelled in 1959. And although the oldsters survived with a shaky victory, the closeness of it broke their hold. Banker Bob Thornton, aged seventy-eight and seeking his fourth term as mayor, was challenged by a former Charter Association colleague, dairy and market owner Earle Cabell, who was twenty-five years Thornton's junior. Cabell charged in his campaign that "a machine made up of downtown landlords, bankers and millionaires is running Dallas." Thornton won by a narrow 3,000 votes. Two other Charter candidates for the city council squeaked through, one by only 223 votes. The real shock, however, was provided by young attorney Joseph Geary, who ran as an independent for the council and decisively beat the Charter Association man.

Part of the credit belonged to Geary's refreshing campaign. Having little money and opposed by all the newspapers, Geary and his friends resorted to such low-budget tactics as standing on an overpass above the main expressway during the morning rush hour, holding a banner "Vote for Joe Geary" and waving at motorists. After a few mornings, the drivers took to waving back, by the thousands. The morning after his primary victory, Geary and company were back with another sign reading "Thanks, folks." Geary also borrowed a 1903 Oldsmobile for touring and talking in neighborhoods—it always drew a crowd. Squads of doorbell ringers were organized among students at Southern Methodist University, where Geary had played baseball.

Major credit for Geary's winning, however, was ascribed to a more fundamental public reaction. He provided a symbol of revolt against the old men of Main Street. His chief source of help was some fifty young lawyers and businessmen from the Exchange Club, to which he belonged. And in the North End precincts, heavily settled with junior executives and young couples, the usual Charter Association majorities of six to one were cut to approximately two to one.

Asked later why he decided to take on the association in 1959, Geary replied, "The association has always chosen who should be on the council. If they didn't anoint you, you just didn't get in. I figured they never were going to choose me, at least not until I was gray haired, around 1980. I didn't want to wait that long."

After the 1959 election, the Charter Association underwent an internal shake-up. The aging Melton was forced to resign as president. And to meet the charge that a handful of Main Streeters made all decisions, a committee headed by realtor W. H. Cothrum formed a network of "grass-roots" neighborhood groups to advise on candidates and platform. The deposing of the old Citizens Association hierarchy proceeded bloodlessly, but as inexorably as a primitive tribe expelling its enfeebled elders.

The extent of change was dramatically indicated two years later, in 1961, by the identity of the two leading candidates for mayor. One was Cabell, trying again after his close defeat of two years before. The other, the Citizens Association entry, was none other than Joe Geary. He had been not only accepted into the fold, but accepted on his own terms—with a veto power over the association's 1961 platform and over its selections for city council candidates to run on the slate with him.

This was not all the humble pie that the once all-powerful Citizens Association had to eat. Some of its long-time supporters, irked by the choice of Geary to head the ticket, bolted to Cabell; others helped form a rival Dallas Charter League that endorsed Cabell and several other independents running against association candidates. On primary election day, these defections made the difference. Cabell received 41,500 votes, Geary 38,700, another candidate 2,100. Thus by a majority of slightly over 700 votes Cabell won the mayoralty in the primary. In lesser setbacks, two other association candidates for the council were forced into runoff elections against independents.

The 1961 returns were but one more indication of the growing belief that the time has come for letting more light and air into the management of Dallas affairs. Even before the 1961 election the city council had begun to admit newspaper reporters—although not the public—to its Monday luncheons as it discussed what action to take at the afternoon council meeting. And at the meetings themselves, the council began casting split votes on some issues, instead of passing everything unanimously, as had been the custom for years.

The reign of the old bulls in Dallas, remarkable as it was, has ended. Yet the revolt is not an ideological one. The young mugwumps do not stand for anything much different from the old ones. They believe in continuing the city's uncorrupted council-manager government much as it has been. Except for one thing. They want a say in it.

In Kansas City, the reign of the old bulls ended on March 31, 1959—the day the city's voters turned their reform administration out of office after nearly twenty years in power. For the reformers it marked the end of a full cycle that had begun back when silent Cal Coolidge was sitting in the White House and tough Tom Pendergast was sitting in his drab office at 1908 Main Street in Kansas City, wearing his hat all day and planning how he was going to outfox the mugwumps.

Just a few months before, Cincinnati had voted in its council-manager charter. Now Kansas City mugwumps had won an election adopting a manager charter, too, and they looked forward to driving the political hacks from city hall. They seemed undisturbed by the fact that Pendergast controlled the city council that would hire the new city manager. Even after Pendergast's council named a sixty-year-old Democratic wheel horse as city manager, the mugwumps made hopeful noises. An article in the *National Municipal Review*, February, 1926, said of the new manager:

> It is recognized that he will appoint Democrats to practically all city positions. But (he) is a pretty capable man who believes that party administration is not inconsistent with efficient government. Mr. Matscheck [director of the mugwumps' municipal

research bureau] thinks he will be strong enough to control the administration.

The mugwumps were soon disabused of this idea. Yet none of them raised a serious challenge to Pendergast for the next six years. Finally a courageous rabbi, Samuel S. Mayerberg, began agitating for a civic clean-up. Although such behavior was not healthy (the Rabbi took to riding in a bullet-proof sedan), other mugwumps joined his crusade.

Secretly at first they set up an organization misleadingly called the National Youth Movement. Working in wards and neighborhoods, they put together an anti-Pendergast network of Republicans and reform Democrats. By 1934, they were bold enough to enter a Citizens-Fusion ticket against the machine candidates. The Fusionist nominee for mayor was Dr. A. Ross Hill, former president of the University of Missouri.

Election day, March 27, 1934, has gone down in local history as Bloody Tuesday. Cars of armed toughs began patrolling the streets before the polls opened. One rolled past the Fusionist downtown headquarters, lacing the front window with seven shots but missing those inside. Another group rushed the Fusionist ninth-ward headquarters, beating the three office workers with blackjacks and gun butts. A hardware merchant was wounded by a stray bullet as he opened his store. A Kansas City *Star* reporter, discovered as he followed three cars loaded with voting repeaters from polling place to polling place, received a pistol whipping. Fusionist workers who tried to protest irregularities at polling places were either beaten or arrested by city police and held in jail all day. A midafternoon appeal to Governor Guy B. Park in Jefferson City for aid in restoring order went unanswered. By nightfall the count showed four murders, two hundred cases of assault, and a Pendergast victory by 40,000 votes.

The Fusionists, as an organization, broke up. But leading mugwumps realized the machine's election-day violence had been a symptom of weakness, not strength, and they set about methodically cutting Pendergast down.

Assisted by *Star* reporters and photographers, a citizens committee collected evidence of vote fraud in the 1936 election and turned it over to United States District Judge Merrill E. Otis and

United States District Attorney Maurice Milligan. A grand jury was called, and the opening of the first sealed sackful of 1936 ballots revealed that ninety-five of them had been altered from straight Republican votes to straight Democratic. In the ensuing trial—a landmark in United States courtroom annals—Milligan obtained fraud convictions against 259 election judges, clerks, precinct leaders of both parties, and policemen.

The mugwumps also turned to the state government for help. Governor Lloyd C. Stark in 1937 named a nonpartisan election board that overhauled the registration and voting system. Two years later the legislature removed the Kansas City (and St. Louis) police departments from local control, placing them under state-appointed boards.

Pendergast completed his own downfall by becoming addicted to horse-race betting on a grand scale. He lost a reported $600,000 in 1936 alone. Attempting to cover his losses, he got involved in a huge insurance companies' bribe that he failed to declare on his federal income tax return. Convicted of tax evasion, he was fined, sentenced to fifteen months in prison and placed on probation for another three years. Upon release, the terms of his probation barred him from politics for five years. Deserted by his wife, the old boss returned to the city he had once ruled, there to live in lonely isolation until his death in 1945.

Even before his departure for prison, the mugwumps had formed a "citizens' audit committee" to find out what had been going on in city hall during Pendergast's reign. The research bureau, the Civic Research Institute, had been on the job since 1921, but it had been unable after 1926 to obtain anything more than fragments of information from the machine's officeholders. The new citizens' audit committee retained an outside firm and its investigation disclosed, among other things, that: there were no records of how many employes the city had—the mayor said about 3,500 were on the payroll, but the auditors found a total of nearly 5,200; one sinking fund was short $8 million; an illegal "city manager's emergency fund" had been created in 1931—since then almost $6 million had passed through it; some $2 million in claims against the municipal government had not been recorded, presumably to make the city's financial condition look more rosy.

These and other revelations received heavy play in the newspapers. Wishing to act while the public was still aroused, mugwumps forced through a city charter amendment requiring a municipal election in 1940 instead of 1942 as scheduled. Harold W. Luhnow, president of the William Volker and Company enterprises and bitter opponent of Pendergast (an avocation that had cost him an 800 percent increase in his personal property assessments), headed a new Charter Party. It captured seven of the eight council seats in the 1940 election and saw its man, attorney John B. Gage, a conservative Democrat, win the mayoralty.

So began the mugwumps' long domination of Kansas City government. Importing trained professional L. P. Cookingham as city manager, they formed a permanent candidate-electing organization, the Citizens Association (described in Chapter Six), which until 1959 never lost an election. Their candidates for mayor were always conservative Democrats, those for the eight council seats usually half Democrats, half Republicans.

Remnants of the Pendergast machine, split into factions, retreated to the Jackson County courthouse and dug in. The mugwumps tried to dislodge them in the late forties with a campaign for a new county charter, but failed. Opportunity seemed to knock again on April 6, 1950, when gamblers Charles Binaggio and Charles Gargotta were gunned down in the First Ward Democratic Club, and soon thereafter the Kefauver hearings publicized Binaggio's role as a First Ward leader and an influential figure among courthouse politicians. This flurry passed, however, without stirring the public to demand sweeping change.

The presence of characters like Binaggio around the opposition camp led the mugwumps in 1949 to establish the Kansas City Crime Commission. It failed to achieve political importance and finally became a desultory operation staffed by a director, an investigator and two office girls.

Repulsed in their attempts to take over Jackson County government, the mugwumps settled down for several years to a live-and-let-live arrangement with the Democratic regulars. The Citizens Association ran Democrats for city office who were acceptable to the regulars. Many leading Democrats in the association gave support to the regulars' candidates in county elections. Contractors having ties with the regular Democrats found they were welcome at city hall and could do business with association-backed officials. In return, the most powerful faction of the regular Jackson County Democrats, led by William H. Sermon of Independence, abstained from entering city elections against the association.

And so, having things pretty much their own way in the city, the mugwumps proceeded to work themselves into a jam. The city manager and enthusiastic businessmen decided that Kansas City should build for the future. Instead of waiting like most cities until things got into a hopeless mess, they believed Kansas City should act now to insure adequate water supply, sewage disposal, freeways, parks and playgrounds, and a jet-age airport. Downtown slums and near-slums should be cleared out and fine new office buildings and parking garages erected in their place, even if a public subsidy were necessary to get projects moving. The city should not wait to be encircled by suburban cities but should annex big chunks of still underdeveloped land, even if this meant a temporary financial drain on the central city.

In this mood, the city administration asked the voters after World War II to approve a total of more than $200 million in general obligation and revenue bonds. The voters said yes by majorities running as high as six to one.

In the same period they approved annexations doubling the city's size and started proceedings that would double it again by 1963 to an expanse of three hundred and six square miles. (Under Missouri law, as in Texas, a city may annex an unincorporated area without its consent.) When the voters turned down a proposed addition of forty-eight square miles in 1952, city manager Cookingham and the council waited two years, then resubmitted the proposal, supporting it with a public relations campaign paid for with city funds. This time they won.

Businessmen and city officials got urban renewal projects under way. The voters agreed to nearly $3 million in general obligation bonds to pay the city's share of the cost.

Everything seemed to be rolling along nicely. But the voters' agreeableness was deceptive.

A few mugwumps sensed that a day of reckoning must arrive. In 1952, former Mayor John Gage had attempted to convince other leaders that the people should be warned of higher taxes if they approved more bond issues. When he lost the argument,

Gage resigned as chairman of the citizens bond advisory board.

As the city began selling bonds to finance its improvement program, it suddenly came face to face with the reality that it did not have enough income to pay the principal and interest on more bonds and still carry on its regular governmental services. Work on some projects ground to a stop; one of these was the jet airport where, although $6 million already had been spent, three times that much was still needed.

There was no use looking to a higher property tax for relief. State law prohibited the city from assessing property at a figure above that set by Jackson County assessors, and the courthouse Democrats, involved in no big improvement program themselves, saw to it that the assessment level was kept low enough to squeeze the association men in city hall.

Cookingham and the mugwumps were not too worried. They could just explain their problem to the people and, as before, the voters would approve what had to be done. The city council decided a 1 percent tax on everyone's earnings would raise enough money. They placed the matter on the March, 1957, ballot and appropriated another $40,000 in city funds for a "campaign" to put it over.

This time the formula did not work. Perhaps it was the economic recession being felt in Kansas City. Maybe city hall had just worn out its welcome. In any event, councilmen and other speakers who tried to explain the earnings tax before usually friendly luncheon clubs and community groups met a chilly response. Sometimes they were shouted down.

The mugwumps realized their campaign was faltering, but the results on election day hit them like a bucket of cold water. The people rejected their earnings tax four to one, 80,000 votes to 20,000. The plan carried in only four of the city's 357 precincts. The mugwumps' dismay was not so much because the city government was still in a financial hole—they could always work their way out of that somehow—but the political implications of the defeat were unmistakable.

The sudden exposure of mugwump weakness failed to jar the aging Citizens Association leaders into action. They never had really sought the support of organized labor, and they did not seek it now. Nor did they flush out the considerable number of businessmen who had remained politically passive for years, letting the association carry the load.

Meanwhile, the splintered factions of courthouse Democrats and other anti-reformers saw their opportunity. They managed to agree on a slate of candidates for the city council in 1959 and campaigned vigorously, led by rousing orator and one-time association supporter Councilman Charles Shafer. Their efforts paid off at the polls. They did not contest three of the council seats held by the Citizens Association. They did contest five others and won them all—two decisively, three narrowly. Their only defeat came in attempting to unseat reform Mayor H. Roe Bartle. The mountainous mayor (top weight 300 pounds) won re-election 54,000 to 41,000.

With a five-to-four majority on the council, the faction Democrats sent professional city-manager Cookingham on his way. In his place they chose a political friend, and soon made clear that his main purpose was to serve as a convenience for the councilmen. Thus the cycle that had started in 1926 rolled full around.

Yet there were differences. This time the strong, shrewd hand of Pendergast was missing. Instead, the councilmen and the factions they represented fell to fighting among themselves. And this time there was a loud, clear voice within city hall, that of Mayor Bartle, to castigate the political hacks. This he did with relish and frequency. After a particularly acid speech over all three local television channels, the council majority retaliated by stripping the mayor of most of his staff, including his bodyguard-chauffeur. The next week, when a load of dignitaries arrived from Washington, Bartle drove the mayoral limousine to the airport himself, ceremoniously helped the VIP's into the car, stowed their luggage and resumed his place behind the wheel, explaining all the way into town that this was the way the city council wanted things. The incident received wide newspaper play, and the mayor soon had his chauffeur back.

Among mugwump ranks all was not peaceful, either. Bartle and others began dropping broad hints to the venerable leaders of the Charter Association that they should retire after a generation of service and let younger men take command. It was also suggested that in the reorganization the name "Citizens Association" might well be discarded and a new name such as "Charter Party" take its place.

These proposals made little headway within the association, and so in 1960, two dozen younger mugwumps—most of them in their forties, a few younger, a few older—took matters into their own hands. They elected a board of trustees headed by forty-three-year-old insurance executive Cliff C. Jones, Jr., and voted to revive the Civic Research Institute—the municipal research bureau that had functioned from 1921 until 1942, when the mugwumps, happily victorious over Pendergast, had let it die.

The revived bureau employed a former Cookingham aide, Charles E. Curran, as executive secretary. The foundation-supported Community Studies, Inc., agreed to help the bureau get off the ground by lending it staff and other assistance. Word was bruited about that once the young mugwumps had their research bureau going, they would turn their attention to forming a candidate-running organization. This would be a successor or, conceivably, a competitor to the old Citizens Association.

And so it appears that, in the 1960s, Kansas City may end up with factions on all sides, mugwump and anti-mugwump alike, unless the veteran reformers can bring themselves to back gracefully offstage.

SAN ANTONIO—RIDERS AND WRANGLERS

Mugwumps have found it a bumpy ride breaking San Antonio in to good government. The first little group that tried it in 1939–40 was led by the Parent-Teacher Association council and young Edward G. Conroy, scion of a well-known San Antonio family. Mayor Maury Maverick humored them by appointing a fifteen-member charter-revision committee and letting them write a charter that would have replaced the commission government of pre–World War I vintage with a council-manager system. But when the charter appeared on the ballot, the mayor opposed it, and it lost by 10,000 votes to 6,000.

Maverick went off to Congress, Conroy went off to the Navy,

and no more was heard about political reform until 1946. Then Conroy and the Chamber of Commerce president, hotel chain owner A. C. "Jack" White, founded the Council-Manager Association. Two years later the Bureau of Governmental Research was born, with Conroy as executive secretary.

The bureau marched forth as a militant champion of the manager plan. White and his colleagues in the Chamber of Commerce also began to needle Mayor Gus Mauermann and his successor, Mayor Alfred Callaghan, with charges of do-nothingism. The city, they pointed out, had no planning department and no master plan. The water system was deteriorating. So was the park system. Property on the tax rolls had not been reassessed for more than ten years. The city commissioners never got around to adopting an annual budget until the year was eight or nine months along. The civil service system was a joke, a plaything of political hacks. Despite the wartime mushrooming of population, the city had annexed no territory; it still covered only thirty-six square miles. Kelly Air Force Base had become a permanent installation with 20,000 or so civilian employes. Oil strikes near the city had brought in more residents. New problems cried for solution. San Antonio, went the jibes, had to wake up.

Stung, Mayor Callaghan publicly upbraided chamber president White for interfering in politics, and challenged the critics to enter someone against him at the polls.

This seemed a pretty safe challenge. The white-collar residents of San Antonio's north end had never showed much interest in local elections. The city hall boys had found it no trouble to control the outcome by herding in voters from the Latin-American districts on the west side and the Negro east side.

Mayor Callaghan's public dare, however, aroused the businessmen. They formed a committee of one hundred, collected a $51,000 campaign fund, entered White for mayor, bought off many of Callaghan's ward leaders and won by a smashing four-to-one majority. Studying the returns, mugwumps found that half the votes had been cast by the white-collar north side, 35 percent by the south side, which was heavily settled by civilians employed at Kelly air base. Voters in the low-income east and west sides, discouraged by the $1.75 state poll tax, accounted for only 15 percent of the ballots. Thereafter the mugwumps concentrated their campaigns in the north and south, largely ignoring the Negro and Latin-American districts.

After White's election, the Council-Manager Association renewed its demand for a popular vote on a charter amendment to effect council-manager government. The four other commissioners (Mayor White sat as the fifth commissioner) paid no attention. They still looked the other way when the association, aided by the P-TA and the League of Women Voters, brought in 13,000 signatures on petitions, far above the legal requirement to force an election. Finally threatened with recall, the commissioners agreed to place the thirteen city-manager amendments on a special-election ballot; but they also placed a dozen similar-sounding amendments on the same ballot and mixed them up together, all unnumbered, so that only a lawyer could know whether he was voting for city-manager government or against it. Mayor White vetoed the hashed-up ordinance and it never came to public vote.

As these shenanigans piled delay upon delay, the mugwumps began to differ among themselves on tactics. One group thought the thirteen council-manager amendments should be boiled into a single amendment that merely established council-manager government in general terms. Another element began to think a strong-mayor system would be better.

The split became so serious that in 1950 the mugwump factions, after at last forcing the commission to give them space on the ballot, submitted two rival reform charters to the voters. Both lost.

This sobered the mugwumps temporarily. They joined forces in 1951, raised another $40,000, ran a full Citizens Committee ticket for mayor and four commissioners, and elected them all along with a charter-writing commission. That October, after another $20,000 campaign, the voters approved the new charter two to one, and San Antonio had city-manager government at last.

C. A. Harrell was hired away from Norfolk, Virginia, as city manager at a comfortable $27,500 a year, and he began instituting civil service, centralized purchasing and other reforms.

There, in some cities, the story might have ended. But San Antonio mugwumps again fell into their old dispute over what kind of city-manager government to have. Mayor White believed he ought to administer the government himself, with the city manager assisting him as a right-hand man. Harrell had the conventional picture of himself as chief administrator answering only to the whole city council. Soon the mayor and Harrell were locked in an open feud.

Harrell and his mugwump allies found another problem—indeed, a pair of them—on their hands following a massive eighty-square-mile annexation in 1952. The territory included the country estates of two big oil men, A. A. Jergins and S. G. Nelson. Enraged at being absorbed into the city, they backed the White faction with a war chest estimated at $100,000 in the 1953 municipal election. The pro-manager mugwumps raised almost as much, but the White slate, supported by the town's biggest real estate owner, department store man Morris Kallison, and by remnants of the old political regulars, gained every seat on the city council. They dismissed Harrell (Cincinnati later grabbed him) and started working on a strong-mayor charter.

Politically, San Antonio was beginning to resemble one of those World War I movies with opposing infantry slogging back and forth over the same churned ground. Now that it was their turn to counterattack, the pro-manager mugwumps began a recall movement against the councilmen—against six of them, that is; the other three had decided they favored city-manager government after all. As the recall petitions gained signatures, the six intended victims found a provision in the charter saying that in case a councilman resigned, the remaining councilmen could choose his successor. So the six began resigning one at a time. Each was replaced by a comrade from the anti-manager camp. The pressing question at each council meeting became—have we got a quorum to accept a resignation?

Since their recall petitions could not keep pace with the resignations, the pro-manager mugwumps dropped the recall effort and pointed toward the 1955 election. Their Citizens Committee, which had taken such a drubbing in 1953, became the Good Government League. They selected as chairman an elderly Ford-agency owner, Frank Gillespie, Sr.

Although they did not realize it at the time, that 1955 campaign marked the turning point for the reformers. It was to establish them and their Good Government League as the dominant force in San Antonio politics. In 1955, however, with the stigma of the 1953 defeat still on them, the pull was all uphill. Gillespie recalls:

> We decided to go for all nine council seats. Getting the candidates was a hectic experience. First we chose the names of five men we thought should be the backbone of the ticket. Four of them turned us down. The other one said maybe. So we tried some more. We got turned down and turned down, especially when we tried to get someone from the Mexican community. At last one man said he would run. Then we got a second. The last day before the filings closed we had seven men, one of whom had agreed that morning. We went to lunch. Two of the men were wavering. Then another fellow came in late and said, "I have been talking to my wife for the last half-hour and she says if I run she's going to leave me." So we had six. Before the lunch was over we managed to replace him, that made seven, and we told them to get an eighth running mate. We didn't put anybody up against the independent on the council, Henry Gonzales. After that about twenty-five of us went out and raised $40,000 for the campaign. All our men won.

The task in 1957 was much easier. Seven of the Good Government League incumbents ran for re-election on the council, and the GGL had no difficulty finding two more to complete the ticket. They encountered almost no opposition.

In 1959, the GGL swept to another nine-to-nothing victory. The reformers triumphed again in 1961. In both elections, however, the resistance was stiffer. And other problems began plaguing the mugwumps. The GGL-dominated city council voted to have the city housing authority accept $17 million in federal funds to build 1,500 units of public housing. Real estate interests poured in cash to block the plan. They circulated petitions forcing a public referendum. In the ensuing campaign, only the Catholic Church and the Mexican community favored public housing. The proposal lost by 12,000 votes to 10,000, a rebuke to the city administration.

A year later, in 1960, the administration, urged on by the Chamber of Commerce, asked the people to approve a $9-million bond issue for an expressway that would have clipped through a corner of Brackenridge Park. Some two thousand women of the San Antonio Conservation Society, abetted by wealthy home owners in the area, raised thousands of dollars for a "save our parks" campaign. The bonds lost by three hundred and thirty votes.[5]

Needing money for new sewers, the city council enacted a sewer service charge on each home owner of 60 cents to $1.25 a month. Cries of pain arose, augmented by Hearst's San Antonio *Light*, which labeled the payments "sewerola." The council retreated a bit, lowering the charges by ten cents a month.

Over the years the citizenry had become accustomed to easy-going government under officials content to let the city drowse along like a dusty Mexican village. When the city-manager regime brought in roaring machinery, dug up streets for new pipelines, and laid miles of smoking blacktop, some inhabitants became annoyed and uncomfortable. They were not used to much municipal activity. A worried housewife, for instance, telephoned city hall demanding: "Did you folks lose a street sweeper? I just saw one going down the street. I've been living in this house for thirty years and I never saw one out here before."

It turned out to be the first time the street had ever been swept.

These public worries and gripes were not, of course, entirely spontaneous. They were helped along by the anti-mugwump politicians headquartered in the Bexar County courthouse. Of the forty-one elected officials there, only two could be called friends of the Good Government League. At city election time, these anti-mugwumps could be counted on to support the opposition groups that ran slates for the city council under names like the San Antonio Citizens Ticket, the Charter Revision League or the Better Government League.

The reformers' major objective in the 1960s is to eject this aggregation from the courthouse. The first step was to elect reform-minded Sam Jorrie as one of the four county commissioners. Jorrie, the hard-driving, fortyish owner of a large furniture store, has constantly fought the other county officials. Collaborating with the pro-reform San Antonio *Express and News*, he helped focus public attention on an independent audit of the tax assessor-collector's office which disclosed that millions of dollars in taxes had never been collected. Jorrie persuaded certified public accountant Charles Davis to run for the assessor-collector's job against the incumbent who had held it for twenty years. Jorrie underwrote Davis' $30,000 campaign; he also arranged to have aerial pictures taken of new housing developments, showing scores of houses that were not even on the tax rolls. Davis won election by a six-to-five margin, giving Jorrie at least one ally in the courthouse.

Meanwhile, the Governmental Research Bureau, renamed the Research and Planning Council and directed by seasoned bureau man John F. Willmott (Conroy departed in the mid-1950s to become city manager of New Rochelle, New York), concentrates on revising the county's form of government. Its immediate goal is a "home rule" state constitutional amendment giving Bexar County the right to draft its own charter. After that, they will talk about whether to create a county-manager government, a county mayor-council form, or perhaps a consolidated city-county government.

In this effort the middle-class reformers can expect little help from the Negroes and from organized labor. Both groups, however, are politically weak and will remain so until San Antonio, a largely nonindustrial city, has more jobs to attract a worker population.

The Mexican Americans, outnumbering the Negroes almost five to one, are potentially an all-important political element, even though they now vote lightly because of the poll tax. At the moment the Mexican rank-and-file seems to like the courthouse politicians with their handout and patronage approach to government better than the efficiency-minded mugwumps. But the mugwumps are courting the Latin community, particularly its business and professional men. The Good Government League includes two Mexican Americans each time on its nine-man slate for the city council; these have been the first Latins ever elected to the San Antonio council. The reform administration has named Latins, and Negroes as well, to city boards and commissions. The Chamber of Commerce has persuaded the Mexican Chamber of Commerce to join it in supporting expressway bonds and other projects.

In the "Anglo"—that is, non-Latin and non-Negro—community, low-income voters show slight affection for the Good Government League; but like the low-income Negro and Latin districts, these precincts also cast a low percentage of votes.[6]

The middle- and upper-class Anglo districts, mostly on the north side, are divided among "liberals" who favor welfare services, rights of collective bargaining, and so forth, and more numerous "conservatives" who oppose these things. This division applies in state and national politics. But on local matters there is no significant difference. Middle-class liberals and conservatives both favor the reformers over the courthouse hacks.

This middle-class support forms the bulwark of Good Government League strength. It appears solid enough to keep the reform element in power for years to come.

The ride for San Antonio mugwumps has been a long and rough one, but they seem secure in the saddle now.

MEMPHIS—NO MO' MUGWUMP BLUES

Ten plagues were visited upon ancient Egypt, the land of its namesake city along the Nile. But for Memphis on the Mississippi, the plagues numbered two—at least in the eyes of its mugwumps. And the city recovered slowly, painfully from both of them.

The first pestilence came in the 1870s. Like good citizens elsewhere, Memphis mugwumps were struggling to free their city of an Irish Democratic political machine, and the prospects, as elsewhere, were for a lengthy tussle. Then the yellow-fever epidemics struck. Eight thousand people died, thousands more fled never to return. The city's hopes of becoming the metropolis of the South were buried along with the victims. Immigrants and northern capital shunned the place for generations.

But as the city lay dazed and fearful of further epidemics, the mugwumps noted that the political machine, along with nearly every other institution in Memphis, had disintegrated. Before the politicians could recover, a quickly formed Citizens League asked the state legislature to take over the city government. Memphis became a ward of the state for fourteen years.

Autonomous again in 1893, Memphis permitted another collection of political mediocrities to gain control until 1909—at which point the mugwumps brought upon themselves the second plague.

Stirring up a reform wave, they won the voters' approval of a new charter creating a commission type of government. Their reform candidate for mayor was a tall, red-headed councilman who ran a harness shop—Edward H. Crump.

Young Crump was not exactly the southern ideal of a candidate. His folks had been poor Mississippi farmers. But Crump staged a good campaign featuring a Negro street band (its cornetist-leader William C. Handy published one of the campaign songs three years later under the title "Memphis Blues"), and Crump beat the incumbent mayor by seventy-nine votes.

His backers' joy soon turned to disappointment. Crump, like a young contemporary in Boston named Curley, showed a bullheaded disinclination to listen to the better citizens' advice. He refused to enforce Tennessee's state prohibition law, and he allowed houses of prostitution to run, holding that the majority of residents did not want a closed town. He also began going after the private power company and talking about public ownership. (He was to continue talking for nearly thirty years, especially around election time, until Memphis Power and Light finally sold out to the city in 1939.)

An alliance including church people, the power company and mugwumps led by editor C. P. J. Mooney of the *Commercial Appeal* moved against Crump in 1915. They charged that Crump should be removed from office for failing to enforce the prohibition law. The state supreme court upheld their contention. Rather than fight the case further, he resigned as mayor. The experience was a painful one for Crump, who was then forty-two years old, and throughout the remainder of his long political career he avoided holding office himself whenever possible.

While Crump withdrew to make money in private business and to build a strong organization based in the Shelby County courthouse, Memphis mugwumps drafted businessman Rowlett Paine to run for mayor in 1919. He served two terms, barely winning re-election, with Crump's last-minute aid, over the Ku Klux Klan entry in 1923.

Crump expected that his rescue act would win him a voice in Paine's administration, but the upright Paine would have none of him. And so Crump prepared for an open fight with the mugwumps for control of city hall in 1927. The result was a slaughter. Crump split mugwump ranks by running an old-family descendant, Watkins Overton, for mayor. He defeated Paine nearly three to one.

Thus began more than twenty years of Crump control. He was unlike any political boss the United States has ever seen, or probably will ever see again—a combination of showman, dictator, humanitarian and hard-as-nails administrator. Unhindered by civil service or voting machines, Crump and his lieutenants built a disciplined phalanx of city and county employes that could deliver any vote total required. Crump's influence at the state capitol in Nashville and in Washington, D.C., sprang from his control over the votes in Tennessee's most populous county; with it he could elect governors, senators and congressmen. A young man wishing to enter politics, if he was bright and personable, could find a role in the Crump organization—and if he was bright, he knew he had slight chance outside it.

To avoid dependence on the business community, Crump built his campaign treasuries by collecting a percentage of each city and county employe's salary. In turn, he won the support of many businessmen by keeping taxes low and running efficient city and county governments. Staffs were well trained. His long black-clad figure often could be seen riding the transit system to make sure service was satisfactory. Corruption was almost nonexistent; the boss tolerated no thieves or bribe-takers. Crump even mollified the church people in the late thirties by cleaning up most of the vice. If any appreciable number of citizens really wanted something—a new school, a playground, a paved street, traffic signal, or some waterfront improvement—they had only to let Mistuh Crump know and he would usually arrange it.

Against this type of competition Memphis mugwumps could make little headway.

In the early 1930s, former Governor Malcolm Patterson rallied a small knot of resistance. This group, steeped in the aristocratic tradition of the Old South, resented Crump's development of voting power among Negroes, who composed more than a third of the city's population. The resistance candidate scraped up 869 votes against Mayor Overton's 23,000. After that there was usually no opponent against the Crump man.

The hopelessness of the mugwumps' position arose partially from a lack of issues. The battle cries of waste and graft that could be used to overturn professional politicians in other cities were useless in Memphis. Nobody could find enough waste and graft to talk about. That left only the matter of principle: that Crump was a dictator, and dictatorship was wrong.

One of the few voices to raise this cry belonged to Edward J. Meeman, editor of the *Press-Scimitar*. A compact bundle of guts and energy, Meeman had been fulminating against Crump's authoritarian rule for years. His speeches and editorials fell mostly on indifferent ears, or frightened ones. Aside from his power of economic retaliation, of which few actual cases were ever recorded, Crump had a habit of issuing statements and running newspaper advertisements about his foes embodying such terms as "cowards," "murderers," "vultures," "mangy bubonic rats," "egg-sucking dogs." While such prose might possess limited political value in Boston or Cleveland, it found a large and delighted public in western Tennessee, and few wished to become its target.

But time, the one opponent no boss can beat, caught up with Ed Crump. The end of World War II found both him and his long-time ally, U. S. Senator K. D. McKellar, sliding into old age. Meanwhile, Memphis had undergone a wartime boom in population, shooting up a third, to nearly 400,000. The flood of newcomers did not know Crump. In addition, a current of reaction against the old political order was running through the state.

Meeman thought he saw his chance in 1948 when a young attorney, Estes Kefauver, decided to defy the Crump-McKellar organization and run for the United States senate. Developments from then on were described thus by one of the mugwumps who took part:

> Meeman had met Kefauver and thought he might serve as a symbol around whom people could rally. Meeman invited about

a hundred down to meet Kefauver in his hotel suite. Forty of us showed up.

The following Saturday afternoon Meeman called seven of us down to the hotel and said he thought we could lick this thing and now was the time to run against Crump—not a head-on local fight but by organizing support for Kefauver. The ones there were Dr. Henry Gotten; two lumbermen, O. D. Bratten and the late Charles Poe; William Barr, his company manufactures paint remover; Lucius E. Burch, an attorney whose family is socially prominent in Nashville; Edmund Orgill of the Orgill wholesale hardware company (he and Burch were interested in Union Now, as Kefauver was, and decided to back Kefauver against the incumbent Stewart, an isolationist); and Ed Dahlstrom of the Graham Paper Company—he's a conservative but joined up after Kefauver promised he was willing to see Taft-Hartley given a fair chance before any move to repeal it.

We decided to issue a report—the first time anybody had issued an independent report on a political matter without consulting Mr. Crump. Some people thought it was wonderful. Some thought we were crazy. Some thought we were going to get beaten up. A new spirit came into the community. Crump in fighting back made it into a personal thing. Our spies told us that Crump had prepared personal advertisements crucifying all of us, but they never appeared for some reason. . . .

Gordon Browning, who formerly was governor with Crump's support, was running for governor again, this time opposing the Crump organization. He spoke at the fair grounds out here. It just happened when he got on the platform that the Frisco railroad cars began switching and bumping in the yards nearby, and blowing their whistles so you couldn't hear a word that Browning said. Things like that always seemed to happen whenever anybody was speaking against Crump. Usually someone in the audience would pick a fight with the speaker and they both would be hauled off to jail.

Anyway, we organized a Committee for Kefauver, worked in the wards and had a panel of speakers who addressed up to thirty

> meetings a night. We also held training schools for poll watchers. The labor unions helped on this. . . .
>
> Both Kefauver and Browning won state-wide, as you know. We got 29,000 votes for them here in Memphis. After that, more people came over to our side. . . . The Browning and Kefauver victories did not break the back of the Crump machine here, but it did give people courage to speak. Nowadays this is all taken for granted. People have forgotten how it was.

Heartened at Crump's defeat by Kefauver and Browning, the same eight men who had formed the Kefauver committee resolved to establish a municipal research bureau, calling it the Civic Research Committee.

Memphis mugwumps, however, never did become much attached to research. They preferred political slugfests. Aided by Governor Browning, who got bills through the legislature for permanent voter registration and other election reforms, the Memphis men staged intensive drives to register voters; with only a third of the eligibles on the rolls, the reformers figured that higher registration would diminish the importance of the 20,000-vote bloc controlled by Crump's city and county employes. The Civic Research Committee followed up with petition campaigns that in 1954 finally succeeded in obtaining voting machines in Memphis.

Crump died in October, 1954. The immediate question became —would Crump's organization die with him? Or would someone else take over and keep it running? Or would Mayor Overton, the Crump protégé, build a new machine of his own? The mugwumps were more worried about Overton than about the other orphaned Crumpites. To eliminate him, they drafted one of their number, hardware man Orgill, to run for mayor against Overton in 1955. Two names appeared on the ballot—that of Overton, whom the Crump organization supported, and that of Orgill, supported by most members of Civic Research and another mugwump group, the Committee for Council-Manager Government.

Orgill defeated Overton and took his seat on the five-man city commission. Obviously he represented only a beachhead. Any significant changes in city government would have to await the arrival of more reformers in city hall. With municipal elections only every four years in Memphis, that meant the target date must be 1959.

When the time came, the mugwumps were ready with a Dedicated Citizens Committee and a new-found sparkplug, industrial chemicals manufacturer Stanley J. Buckman. The committee ran a "unity ticket" composed of three incumbent city commissioners who had pledged themselves to a good-government platform, and two newcomers. (Mayor Orgill, originally scheduled to head the ticket, had to withdraw after serious surgery.) With the backing of both the *Press-Scimitar* and the *Commercial Appeal* and a campaign organization whipped into a constant lather by Buckman, the "unity ticket" galloped into office. It took the mayoralty and the four other commissioner seats by wide margins.

The reformers promptly decided to make their Dedicated Citizens Committee into a permanent candidate-running body, bearing the somewhat less exalted label of Citizens Association of Memphis and Shelby County. Its goals included city-manager government, possible city-county consolidation, stronger civil service, regional planning. By 1961 the association had nine hundred members (at five dollars a year), divided among eighteen subdistricts blanketing the city and county. There seemed a fair prospect that it would dominate city elections at least throughout the sixties.

Memphis mugwumps are discovering, however, as other mugwumps have discovered, that gaining control of the county courthouse is a more difficult task. An attempt in 1956—a slate for county offices offered by the brand-new Good Local Government League—met crushing defeat at the polls. In 1960, the Citizens Association headed by Buckman tried again. It did somewhat better, electing a minority of four to the nine-man county court (board of county commissioners). But the majority remained under control of a former Crump man, suburban banker Paul Barrett.

Barrett gained his triumph by employing an old Crump device —forming an alliance with Negro leaders. After losing in 1960, the mugwumps concluded that Negro support is an advantage, not a disadvantage, in Memphis, and they began recruiting Negro members into their Citizens Association.

This hesitant step is but one of several the reformers must take if they are to wipe out the last traces of Mistuh Crump. The imperious old man kept the town's citizens in political swaddling clothes for a generation. The populace still faces awkward years of growing up, of learning to use the processes of proposing, debating, listening, compromising and persuading in order to get things done.

The mugwumps in Memphis need to learn this as well as others. Not long ago one of them said: "I actually think the best way to run this town is to have seven or eight men do it."

Ed Crump is dead, his machine has fallen into fragments, but his philosophy still hangs around the neck of Memphis. Fortunately, this won't last forever, either.

NEW ORLEANS—THE CHOSEN INSTRUMENT

Well before Huey Long appeared, New Orleans mugwumps, like those in Cleveland, Cincinnati and other less exotic cities, were fighting the spoils system, graft and government by hack. But living as they did in a port that prospered from the ships, the riverboats, the men who worked them, and the outlanders who came to town to buy, sell and cavort, New Orleans mugwumps found other evils to attack—block after block of whore-houses, gambling joints, saloons, speak-easies, dives of all kinds, and a tolerant tradition of accepting these establishments as an indigenous part of New Orleans.

The reformers, many from southern aristocratic families, won occasional victories over the Tammany-type regulars roosting in city hall. Aided by reform Governor John M. Parker, they elected a reform mayor, Andrew J. McShane, in 1920, along with a majority on the five-man city commission-council. McShane, however, could not keep his team united, and the reform administration lost out after one term to a faction calling themselves the Old Regulars.

The reformers' feud with the regulars shrank to insignificance in the late twenties when Huey, the Kingfish, arrived. The mugwumps disliked the regulars. But they hated Huey.

The Kingfish had the talent for exciting undying enmity or undying loyalty. Loyalists pointed to his new highways, bridges, schools, free textbooks, his concern for the poor, his defiance of the Bourbons. His enemies saw the ruthlessness, the vote frauds, the corruption. New Orleans and the state became divided into two camps, the Longs and the anti-Longs. When Huey was assassinated in 1935, brother Earl took over the leadership, and the division continued.

During the 1930s, the reformers had little luck at the polls. The Longites won most elective offices in New Orleans; and when they did not win, the Old Regulars did. But the mugwumps kept working. In 1933, architect Charles Favrot sold a small group of leading citizens on forming the New Orleans Bureau of Governmental Research. Favrot became its president, wealthy cotton broker Edgar B. Stern the vice president.

More important centers of action were the *Times-Picayune* and the *Item* newspapers, and a group of prominent men, many of whom served on the board of trustees of Tulane University. These elements engineered the anti-Long movement.

The first break came in 1939, not locally but at the state level, when the post-Huey organization got trapped in fraud scandals that sent Governor Richard W. Leche, Louisiana State University president James Monroe Smith, and others to jail. New Orleans mugwumps led in forming a People's League and drafting lawyer Sam Houston Jones of Lake Charles to run for governor on a reform ticket. Among those active in the campaign were three young law partners—Hale Boggs (later a congressman), Jacob Morrison and his younger half-brother deLesseps, nicknamed "Chep."

When Jones won the governorship, he brought the two-man staff of the New Orleans Bureau of Governmental Research to Baton Rouge for three months to help prepare the state's first modern budget. More significant politically, Jones submitted and the legislature passed bills requiring voting machines in New Orleans and placing the state employes and New Orleans city workers under civil service. In 1943, the *Times-Picayune* published a series of articles charging that the administration of Mayor Robert Maestri, a Long follower, had padded the city payrolls by a million dollars before the 1940 and 1942 elections.

Despite these gains, the mugwumps had little hope of ousting Mayor Maestri in 1946, but they rounded up a candidate—an inexplicable choice named "Bathtub Joe" Fernandez, whom Huey Long had once sent to Washington as First District congressman. A week before the filings were to close, executive editor Clayton Fritchey of the *Item* learned that Bathtub Joe had made a deal with Maestri to withdraw from the race on the last day of filing. When Fritchey's story appeared, Bathtub Joe withdrew at once. This left the anti-Longs five days in which to find a new champion.

At this confused moment, thirty-four-year-old Lieutenant-Colonel Chep Morrison returned from the wars. He had some political background—as a reform campaigner in the middle-class twelfth ward, as a member of the state legislature where he had introduced the New Orleans voting-machine bill—and he was enthusiastic and willing to run. The anti-Longs chose him as an eleventh-hour substitute.

Morrison campaigned hard. And the mugwumps, particularly the women's division, gave their handsome young candidate full backing. A feminine brigade marched the streets with brooms over their shoulders in imitation of the "clean-up squads" of Kansas City women who had campaigned against the Pendergast machine six years earlier.

The count on election night showed Morrison with better than 67,000 votes, Maestri with 63,000. It was hard to tell which side was more amazed.

Some mugwumps found their triumph a bit unsettling. Here they were in charge of a major city with an inexperienced mayor and little else. United States history was replete with similar reform "successes" that had fallen flat within months after taking office. The Bureau of Governmental Research pitched in by making thirty separate recommendations on how the city government could be improved.

It turned out that nobody needed to worry about Morrison. He proved himself one of the smartest political operators that New Orleans or any other city had seen.

In 1948, Earl Long won the governorship and struck back at Morrison (who had supported Long's opponent) by having his obedient legislature pass special bills handing control of the New

Orleans police force back to the safety commissioner, cutting city revenue and gerrymandering its election districts. It happened that Morrison was having local political difficulties at the time. Long's crude tactics came to his rescue. The resentment they engendered in New Orleans insured Morrison's re-election in 1950.

Discovering he had alienated not only his enemies but many friends in New Orleans, Long sought to make amends by letting through the 1950 legislature a constitutional amendment giving New Orleans permission to write its own home-rule charter; the amendment also barred the legislature from passing special bills applying to only one city.

Even before the state's voters ratified the amendment in 1952, the mugwumps had started writing a charter, drawing heavily upon the Bureau of Governmental Research for advice. The charter, creating a strong mayor-council government replacing the five commissioners, was adopted and went into effect in 1954.

These developments strengthened the mayor's political position, but it was in the local wards that Morrison displayed the skill that meant his survival. Probably no one was a better authority on this than the mayor's frustrated rival, James E. Comiskey, head of the Old Regulars faction of New Orleans Democrats.

In the 1960s, Comiskey is one of a vanishing breed—the Irish big-city political leader of the old school. A large man, still handsome with silver hair and black eyebrows, a deep pleasant voice, he can usually be found at his wholesale liquor warehouse on Poydras Street, behind a desk semicircled with a thick stand of bottles, including his own brand, Old Comiskey (bottled in Kentucky, six years old, eighty-six proof). When interviewed in the late 1950s, he talked readily about his political organization:

> We have a leader in each of the seventeen wards and a captain in each of the three hundred and twenty precincts in Orleans Parish. We have a men's organization and a women's organization which is less active. . . . The men in each ward elect a chairman. Then there's the Old Regulars steering committee made up of five ward leaders and me, the city chairman . . .
>
> Each ward leader picks himself a headquarters, sometimes in

> the basement of a home, maybe in the back of a shop. . . . Nearly all the ward leaders are on the public payroll, usually with the alcoholic-beverage control board, the attorney general, the state banking department or some other non-civil service state job. Two of us are local tax assessors elected by the people of our district—me from the third. I was born there. My parents and grandparents lived there, too, all of us not a stone's throw from each other . . .
>
> About half of the precinct workers are on the payrolls of state or local government.
>
> The Morrison organization is similar to ours. . . . Some of our old leaders have switched over to Morrison. He took a half dozen of my leaders away in the past five years, mostly by offering them lucrative positions. He has gained control of the parish [county] Democratic Committee by the same method. This committee sets the dates of elections and the polling locations, it appoints the election commissioners and names the three hundred and twenty custodians of the voting machines at twenty dollars a day . . .
>
> Morrison's got a good organization, all right, and he runs the show. He is boss. Don't let anybody tell you different.

The Morrison organization, the CCDA (Crescent City Democratic Association), won lopsidedly in the 1958 municipal elections just as it had for a decade. Morrison men took all city council seats except one.

The next year, however, Morrison ran again for the governorship (he had lost to Earl Long in 1956). This time he led his major opponent—songwriter and former governor Jimmie H. Davis—in the first primary, but in the two-man runoff Morrison lost decisively. Davis, while trailing the mayor 70,000 to 103,000 in New Orleans, made inroads among middle-class voters, who regarded Davis as being anti-Long and pro-good government. This 1960 setback apparently did Morrison no good. Later that year, in an election for eight judgeships, the Old Regulars won seven contests, Morrison's CCDA only one. It was CCDA's worst showing at the polls. And the mayor's organization was staggered again in 1961 when Comiskey's son, James A., beat its candidate for councilman-at-large.

Morrison was being harried on another front. A mugwump element that deplores the city's sinfulness exists today as it did a generation or two ago. The struggle revolves, naturally enough, around the police and law-enforcement agencies.

A peculiar atmosphere of precarious control, of violence just below the surface, has long hung over the New Orleans police department. In the 1890s, a police chief was murdered by supposed Mafia members. In 1917, the police superintendent was beaten to death in his office by a huge policeman he had discharged. In the 1950s, the department was regarded, like Chicago's, as having an unusual number of links with the underworld that is nominally its foe.

On New Year's Eve, 1950, a contractor-engineer named Dunn from Memphis entered a joint in the Vieux Carré, the French Quarter, apparently received knockout drops in a drink, and never came out alive. The incident, coming on the heels of other Mickey-Finn cases, caused an uproar. Not only were such things illegal, but they were bad for New Orleans tourist business. Mayor Morrison appointed a citizens committee to see what could be done to clean up the Vieux Carré.

The city got another jolt the following year, when two days of Kefauver committee hearings brought out the names of local gambling figures and revealed a former police superintendent with an interest in several gambling casinos and drawing a $100-a-week retainer from a horse-betting wire service. Other witnesses described how a former chief of detectives accumulated $150,000 in six years. The hearings disclosed that the slot-machine operators association made political contributions to all sides in New Orleans elections (the association president said the group had even given $8,000 to the campaign of reform Mayor Morrison).

An aroused group of businessmen, lawyers and clergymen agreed that New Orleans needed a crime commission. They gathered a following at dinners addressed by Spruille Braden of the New York Anti-Crime Commission and Virgil Peterson of the Chicago Crime Commission. In February, 1952, the Metropolitan Crime Commission of New Orleans, Inc., was born.

It grew with painful slowness. Everybody was against crime, but nobody came up with the $40,000 for the commission's annual expenses.

Meanwhile, a grand jury asked the mayor and commission-council for money to employ investigators so that it could look into allegations of police graft, gambling, and allied matters. Instead, the commission-council voted to conduct the investigation itself. It authorized a Special Citizens Investigating Committee (SCIC), and asked three other groups—the Bureau of Governmental Research, the new Metropolitan Crime Commission, and the Society of Former Special Agents of the FBI—to name one man each to the committee. The commission-council gave the SCIC subpoena power and a $50,000 bank account.

The SCIC brought in former FBI man Aaron M. Kohn from Chicago, where, following the murder of politician Charles Gross, he had been helping a Chicago city council committee probe gangland's relationship to politics.

Kohn soon found life in New Orleans more exciting than it had ever been in Chicago. Using undercover men, he compiled an 1800-page report about illegal liquor, prostitution, betting, and police pay-offs, then aired the information in twelve days of stormy hearings. A combination of court injunctions and political heat silenced him and the SCIC. In March, 1955, Kohn was sent to jail for ten days after refusing to reveal the name of a police sergeant who had given him documents detailing police graft collections. His stay was enlivened by a mass meeting on the city hall steps of nearly two thousand persons demanding his release.

Kohn, a stubborn man, took over as managing director of the crime commission despite its anemic bank balance. He opened an office and settled down for business. A number of ardent anti-Long mugwumps were not pleased at this development. They believed the Crime Commission's final effect would be to embarrass the Morrison administration and give ammunition to the Long faction and the Old Regulars for a comeback. Some of this feeling appeared within the Crime Commission itself; a few members resigned, declaring the commission was playing too rough. Undeterred, Kohn and the commission continued gathering evidence against lottery operators, demanding dismissal of law officials it considered unfit, and generally goading New Orleans to improve its police department.

In this effort to wake up the town, the Crime Commission received help from unexpected quarters. One was sixtyish bail-bondsman Peter Hand, one-time slot machine operator, former member of the state legislature, and an old friend of Governor Earl Long. He appeared on television station WYES one July evening in 1959 and answered questions by three reporters from the *States-Item* and *Times-Picayune*. With an air of refreshing frankness, Hand told of widespread bribery in the state legislature; he estimated the cost of getting a bill through the body at $500 and up. Then the questioning turned to local affairs:

Q. Mr. Hand, I think they said that you once were a handbook operator.
A. That is correct.
Q. For our viewers who may have lived sheltered lives, where I count myself, what is a handbook operator?
A. Well, a man that operates one of these bucket shops. . . . You have a board man and you take bets on horses and races.
Q. Isn't that illegal?
A. Yes, sir, but you get around that point in certain ways by taking care of certain people.
Q. What do you mean certain people?
A. Well, the law for one, and such things as that. You make a political donation at the proper time and you go on and everything is all right. Nobody will be bothered.
Q. Is it possible to operate a handbook or an illegal gambling game without the consent of the authorities?
A. Absolutely not.
Q. How long could you stay in business if—
A. About twenty minutes . . .
Q. What do you think of the gambling situation now? Is it under control or what is your—
A. Absolutely not . . .
Q. Mr. Hand, I understand that you attended both the Tulane

and Loyola law schools for some periods. Why didn't you continue with this study and become a lawyer?

A. Well, at the same time that I attended these two universities, I was operating a handbook in the business section of the city, and most of my business was with lawyers and doctors; and at the end of the day I'd look at my receipts taken in and find a lot of, fifteen or twenty, checks and when I'd send them to the bank—NSF. So I said to myself, if I got to go to these schools to learn how to be a lawyer that don't have enough to pay a two-dollar or five-dollar check, well—

Q. Have you ever regretted your decision to leave school to be a full-time handbook operator?

A. Never, never! I made a lot of money booking and in other games.

Q. Have you ever been in the slot-machine business, Mr.—

A. Yes, sir. I was in the slot machines from 1940 to 1946 with the syndicate, and it was very profitable. My take was three thousand five hundred dollars a month . . .

Q. You say syndicate. What do you mean by a syndicate?

A. Well, a syndicate is other people than local people . . . Costello and Kastel had the biggest interest. They are out-of-towners . . .

Q. How many machines did you have, Pete?

A. Sixteen hundred.

Q. Sixteen hundred! How did you get by with all those machines in town?

A. Well, those machines were sort of legal. We went to court and won a decision in the lower court, and then we went in the Supreme Court and proved it wasn't slot machines, until 1946, and then Morrison proved otherwise . . .

Q. Do you feel that someone can successfully operate a handbook today under conditions as they are today?

A. Absolutely! You don't think all the handbooks are closed, do you?

Q. You seem to intimate that they are open and running right here in the city of New Orleans.

A. Absolutely . . . I couldn't tell you how many books are operating, but I would say that you have at least forty or fifty books in buildings and I'd say you have the rest in phone services and in homes.[7]

How much of Mr. Hand's account was fact and how much fancy nobody was quite sure. The telecast, in any event, caused a stir, especially after the Crime Commission reprinted it.

All the spotlights aimed in its direction seem to have had an effect on New Orleans' police department. Most observers, including the Crime Commission, agree that the department has been improving.

The same may be said of most other city departments. The advances, however, have not been spectacular. Morrison, the young lawyer turned reform politician, has gathered few laurels as an efficiency expert. He built a reputation not as an administrator-mayor but as a promoter-mayor. During his regime, he led the parade for dramatic physical changes in New Orleans, including expressways, a new bridge across the Mississippi, a central railroad terminal, new downtown office buildings, and the clearing of seven blocks of central slums for an impressive civic center with an eleven-story city hall, state office building, library, supreme court building and civil courts building. The mayor's able public relations staff has given him credit for growing trade with Latin America and for the multimillion-dollar string of petrochemical industries springing up for fifty miles along the Mississippi, drawn perhaps by Chep's salesmanship, drawn certainly by the three hundred billion gallons of fresh water that flow by each day into the Gulf.

Back in 1946 the mugwumps were looking primarily not for an administrative genius or a promoter. They wanted someone who could kick the Old Regulars and the Long forces out of power in New Orleans. This Morrison did. But after sixteen years, his era was scheduled to end. The 1954 city charter and its clause limiting mayors to two successive terms meant that he could not file for re-election when his term expired in 1962. This signified one inevitable change.

Another probably will be the disappearance of the basic cleavage, Longs versus anti-Longs, that has shaped state and city politics for thirty years. The death of Earl Long in 1960 left Huey's son, United States Senator Russell Long, as heir to the dynasty, and unlike his father and his uncle, Russell does not generate the kind of love and hate that can divide a population into warring halves. Losing the Longs as a devil-image can have unforeseeable repercussions among New Orleans mugwumps and their political alignments.

Another imponderable is Morrison. He had hoped to run for mayor again in 1962, but the voters at the 1961 election refused (62,700 to 61,200) to change the city charter so that he could file for another term. Rebuffed, Morrison resigned in mid-1961 to become President Kennedy's ambassador to the Organization of American States. This left New Orleans mugwumps in an uncertain position. Was Morrison really long gone? Or would he try to keep his Crescent City Democratic Association alive, managing it as a political commuter? Even if he tried, could he succeed?

It looked very much as if New Orleans mugwumps would soon have to cope with the same old problem again—finding someone to serve as the chosen instrument, someone who could beat the hacks at their own game.

11

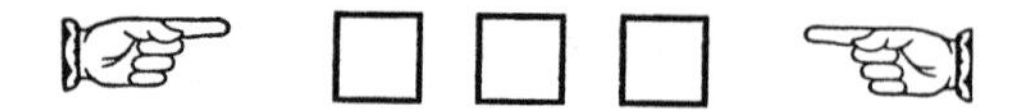

The Tidy Towns

Milwaukee • Cleveland • Los Angeles • Seattle

There seems to be no single road to good government, and no single way to preserve it, once attained.

Milwaukee got there by way of an Irish Socialist mayor who could get along with German neatness and Yankee frugality. Cleveland arrived via a wealthy Progressive mayor and a mugwump revolt that succeeded, then failed, yet did not fail completely. Los Angeles had its transplanted Midwest mugwumps who fought a railroad and stamped out political parties before they could get started. And Seattle achieved good government when a handful of young Republicans had time to sit in their law offices during the depression and get mad about the Democratic hacks who had taken over the County-City Building.

MILWAUKEE—UP FROM PENURY

Chicago and Milwaukee are less than a hundred miles apart geographically. Politically, they are on different planets.

Chicago is proud of its Crime Commission; Milwaukee is proud of its police force. Chicago struggles to eliminate racketeers from its political councils; Milwaukee would hardly know a racketeer if it saw one. In Chicago small-scale graft causes no more stir than a tip to a hat-check girl; in Milwaukee a municipal employe discovered accepting a five-dollar bribe would be pilloried on the front page of the *Journal* and bounced out of city hall. For Chicago, in other words, honest government is something to hope for, some day. In Milwaukee it is something they have known for forty years.

Chicago patriots resent such comparisons. To manage affairs neatly in a humdrum little city off the beaten track, they say, is much simpler than in a shifting pulsating industrial center six times as large. The Chicagoans undoubtedly have a point. But other factors than size lie behind the Milwaukee story.

Milwaukee's political make-up can be traced to the two main streams of immigrants who peopled the city. First came the New Englanders with their mugwump ideas of right and wrong. The second stream, from Germany, included many Socialists fleeing after the collapse of the 1848 revolutions. For all their differences, these two groups possessed something in common: a moralistic approach to government. They shared a belief that the exercise of governmental power is a sacred trust. This righteousness for which Milwaukee was later to become noted was not too evident during Wisconsin's roistering lumbering days. Mayor David Rose, who was finishing his fifth term in 1910, had had a wide-open town, with gambling, prostitution and plenty of boodle around city hall.

One might have expected it would be the puritanical progeny of New England who would throw such rascals out; but it was the Socialists who brought reform to Milwaukee. Led by Victor Berger (who with Eugene V. Debs was then organizing the national Socialist party), the Milwaukee Socialists entered a slate in the 1898 city election and received less than three thousand votes. They were back two years later, however, with several thousand more, and the total mounted at each election until in 1910 the Socialists swept the ticket. Berger went to Congress, Emil Seidel became mayor, and an obscure young lawyer named Daniel Webster Hoan was elected city attorney.

The Socialist victory galvanized the businessmen into action. They joined with the old city hall regulars to defeat Seidel in 1912. The following year a mugwump element started the Citizens Governmental Research Bureau. They also launched a Voters League. Going to the legislature, they obtained a bill removing party labels from the Milwaukee ballot; thereafter, confronted only by a list of names, the working-class voters had trouble identifying Socialist candidates.

This counteroffensive stopped the Socialist advance. For twenty years the Socialists were unable to gain a majority in the city council. But the mugwumps could not stop Dan Hoan. And after a while they did not want to very much.

As city attorney, Hoan had gained a certain mugwump admiration by making life difficult for the utilities. He sued the gas and electric companies to win lower rates. He forced the railroads to eliminate grade crossings in the city and made the traction company pave between its tracks. In another suit he established the city's right to regulate billboards.

After his election as mayor in 1916, Hoan won over more of the thrifty burghers by his careful handling of city funds. He established centralized purchasing in 1917, as the mugwumps were urging; soon the city was paying cash for its supplies and taking a discount. Only the bankers objected when the mayor ceased depositing city trust funds in their institutions at 2 percent interest, placing them instead in short-term federal securities drawing a higher return. Property owners who were short of cash to pay taxes did not need to go to banks or loan companies; the city would give them a six-month extension—with interest at 6 percent.

By thus saving a dollar here and earning fifty cents there, Hoan soon had the city on a pay-as-you-go basis, even for many of its capital improvements. So absorbed did Milwaukee's administration become with saving money that in the 1930s it even declined federal works projects because it did not wish to put up matching funds.

During Hoan's twenty-four years as mayor, Milwaukee acquired a nation-wide reputation for economically providing its people with good police, fire protection, sanitation, parks and other services. The mayor, of course, did not accomplish this all alone. He never had a majority on the city council except briefly in 1922 and again in 1932–36; on both occasions two members of the Nonpartisan opposition joined his Socialist minority to give him working control. Hoan, to put his program across, needed the support of mugwumps, men of property and the press—and this he could generally obtain. Professor Joseph P. Harris of the University of Wisconsin wrote after Hoan had beaten his Republican opponent in 1928: "Hoan made no campaign whatever and carried the wealthy conservative wards. He is commonly looked upon by the conservative groups of the city as being one-tenth Socialist and nine-tenths a lawyer and businessman, and a good one."

Even Milwaukee, however, could become bored with Dan Hoan and his good government. In 1940, a little-known young assistant city attorney, Carl Zeidler, had the brashness to challenge old Dan for re-election. A handsome blond Republican, Zeidler staged a flamboyant campaign. Pretty girls in evening dresses passed out literature at his meetings, and sometime during the evening he would usually sing "God Bless America" in a clear baritone. He beat Hoan by fifteen thousand votes.

Carl Zeidler did not remain long in city hall. When World War II came, he joined the Navy and disappeared at sea on a tanker, apparently torpedoed. His successor, elderly real estate man and saloon owner John L. Bohn, remained safely, almost inertly, in the mayor's chair until 1948. Then another Socialist entered the scene.

He was Zeidler's younger brother Frank. The Socialist party, once a tightly knit and disciplined organization, by this time had dwindled to a few old men. Instead of trying to revive it, the thirty-five-year-old Zeidler and his friends called a meeting of some fifty liberals and labor leaders and organized the Municipal Enterprise Committee. Zeidler, who had made a weak showing in the 1944 primary, became their candidate for mayor. Mugwumps and the press attacked the committee as a Socialist front, but Zeidler rolled to victory by 124,000 to 97,000.

Like Hoan, Zeidler soon won over many mugwumps—won at least their tolerance—by working hard to be a good mayor. In 1952, the powerful Milwaukee *Journal*, which had opposed him four years earlier, supported him for re-election. Only real estate interests annoyed by the mayor's housing program offered serious opposition. His margin on election day was an overwhelming 92,000.

The 1956 election found the anti-Zeidler forces better organized, with money to run newspaper advertisements declaring that mobs of juveniles crazed with liquor and dope were roaming the city, and a whispering campaign that Zeidler was a "nigger lover." With the *Journal* again on his side, the mayor won by a reduced majority of 23,000 votes.

During these years there existed between the mugwump-business element and Zeidler what could be described as a working truce. Neither quite trusted the other. Relations were civil rather than cordial and close.

Something of the same atmosphere had prevailed during Hoan's long tenure. But the two eras were different. Hoan's thrifty stewardship was the kind of government that Milwaukee's leaders then felt they wanted and needed. Hoan ran city hall well. He did not bother them, and they did not bother him. Close relations were unnecessary.

When Zeidler took office in 1948, however, Milwaukee was entering a new age. Her leadership was beginning to split over what kind of city and what kind of government they wanted.

Nearly everyone admitted the town was starting to show its age. The commercial buildings were old. Neighborhoods of little frame houses on little lots had gone to blight. Local newsman Richard S. Davis described Milwaukee as sitting "in complacent shabbiness on the west shore of Lake Michigan like a wealthy old lady in black alpaca taking her ease on the beach."

This picture did not disturb some of the leading citizens, but others formed the Greater Milwaukee Committee to overthrow the pay-as-you-go policy that Hoan had painstakingly developed during his quarter-century in office. The committee, composed of a hundred and fifty big property owners, urged instead large-scale borrowing through bond issues to build a stadium for the Braves baseball team, a new zoo, a sports arena, an airport terminal building, a new museum, an addition to the library, and a new city hall annex adjoining the quaint German-postcard structure that had housed municipal offices since 1895. Milwaukee voters approved the multimillion-dollar bond issues for these public structures with hardly a murmur.

Private redevelopment, however, was another matter. When the Marine Bank, the city's third largest bank, sought to put up a new $17-million building with parking and a plaza, it found the powerful First Wisconsin Bank and allied interests trying to block the project. The battle scene was the city council, which had to approve granting the Marine Bank a "freeze" on the assessed value of the property for seven years—a concession permitted by the 1943 state redevelopment law in order to stimulate new private construction. After a strenuous behind-the-scenes fight, the Marine Bank won the council's approval of its undertaking.

The battle of the banks led to the formation of a new top-brass committee, the Milwaukee Development Group, headed by respected Edmund Fitzgerald, retired chief executive of Northwestern Mutual Life Insurance Company, headquartered in Milwaukee. Fitzgerald and a score of other leading business and financial men founded the development group in August, 1959, with the firm, if unannounced, intention of shoving the town's Silas Marners out of the way and getting on with urban renewal. One observer close to the group explained: "We've had too many high-level obstructionists. This is a tight-fisted town, especially some of the big men. Many of them are holding onto their first nickel. They just are not bold and venturesome."

The Fitzgerald group retained the Citizens Governmental Research Bureau, directed by Norman Gill, to study the economic possibilities of building high-rise apartment towers around the periphery of downtown, erecting new hotels and motels, and redeveloping the Lake Michigan waterfront.

The movement gained an ally at city hall in 1960. Mayor Zeidler, upon his doctor's advice, had decided not to run for re-election. Congressman Henry Reuss, a scholarly Harvard-educated liberal and member of an old Milwaukee banking family, filed for the vacant office and was regarded as a sure winner, especially after he led the field in the March, 1960, primary. In the run-off a month later, however, another Democrat—insurance-man and State Senator Henry W. Maier—came from behind with a lectern-thumping television campaign and swamped Reuss, 132,000 votes to 97,000.

The new mayor, surrounding himself with a brain trust of former college professors and professional administrators (even his bodyguard had an M. A. degree), set out to improve diplomatic relations with the city council; and he let the business leaders know he was ready to cooperate in a Milwaukee renaissance.

Milwaukee has all the political tools to remake herself from the dowdy old lady by the lake into, if not a glamour girl, at least a well-preserved matron. Like Pittsburgh, Milwaukee possesses the means for arriving at an effective consensus. She has a highly responsible press, led by the *Journal*, which is one of the nation's most prosperous newspapers (and largely employe owned); it watches over local government like a strict parent. The press works closely with the Governmental Research Bureau, whose director Gill quietly and constantly feeds suggestions to the city council and county supervisors. Integrated with the press and the research bureau is a circle of citizens holding key positions in the life of the city and its decision-making apparatus.

Perhaps most important of all, there is the Milwaukee tradition that a city should be governed well.

When "good government" meant honesty, conscientious service, and watching the pennies, that was the kind of government that Milwaukee had. Now that good government is coming to mean something else—the creation of instruments through which the people can free their city of squalor and inconvenience and ugliness—Milwaukee can probably be counted upon to achieve that, too.

CLEVELAND, INC. (ESTAB. 1796)

Cleveland resembles an old well-run firm. There is some gossiping around the water cooler, a veiled jockeying for power at the upper levels, but aside from these minor distractions it moves serenely along, with everyone performing his duties as prescribed by long custom. Business is run by the businessmen; government is run by the bureaucrats protected by civil service and a tradition of good government; politics is handled by the two leading newspapers, the *Press* and the *Plain Dealer*, in concert with conservative Democratic leaders.

As for the mugwumps—mostly Republicans who go home at night to the suburbs—they have learned in recent decades to accept their place in the outer office, free to drop ideas into the suggestion box, but seldom invited to board meetings. Cleveland's mugwumps find themselves somewhat in the position of a faithful employe who years ago was moved up to manager, bungled the job, and has been permitted to stay around in a minor capacity ever since.

The Cleveland mugwumps' era of glory came in the 1920s, preceded by a generation of vigorous reform and civic building.

The reform wave started in 1896. Mayor Robert McKisson, who had long annoyed the good citizens by hiring an army of city street workers just before elections, finally went too far by calling a municipal election upon only two weeks' notice and then keeping the polls open only four-and-a-half hours.

An indignant young Western Reserve University law professor, Harry A. Garfield, son of the late president, called a half-dozen other young men to his office, and they persuaded fifty of the city's leading figures to organize the Municipal Association. Among the fifty were Samuel Mather, head of Cleveland's number-one family, and traction magnate Tom L. Johnson.

Four years later Johnson defeated McKisson for mayor and began the stormy eight years in office that were to make him one of the famous United States mayors. As Johnson, a Democrat, fought Republican boss Mark Hanna and the light and transit companies, he caused a split within mugwump ranks. Some admired his graft-free administration and his fight against the utilities. Others saw him as a dangerous radical and an enemy of the Republican Party. In 1909, the mugwumps' Municipal Association joined the coalition put together by rising young Republican boss Maurice Maschke to defeat the great Tom L.

Within two years Johnson was dead—some said of heartbreak—but his protégé, attorney Newton D. Baker, recaptured the mayoralty in 1912, carrying on with a Johnsonian program until he went to Washington in 1916 to become President Wilson's secretary of war. This left the field relatively open for Maschke and his Republican organization.

The mugwumps had got along reasonably well with Baker, but the Maschke crowd was something else. As soon as the fighting was over in Europe, the mugwumps declared war on the political hacks who had gathered around the city and county offices. In 1919, a special grand jury called for removing the county prosecutor and the city police commissioner. The next year the chief justice of the municipal court was charged with murder, twice tried and acquitted. Thereupon the mugwumps brought in Dean Roscoe Pound and Professor Felix Frankfurter of Harvard Law School to survey what was wrong with the Cleveland police and courts.

Amid the turmoil, an irrepressible Western Reserve professor, A. R. Hatton, began agitating for a city-manager government with a city council elected by proportional representation. Voters approved the manager-P.R. plan in 1921, making Cleveland the largest United States city at that time (800,000 population) ever to have adopted it. Mugwumps in New York, Philadelphia and elsewhere, dedicated to the manager-P.R. plan, rejoiced and watched for the millennium to come in Cleveland.

But unlike their contemporaries in Cincinnati, the Cleveland mugwumps showed no willingness to form a municipal party and get into politics to hold their gains. Hatton and a handful of others tried vainly to round up a slate of candidates for the new council and to form a campaign organization. As a result, Maschke was able to maneuver just as Tom Pendergast was to do in Kansas City a few years later, seizing control of the city council and with it the mugwumps' newly created manager form of government. Maschke obtained the cooperation of the Democratic leader, Burr Gongwer, by giving him 40 percent of the city hall patronage plus a large slice of the city's insurance business.[1]

The mugwumps, their victory turned sour, never could elect more than four or five of the twenty-five-man city council. And the majority of the council were a sorry lot. Some of them, unconcerned by conflicts of interest, made extra money, just as they had in pre-manager days, by appearing in police court as defense attorneys. Others were hired by business firms that had been found breaking city regulations to plead with city boards and enforcement officials. One councilman made a comfortable income representing dismissed policemen and firemen before the civil service commission, a body that he helped appoint and whose payroll he approved every two weeks.

While the councilmen played their games, the city manager—a strong-willed dynamo named William Hopkins, who had built the Belt Line railroad around Cleveland—ran the government. He had been picked by Maschke and Gongwer, yet the mugwumps backed him because they desperately wanted their manager plan to prove a success. Hopkins, with his great capacity for details and deep love of the limelight, handled city affairs almost singlehandedly. For five years he received mostly applause. When the regular politicians tried, as they did at nearly every election, to throw out the P.R. voting system or the city manager plan, Hopkins and the mugwumps turned them back—although only by narrow margins.

But in the late twenties Hopkins broke with Maschke, and that meant his end. The council discharged him. The mugwumps had tried to forestall this by belatedly organizing in 1929 a Progressive Government Committee, recruiting candidates for the council and raising a $70,000 campaign kitty. This was enough to purchase the aid of Democratic leader Gongwer but not enough to beat Maschke. (The victorious Maschke canceled his alliance with Gongwer and the Democrats, cutting them off from patronage—a move that he soon was to regret.)

The battles to preserve the manager-P.R. system during the twenties drew many recruits into the mugwump organizations. The old Municipal Association, which had been remade into the Civic League in 1913, was reorganized again in 1922 as the Citizens League. Starting with a thousand members, it had grown by 1930 to five thousand, its all-time high point (the present membership is three thousand). In addition to the Citizens League, the reformers also established a Municipal Research Bureau in 1920. But as the bloom wore off the reform movement, the research bureau folded in 1928.

What finally destroyed the manager-P.R. plan were two events over which the mugwumps had no control—the depression, and a series of scandals involving the city council.

Newspaper reporters stumbled across evidence of graft and turned it over to one of the few Democrats holding office, prosecutor Ray Miller, of the Notre Dame football-playing Millers. The crusading prosecutor (who has since become chief of the county's dominant Democratic party) blew the lid off city hall by convicting the respected Republican leader on the city council, Liston Schooley; he and his son pleaded guilty to pocketing $30,000 in a city land deal. Other Republican councilmen were brought to trial for other land transactions and for accepting bribes. These exposures caused deep public shock. Perhaps because they were Cleveland's last major political scandals, they are still talked about today.

As if this were not enough to wreck Maschke's Republican organization, the economic depression struck, bringing a Democratic swing.

Unluckily for the mugwumps, their fortunes by now had been tied to those of Maschke. The reformers wanted to preserve the manager-P.R. government as a matter of faith. Maschke wanted to preserve it because he controlled it. Consequently, when the Democrats loosed another attack on the manager-P.R. plan in 1931, as they had been doing intermittently for six years, the mugwumps found themselves waging a defensive campaign side by side with their old foe. They proved no match, however, for the Democrats led by Miller and former Mayor Newton Baker, now a wealthy corporation lawyer and elder statesman for the local Democrats. The voters tossed out the eight-year-old manager government by 61,000 to 52,000. The mugwumps' noble experiment was over.

Cleveland mugwumps never fully recovered from this setback. The blow to both their self-confidence and their reputation among the public had been severe. The Citizens League settled down to becoming a watchdog over local government, issuing reports on candidates and analyzing budgets. It left the recruiting of mayoralty candidates to editor Louis B. Seltzer and his Cleveland *Press,* sometimes in conjunction with the less influential *Plain Dealer*. The city had its succession of "newspaper mayors" —Republican Harold Burton, followed by Democrats Frank Lausche, Thomas Burke and Anthony Celebrezze—all independent-minded executives who made it a point, despite their show of lone-handedness, to keep in close touch with the editors.

It made a barren environment for the mugwumps. With no scandals to pounce on, no glaring inefficiency to criticize and the press content with the status quo, they had little fodder for crusades.

In Pittsburgh, Philadelphia or New Orleans, the mugwumps could rise up after World War II and demand that the city eradicate the rot in its midst, physical and political. But Cleveland did not have much rot of either kind. Early in the century it had built its civic center of public buildings, a $38-million group planned by noted architect Daniel Burnham and modeled after centers some Clevelanders had seen in European cities. Shortly afterward, the Van Sweringen brothers poured $60 million into a cluster of business buildings centering on a huge union railroad terminal.

Thus ahead of its time in downtown redevelopment, Cleveland paid the inevitable penalty. Today the grand structures have become a bit old-fashioned. Yet they possess a dignity that, combined with the city's spacious streets, gives an effect of solidity and assurance.

This, however, has not prevented Cleveland from catching some of the postwar fever for urban renewal. With nearby Pittsburgh and other cities making a to-do about slum clearance, Mayor Burke in 1952 named a committee of leading citizens and asked them to see about tearing down tenements and modernizing the downtown. Within two years the committee became the Cleveland Development Foundation, promoting a half-dozen projects to clear out broken-down neighborhoods and replace them with middle-income apartments. The foundation retained architects, lawyers and engineers; it speeded negotiations among federal urban-renewal officials, city officials, private builders and banks; and most important, it persuaded eighty-six Cleveland firms to put two million dollars into a revolving fund for loans to developers so that they could get projects moving.

As a long-range goal, the foundation and the city-planning department agreed on clearing slums and erecting new housing on some 750 acres within the city and, in the process, thinning the population. Far from wanting the city to grow, the planners hoped to see Cleveland with 14 percent fewer people in 1980 than it had in 1960.

This planned elimination of thousands of housing units, especially in the congested low-income neighborhoods, was bound to pose a major problem: Where would the displaced slum dwellers, mostly Negroes, go? Into the white suburbs? Into special black suburban developments? On to other cities?

City planners and foundation officials admitted they did not have the answer. But like planners and officials elsewhere, they decided to go ahead and tear down the slums anyway, trusting that the relocation problem would be solved somehow, some day, by somebody.

The foundation also put its considerable influence behind the Mall Center plan for downtown Cleveland. This project, which was planned to extend twelve blocks along Lake Erie, called for a huge exhibition hall, a four-thousand-car underground parking garage, a thousand-room hotel, a thirty-four-story office tower, and lengthening the runways of the adjoining lakefront private-plane airport to 5,200 feet. All this was expected to cost $50 million from private sources plus $15 million in city funds.

While the big boys of Cleveland were giving attention to the Development Foundation, their number two and number three subordinates continued, as they had in the past, to participate in the Chamber of Commerce and the Citizens League. There they were joined after World War II by an energetic young group who started stirring up the town.

One was Seth Taft, son of Cincinnati's reform politician, Charles P. Taft, and nephew of the late Senator Robert Taft of Ohio. Seth, an attorney in his mid-thirties, became president of the Citizens League in 1957.

Two years earlier he and league director Estal Sparlin had begun reviving an idea that, eventually, could go far toward restoring mugwump prestige in Cleveland and Cuyahoga County. The plan, which had been sleeping since it was raised and dropped several years before, was to create a county-wide metropolitan government. Sparlin and Taft enlisted the aid of business executive Don Carmichael, along with Taft's law associate Bayless Manning, former Cleveland *Press* reporter Oliver Brooks, and a handful of others from the "junior fifty club"—a group of young business and professional fellows who had campaigned for Senator Taft's re-election in 1950 (their name was in mocking imitation of Cleveland's venerable, wealth-encrusted and civicly torpid Fifty Club).

This nucleus first interested an array of city and county officials in the metro idea, aligned a hundred business, civic and political organizations as sponsors, then persuaded T. Keith Glennan, president of Case Institute of Technology, to call a meeting of Cleveland's top businessmen to raise money for a nonprofit corporation that would promote metro. The outcome was the Cleveland Metropolitan Services Commission, probably the most ambitious home-grown effort of its kind thus far in the United States.

The organizers sent letters to more than two hundred local companies informing them they were expected to contribute from $250 to $17,500 each for the metro commission. This drive, plus $125,000 from the Ford Foundation, netted a half-million dollars. With this the commission of public and civic officials employed a staff of fifteen youthful political scientists, economists and public relations men. They produced more than thirty reports describing Cuyahoga County's problems on everything from fire protection and transit to water supply, sewage, land use and planning.

Even before the metro commission's alloted life span, and its half-million dollars, expired in June, 1959, the county commissioners asked the people to vote on whether they wanted a commission to write the new charter. The answer on the November, 1958, ballot was an overwhelming yes.

Yet a year later, when the proposed metro charter was written and submitted to the same voters, the answer was an overwhelming no. It lost narrowly in the suburbs, heavily in the city. In addition to the Negroes, who feared that a union with the white suburbs would weaken their political influence within the city, many municipal workers voted against the charter because it eliminated the civil service commission, replacing it with an appointed personnel director. Mayor Celebrezze and some of his cabinet did not like the plan because it would remove his city departments of airports and public utilities to the new metro government.

Picking themselves off the floor, the Sparlin-Taft contingent sought to salvage something by asking Celebrezze to head a committee of twenty-five mayors, county officials and citizens which was to write another metro charter that would be more politically palatable. Celebrezze accepted the invitation, and the committee went to work in 1960. The charter it produced evoked satisfied nods from most mayors and disdainful sniffs from most county officials, both for the same reason: it transferred few important powers from the cities to the county government.

Meanwhile, the Cleveland Development Foundation insured that the metro idea would stay alive by granting the Citizens League $25,000 a year for continued research and reports.

If Cleveland mugwumps should succeed in producing a metropolitan government plan that can win approval, their political stock in the community will enjoy an upturn. The mugwumps can use it. Anything is welcome that will blur the still lingering memories of their city-manager-government fiasco of the 1920s.

Whatever decisions the editors and political bellwethers reach on metro or Mall Center or slum clearance or other mugwump projects, those decisions undoubtedly will be made in orderly, deliberate fashion behind closed doors with no raising of rude voices—at least none audible to the outside. Because that is the way things are done in Cleveland.

LOS ANGELES—AFTER REFORM, WHAT?

The little city of Los Angeles in the late nineteenth century was peopled mostly with New Englanders, New Yorkers, and Midwesterners. They attended a Methodist, Congregational or other Protestant church each Sunday. They saw the world through Calvinist eyes as a place for working hard, making money, fighting sin and voting Republican. Like their mugwump brothers of the East, they had little love for the robber barons of the big corporations. Mixed with this was a strain of agrarian radicalism brought from the Populist strongholds of the farm belt.

The Los Angeles mugwumps had only one foe to fight. That was the Southern Pacific Railroad, which held not only their city government but the entire state in its grip. In older and larger San Francisco to the north, mugwumps also disliked the railroad, but they had a traditional mugwump rival as well—the Irish Catholic politicians who in the latter nineteenth century had set up shop in San Francisco just as they had in most other large cities. Los Angeles, however, had no sizable minority except the Mexicans, and they took almost no part in politics.

As long as the Los Angeles mugwumps were few in number (the city had less than 100,000 population during the 1890s), they made slight headway. A group of Protestant ministers led a futile crusade against the railroad's hand-picked officials in city hall. A few years later, in 1893, the mugwumps formed a Citizens League that got nowhere in obtaining a new city charter. One of their leaders, Dr. John Randolph Haynes, tried another tack in 1895, organizing a Direct Legislation League to promote the initiative, referendum and recall.

The reformers enjoyed a small glow of triumph in 1896 when the city's gambling establishments were shut down. A bit later they obtained Sunday closure of saloons. A more significant victory came in 1903 as Dr. Haynes' initiative, referendum and recall were made part of the city charter. This was followed in 1906 with the first open sign that Los Angeles and the state were growing too big to fit into Southern Pacific's pocket much longer.

It began, as so many reform movements have, with a few young men getting together for lunch. In this case they were a newspaperman and three lawyers—Edward Dickson, editorial writer for the city's oldest Republican paper, the *Express;* Meyer Lissner; Marshall Stimson; and Russ Avery, who was president of the Los Angeles Voters League. After a few months of luncheon conferences, they invited business and professional men to a meeting at the Chamber of Commerce and organized a slate against the Southern Pacific candidates in the coming city election. They had the support of Dickson's boss, wealthy *Express* publisher Edwin T. Earl. This automatically evoked the fierce opposition of Earl's dedicated enemy, Harrison Gray Otis of the Los Angeles *Times.* The reformers, roared Otis, were splitting the Grand Old Party.

More opposition came from the small but fast-growing labor unions led by the Socialists. Like Otis, they had not been invited into the reformers' early councils.

This opposition from the conservative right and Socialist left proved a flimsy obstacle. An avalanche of votes carried seventeen of the twenty-three reform candidates into office. It marked the beginning of the end of Southern Pacific domination in the state. From the east came well-publicized congratulations sent by President Theodore Roosevelt and Progressive Senator Robert La Follette of Wisconsin.

The following January, Dickson chanced to sit next to Chester Rowell of the Fresno *Republican* in the press gallery as they covered the legislative session in Sacramento. Dickson's description of the S.P.'s defeat in Los Angeles led Rowell to join him in starting the Lincoln-Roosevelt Republican Clubs—a movement that three years later wrested control of California's Republican party from the railroad and placed it in the hands of the Progressive Republicans and their governor, Hiram Johnson.

The majorities that put Johnson into the governor's chair came not from his own San Francisco but from Los Angeles. There the reformers were in full cry. The S.P.'s last important officeholder, Mayor Arthur C. Harper, had been exposed as taking money from the underworld. When the mugwumps started a recall movement, he resigned. Emulating Boston mugwumps of the period, the Los Angeles men organized a Good Government Association and a City Club. They joined with the Chamber of Commerce to push through city charter amendments abolishing the elected-by-wards council and creating a smaller council of nine elected at large, as Boston was doing.

With the Southern Pacific machine routed, the only remaining threat to the mugwumps was the Socialists. Their power among the working-class voters had risen fast. In 1909, their unknown candidate, Fred Wheeler, came within 1,600 votes of being elected the city's first Socialist mayor. Two years later another Socialist, Job Harriman, seemed headed for certain victory—he led in the mayoral primary—but four days before the election the two McNamara brothers confessed to dynamiting the anti-union Los Angeles *Times*. The confession turned thousands of voters against labor. When the Socialists tried again in 1913, Harriman finished a feeble third.[2]

Having gained control of city hall, the reformers set their sights on Los Angeles County government. At their request, Johnson and the legislature passed a state constitutional amendment permitting counties to write home-rule charters. The California voters ratified the amendment in 1911; the next year Los Angeles County adopted a new form of government.

This string of victories had attracted nation-wide attention. When the National Municipal League held its 1912 convention in Los Angeles, the occasion recognized six years of thoroughgoing reform such as few cities had seen.

It was, in a sense, too thoroughgoing. The reformers had nothing left to reform. Mugwump organizations slowly began to disintegrate, amid bickering and personal quarrels, and only occasionally thereafter did the progressives unite for a brief campaign. Usually these involved the municipal water and power department. Conservatives, led by the Southern California Edison Company and publisher Harry Chandler (General Otis' son-in-law and successor at the *Times*), fought public power at every step —first when city-owned power plants were built along the 250-mile Owens Valley aqueduct to generate electricity from the water descending three thousand feet from the High Sierra, again in 1922 when the city purchased all private power distribution lines within Los Angeles, and in 1928 when the Swing-Johnson bill was before Congress to construct Boulder Dam on the Colorado River. The progressives arose each time to aid the cause of public power, and they formed ranks again in the early 1920s as Los Angeles adopted a new city charter. But the most spectacular revival of the reform spirit came in the 1930s.

Like many another city, Los Angeles had a police department graft ring, a circle of veteran captains and higher-ups who handled pay-offs from gambling, prostitution and illegal liquor operators. Mayors and police chiefs might come and go, but the ring went on forever, weathering flurries of reform. One such flurry came in 1931 and 1932. A young business-and-professional element calling themselves the Minuteers, or Minute Men, demanded a clean-up of the police department, district attorney's office and the courts. When nobody paid much attention, they appealed to the governor and legislature in 1933 for an investigation like the recent Seabury hearings in New York that had upset the Walker administration. The legislature and governor paid little attention, either. The Minute Men faded temporarily.

The Los Angeles situation got a bit rougher after Frank L. Shaw was elected mayor in 1933. The public did not become excited, however, until Shaw had started his second term in 1937. On that year's grand jury was thirty-seven-year-old Clifford E. Clinton, the politically untutored owner of a depression-era "golden rule" cafeteria where diners were asked to pay as much of their checks as they could afford (10,000 patrons walked out without paying in a three-month period, yet Clinton prospered and soon had two cafeterias).

Clinton took his jury duties seriously. He went to bawdy houses and gambling joints personally gathering evidence, much as the crusading Reverend Mr. Parkhurst had done in New York in the nineties. But Clinton found most of the other grand jurors bored with his findings. When the jury's term expired at the end of the year, Clinton and three other jurors wrote a minority report. The Superior Court judge in charge of the jury declined to accept it, but another judge, Fletcher Bowron, did.

Meanwhile, a group of church ladies had called on re-elected Mayor Shaw and begged him to do something about vice and gambling. The mayor blandly assured them that he would cooperate with any citizens committee wishing to make an investigation.

Hearing of the mayor's offer, Clinton gathered a group at the German Methodist Church one evening, and they organized themselves into the Citizens Independent Vice Investigating Committee, CIVIC for short. They called upon the mayor and found the atmosphere chilly. So Clinton and his collection of church people, lawyers and doctors continued on their own to dig up facts about sin and apparent graft. Clinton purchased radio time and went on the air four times a day with his exposés and calls for reform.

To judge from the public response, Clinton might as well have been shouting into the wind. He became that character who was always talking on the radio. Then somebody blew up Harry Raymond.

Raymond, a former policeman turned "private eye," had been scheduled to appear in a court suit on January 22, 1938, when it was expected he would testify that Mayor Shaw had received campaign contributions from gamblers. One morning a week before the trial, Raymond stepped on the starter of his car. In a split second the car was junk, and Raymond was carted to the hospital with 150 fragments in him. The press and public awoke with an indignant roar.

Months later Raymond was well enough to appear at the trial in which police Captain Earle E. Kynette and patrolman Roy J. Allen were convicted of attempted murder, assault with intent to kill, and malicious use of explosives. During the trial the records of Kynette's Special Intelligence Unit, or "spy squad," were brought into court. They included dossiers and recordings of wire-tapped conversations of three hundred respectable citizens, including Clinton, numerous ministers, Judge Harlan Palmer, who published the Hollywood *Citizen-News,* and County Supervisor John Anson Ford, who had run against Shaw as a reform candidate in 1937. The disclosure of this Gestapo system further aroused the public.

Clinton's CIVIC and a suddenly formed Federation for Civic Betterment circulated recall petitions against Mayor Shaw and, with only thirty-six days to go before the election date, drafted a reluctant Judge Bowron to run for mayor. Although opposed by the *Times* and only half-heartedly supported by the other four downtown dailies, they won election for Bowron by a two-to-one majority.

Once Bowron was in office, the reformers dispersed and went back to their private affairs. This, it will be recalled, was the classic pattern of good-government uprisings of the nineteenth century. As soon as the reformers were out of sight down the street, the party hacks flowed back into their former positions. Bowron's problem, however, was not party hacks. Los Angeles, like California generally, had no parties in the usual sense. Hiram Johnson and the Progressives had hammered home the idea way-back-when that *all* political parties were evil; and to make sure that strong parties could not be built, they had enacted the cross-filing system permitting a candidate for state or national office to file on the primary ballot of not only his own party but all others.

Rather than party hangers-on, Bowron had to worry about the crooks, incompetents and thugs who had infiltrated the city government, with their ties to gambling and vice operators. The mayor took the offensive. He bluntly demanded the resignations of all members of the citizen commissions who supervised the major city departments. The commissioners, even those whose terms had several years to run, complied. The mayor reappointed some, but he cleaned out the civil service, police and pension commissions. At Bowron's suggestion, the police chief and twenty-three others of his high command retired to private life. Over in the civil service department, the new commission liquidated an inner circle that was peddling copies of civil service examinations, with answers, at $50 and up, civil service positions at $400 up, and police captaincies for $1,500.

These events—the bombing, trial, recall, and graft disclosures—gave an impression of a government rotten to the core. Actually, the soft spot had grown primarily around a band of rascals who had succeeded in infesting the city council and certain departments. But fundamentally the great body of Los Angeles city and county government had developed along quite different lines, shaped by the Progressive doctrines of nonpartisanship, merit systems, modern budgeting, accounting controls, and the concept that governmental administration is not a handmaiden of politics but a separate and skilled trade, a profession whose practitioners should be well paid and given a reasonably free hand. These doctrines became embedded beliefs among the public. A tradition of professionalism grew up around Los Angeles government.

It was accompanied by another tradition, one of innovation. The 1913 charter, which the mugwumps had helped write for Los Angeles County, was far ahead of its time for a county government. It provided for civil service, nonpartisan elections, the short ballot (each voter made only four choices—for sheriff, assessor, district attorney, and the county supervisor from his district), and it established the first office of public defender. At about the same time, the Los Angeles city police department hired the first policewoman in the United States.

This willingness to experiment showed itself again in the city charter adopted in 1924. To the horror of eastern mugwumps, the charter writers ignored both the city-manager and the strong-mayor plans, creating instead a collection of seventeen largely independent departments, each governed by a commission of five citizens appointed by the mayor, each commission employing a manager to run its department.[3] A member of the charter commission explained: "We felt that no one man has the strength or the varied enthusiasm to undertake the whole management of a large city. What we have done is to take the city-manager principle and apply it to smaller, more easily handled units." Although New York mugwumps today are urging a similar principle for decentralizing their city government (see Chapter Nine), this was heresy in 1924.

The county supervisors blazed another new trail in 1938 by creating a chief administrative officer and giving him a large staff of analysts. They were to advise the board of supervisors. While the CAO, as he is known, is technically still only an adviser, his job has evolved into that of virtual county manager.

A clause in the 1913 charter gave the county the right to provide municipal services for any city. The county was already assessing property and collecting taxes for several surburban cities on a contract basis; the county, that is, did the work and the city paid a fee for it. In the years following, this contract-services system was expanded to include public health, street work, building permits and a score of other services. In 1954, when the huge "bedroom" city of Lakewood was incorporated, the county agreed to provide virtually all of its services, including police protection. Since then two dozen more cities around Los Angeles have contracted with the county for the Lakewood Plan package of services. In 1961, the county had nearly a thousand service contracts with most of the seventy-one cities in the county. As a method of coping with the metropolitan mess of duplicating and crisscrossing functions, the system is being watched by other major cities.

The fast spread of the Lakewood Plan could take place, of course, only in an area where the public had confidence in the men administering it. That kind of faith in the professional competence of both Los Angeles county and city bureaucrats has taken root in the decades since the Progressive take-over. The feeling by now extends even to law agencies. There is a belief that these civil servants can be trusted to do a good job so long as they are protected from bad bosses—from corrupt mayors, councilmen or other elected officials working in collusion with corrupt outsiders.

This faith has had a curious effect. Among the bureaucrats, it seems to have been taken as a challenge to which they must rise. The people expect them to watch out for boodlers, angle-shooters and fast shufflers; and, by heaven, they will. And when any problems of government appear, the people expect them to come up with the answers. And they will. The community appears to want the bureaucrats to be the paid guardians of the public conscience, the paid assemblers of facts, and the paid finders of solutions.

This leaves Los Angeles leading citizens with a simple role. They merely must stand guard and make sure no evil forces get in to attack the toiling bureaucrats. This the leading citizens accomplish without the aid of any strong mugwump organizations. Indeed, they do it with no real organization at all. Just something called the "downtown club."

This amorphous circle includes mostly men of property. They pay only spasmodic attention to the local government as long as it runs uneventfully. The bureaucrats try to see that it does. The downtown club perks up, however, at anything—freeway routes, urban renewal, transit proposals, new public buildings—that may affect the values of downtown real estate.

And the club likes to decide who will be mayor. Since the mayor appoints the 115 citizens who sit on the commissions that run the city departments, it gives the downtowners a feeling of security to have their man doing the appointing.

The downtown club decided in the early 1950s that Fletcher Bowron, after fifteen years, had been mayor long enough—a decision apparently precipitated by Bowron's insistence on going through with a public housing program opposed by real estate interests. The downtowners brought back Republican Congressman and one-time accountant Norris Poulson from Washington as a champion of free enterprise (Bowron, a lifelong Republican, had always thought he was in favor of free enterprise, too), and ran him for mayor against Bowron in 1953. Poulson won decisively.

The downtown club has what might be called a concentric membership. The inner ring, although sometimes segmented by quarrels, usually presents the same circle of faces—the presidents of a few insurance companies, industries, retail firms, law offices, and representatives of the Los Angeles *Times-Mirror* and, generally, Hearst's Los Angeles *Examiner*. The outer ring of other prominent business and professional men shifts somewhat in make-up, depending upon the matters involved and the interests at stake.

While the downtown club itself has no formal existence, its members belong to or financially support other organizations that do speak up now and again on municipal affairs.

The Chamber of Commerce State and Local Government Committee has been headed by municipal bond attorney James L. Beebe since he founded the committee in 1932. Forty or fifty members gather for lunch every Wednesday, listen to a local official or other speaker, and perhaps pass a resolution supporting a bond issue, urging a better mass transit system, or opposing a local fair employment practices commission.

The chamber committee relies for what research it does on the California Taxpayers Association, which assigns one or two men part-time to Los Angeles municipal government. The Cal-Tax office also serves as headquarters for the Citizens Budget Committee—a loosely allied front of some fifty community, business and service clubs. The committee usually sends the city council, the county supervisors and the school board a statement of advice at annual-budget time.

A somewhat more aggressive group, the Property Owners Tax Association, has been watching tax dollars since 1932. Its financial support comes from certain oil companies, utilities and large suburban land owners. The association's two-man staff spends full time at political infighting around Civic Center (the Los Angeles term for several square blocks covered by municipal and state government buildings). The association's regular opponents are the organized public employes—the Affiliated Teachers of Los Angeles, the smaller but militant American Federation of Teachers, the Police and Fire Protective League (composed of policemen and firemen) and other groups of city and county workers. Their requests for more pay and pensions always bring the Property Owners Tax Association out swinging.

The Downtown Businessmen's Association, a promoter group, is nourished with $150,000 a year from worried owners of downtown property and retail merchants. The three-man staff pushes urban renewal, faster transit, new freeways and anything else that may halt the drop in downtown retail trade and property values.

A luncheon forum group, Town Hall, sometimes assigns a committee to report on ballot propositions in forthcoming elections or on local controversies such as the city's gift of Chavez Ravine to Walter O'Malley's Dodger baseball club. Although Town Hall's members are overwhelmingly conservative (they favored a state right-to-work law in 1958 by nearly four to one), these occasional reports have been objective in tone. They are too infrequent, however, to have appreciable effect.

Indeed, Los Angeles is spectacularly devoid of any citizen organization resembling the Seattle Municipal League, the New York Citizens Union, the Cleveland Citizens League or Milwaukee's Bureau of Governmental Research—the kind of organization that keeps track of what is going on in local government and tells the public about it, an organization whose reports enjoy the respect and confidence of a majority of the newsmen and the people. When it comes to governmental matters, the average Los Angeles citizen does not know whom to believe—about anything. The extent of this confusion was revealed in surveys taken in the 1950s by the private polling agency Facts Consolidated. The polls were made largely in white-collar home-owning neighborhoods where mugwump influence, in other cities, would tend to be strongest. Those interviewed were asked how much weight they would give to recommendations from different sources on how to vote on ballot propositions. Probably in no other major city would the replies from a cross-section of middle-class citizens have resembled the following:

Recommendation would carry:	a lot of weight	no weight
Your own church	38%	44%
The P-TA	34	41
Chamber of Commerce	14	62
Republican Party	12	73
Democratic Party	9	74
AFL	9	76
CIO	5	83

Los Angeles churches are not especially political. They take no more part in local governmental affairs than churches anywhere else, which is to say they take almost no part at all. For them to head the list of respected advisers on public questions could only indicate to what extent the city's middle-class voter floats in an informational vacuum.

The citizen has found this suspension uncomfortable. He has had an undefinable feeling that "they" are not leveling with him, that he has been cozened into voting for this and paying for that, while no one ever consults him. The feeling is seldom verbalized except among groups in outlying sections like San Fernando Valley or the Harbor area, or among faculty men at UCLA, USC or one of the smaller colleges. Pandering to this sense of exclusion is a peculiar Los Angeles phenomenon—a local species of television "newscaster" with little journalistic experience (most of them are former actors) who take delight in nightly shocking their thousands of viewers with dark hints of corruption among city and county officials.

Until recently, however, there was no sense of discontent among the downtown club and their friends. They were satisfied with the status quo. Their civic energy, which in another city might have gone into reform, was drained off in a different direction—into forming nonprofit corporations to build and run cultural monuments of various kinds. Mrs. Norman Chandler, wife of the *Times* owner, frequently led these drives to obtain land, official backing and often subsidies from the city or county government to make an enterprise possible; she has been aided by some of the city's *nouveau riche* (Los Angeles has hardly any other kind of *riche*) willing to underwrite the project with their oil millions, savings-and-loan millions or real estate millions. Once one of these campaigns gets under way, the air around Civic Center fairly crackles with political pressure until the bureaucrats, the county supervisors and the city council have come through with the necessary approvals. In addition to the Hollywood Bowl, the nonprofit corporation device has been employed recently for a $5-million art museum, a $4-million film museum, a $23-million music center (Mrs. Chandler at first wanted a $50-million one) and a $6-million zoo.

Aside from their occasional descents on Civic Center to push through one of these undertakings, the leading citizens have left local officials more or less alone. They did not complicate the bureaucrats' lives by forming vigorous mugwump organizations to observe them, correct them or needle them into changing their ways. There was no demand for such an organization. And while the business-professional men out in San Fernando Valley, San Pedro and elsewhere might complain about the downtowners' control of the mayor and other officials, the suburbanites have been too scattered and too far from Civic Center to create a permanent resistance movement.

That has been Los Angeles government: an army of career professionals operating a $1½-billion complex of services with a minimum of disturbance; a downtown circle of influential men who seldom intervened except to pass a bond issue, to elect a mayor, or to drop a word now and then to councilmen, supervisors and budget directors; and millions of citizens who sometimes groused but never very loudly, and voted pretty much as the Chandler and Hearst newspapers told them to.

The system, while not exactly democratic, seemed tidy.

But on the night of May 31, 1961, the system underwent a rude shock. As the ballots were counted from that day's city election, it became clear that former Democratic Congressman Samuel Yorty—regarded as a political has-been, possessing almost no organization, disavowed by leaders of his own party, supported by none of the four downtown daily newspapers—had beaten two-term incumbent Mayor Poulson by 16,000 votes.

Yorty went into office declaring the "downtown clique" was "out."

Actually, the downtown club was not even on the canvas, let alone out. But it had been shaken up. Its smugness was shattered. As the process of recuperation gets under way, the idea might just possibly percolate through to the club that it must enlarge its membership, and its outlook. With Mayor Yorty appointing anti-downtown majorities to the five-man commissions that govern the city departments, the leading citizens could lose their long indifference to the details of how municipal departments are run. Their complacency might change to concern. City hall, instead of being a comfort station for Los Angeles men of property, could become the focal point of a critical scrutiny, a mugwump type of constant surveillance. This would require creating the kind of organizations that Los Angeles has not known for a generation or more—independent citizen agencies that continuously seek out facts about local government, analyze them and report them to the people.

The Los Angeles mugwump, after decades in limbo, may be on the verge of a comeback.

SEATTLE—THE TIGHT-ROPE ACT

As long as a mugwump organization is a hopeless minority of dedicated reformers fighting uphill for better government, its problems are relatively simple. It is only after the reformers reach the top that real complications set in. What had been a doughty little band of knights-errant swells into a heterogeneous army of occupation. The single-mindedness, the easy black-and-white objectives of the campaign years vanish, and in their place come the confusing demands of power and its wise exercise.

Los Angeles before World War I was a case in point. A half-century later Seattle provided another.

Early Seattle mugwumps created a few temporary organizations that never lasted long.[4] Like Los Angeles, the city had no Irish Catholic political machine to solidify a mugwump opposition. Seattle, however, had its share of hacks who found the pickings especially good among the flourishing vice businesses catering to the Scandinavian lumberjacks, fishermen, sailors and miners. Police pay-offs were a fixture in Seattle politics until the mid-1940s.

One of the more colorful operators was Mayor Hiram Gill, and it was in hopes of retiring him to private life that three young attorneys—Hugh M. Caldwell, C. J. France and William E. Bebb—revived the old (1894–95) Municipal League in 1910.

The league, as a luncheon-forum group, waxed and waned for the next three decades. When its leaders, mostly Bull Moosers, invited Theodore Roosevelt to make his principal Seattle address before the league, its membership shot above 1,500. The roster dwindled, but rose again in 1925 and 1926 when the league twice campaigned for a city-manager charter and narrowly lost—the last time by only 111 votes. Thereafter the league shrank once more as it continued its weekly noon gatherings and passed resolutions in town-meeting style. These had slight effect on local affairs, possibly because they often veered direction from week to week, depending on who attended the luncheons. Superintendent J. D. Ross, for instance, whose municipal light department was battling with the private Puget Power and Light Company, saw to it that enough City Light employes joined the league so that they could pack meetings when necessary to block anti–City Light resolutions—or to rescind any that might have slipped through the week before. Many conservative leaguers, irked by these periodic invasions, dropped out of the organization.

Still more mugwumps withdrew from politics during this postwar period because Seattle's government, like that of Boston, New York, Chicago, San Francisco and other cities, took on an atmosphere of buffoonery. Candidates for mayor competed for headlines by donning weird costumes and jumping off the dock into Elliott Bay. Among those winning the mayoralty were a lawyer indicted for bootlegging, a supposedly hard-headed banker who approved the city's paying $15 million for a decrepit streetcar system worth half that amount, an advertising dentist, and a university professor's wife. The Seattle *Times,* in an elaborate spoof of the situation, ran orchestra leader Victor Meyers for mayor in 1932. Under the tutelage of an irreverent reporter, Doug Welch, he advocated hostesses on every streetcar and appeared for his major speech at the Chamber of Commerce wearing a sheet, leading a goat and declining to say a word because it was his day of silence. The winning candidate that year was John F. Dore, a criminal attorney facing disbarment proceedings.

The following November a horde of depression-ridden barbers, meat salesmen, insurance agents, lawyers and whatnot filed on the Democratic ticket. They rode the Democratic landslide into nearly every job in the county government. Another beneficiary of the one-sided vote was bandleader Meyers, who was elected to the first of his several terms as the state's lieutenant governor.

With both the state and county governments and, to a growing extent, the city government in Democratic hands, a Republican element of mugwumps began to reorganize. Ralph P. Potts and Albert King, with a half-dozen other young lawyers, formed the New Order of Cincinnatus in 1933, and began recruiting men aged twenty-one to thirty-five. The group spread rapidly in white-collar districts. By the following spring of 1934 they felt strong enough to enter youthful David Lockwood in the councilmanic election. Lockwood won.

The other councilmen greeted the reform newcomer with no enthusiasm. They made him chairman of their efficiency committee, which had not met in years. It proved all the springboard that Cincinnatus needed. Lockwood called meetings of his committee and introduced cases of inefficiency he had discovered in city departments. Since almost any part of the city government could be investigated for purposes of "efficiency," Lockwood made headlines week after week with his findings. All his motions to change departmental operations were voted down, but that did Cincinnatus no harm politically. The next year the New Order elected three more council members—attorneys Arthur B. Langlie and Frederick G. Hamley and clubwoman Frances F. Powell. Although still outnumbered five to four on the council, Cincinnatus had shown such pull at the election booth that the five other councilmen meekly voted for nearly all Cincinnatus measures. Their votes made no practical difference. Mayor Charles Smith either vetoed the ordinances or passed word to his department heads that they could ignore them. Cincinnatus decided it would have to take over the mayor's office.

By this time the two-year-old New Order was riding high. It had district organizations in most parts of the city and a total of 1,500 members. There was an organization in town, however, that had a great many more members—Dave Beck's Teamsters Union—and it gave Cincinnatus a rough time in 1936. Because Councilman Langlie was the only leader among them old enough to run for mayor (the city charter set the minimum age at thirty-five), he became the Cincinnatus nominee. Beck, who wanted a friendly police department to help him in his drive for power, supported former Mayor (1932–34) Dore.

Langlie lost, but the race was close. The other two Cincinnatus candidates, however, running for city council, took a surprising shellacking. Cincinnatus began to falter. Then the following spring, Councilman Lockwood was unseated by an ultra-liberal University of Washington English instructor, Hugh DeLacy.

Langlie and others of the inner circle met and concluded that the Cincinnatus label had lost its political appeal. They announced to the press that the New Order was dead and buried.

The only thing that disappeared was the label. Langlie filed again for mayor in 1938 and decisively beat Dore and Meyers. Two years later he won re-election almost unopposed. And the Cincinnatus reform program continued with the adoption of centralized purchasing, a police training program, and a major overhaul of the city's worn-out transit system.

Throughout this period the Municipal League had remained an impotent luncheon club of only a few hundred members. Its rejuvenation began in 1938. The first step was to discard the old town-meeting format and to vest control, instead, in a board of twenty trustees. The trustees employed a full-time executive secretary, an office girl and a finance-membership solicitor. With this hired help and a new determination among the trustees to challenge the organized Democrats in the County-City Building, the membership started to climb. Beginning with fewer than three hundred in 1938, it doubled in 1939, nearly doubled again in the election year 1940 and rose steadily thereafter.

The total was nearly two thousand in 1944 when C. A. Crosser, a municipal research veteran from Toledo and Des Moines, became executive secretary. By this time a news editor and a part-time legal counsel had been added to the staff. Crosser, a tireless workhorse, expanded the program of the league committees until one or two of them were meeting every day to push along some league study or project.

The biggest of these undertakings was the new city charter adopted in 1946, which strengthened the hand of reform Mayor William F. Devin. An attorney who had been elected police judge and had cleaned out the gamy smell from the city traffic-violations bureau, Devin became mayor in 1942 (Langlie had been elected governor in 1940). The new charter gave Devin authority to hire and fire the police chief, and he used this power to install a police administration of Young Turks who had attended the FBI school and Northwestern University long enough to acquire the spit-and-polish approach to police work.

While Devin's administration did not accomplish the impossible by eliminating all police graft, it did break up the official channels through which envelopes had flowed to the front-office brass and across the street into the council chambers. The charter also aided the mayor in professionalizing the health department and other offices. The league did its bit with the city council, building alliances with friendly councilmen, trying to isolate unfriendly ones—a policy that over the years brought the desired results.

The King County government, also centered in Seattle, proved a tougher nut. Its thirty departments and their non-civil service employes were an important part of the Democratic state organization. Any frontal attempt to remake the county government into a nonpartisan professionalized operation was bound to meet stiff resistance.

And so the Municipal League had to content itself with waiting for exposed targets—an illegal insurance policy, a proposal to pay $75,000 for a building that had been appraised at much less, a suspiciously high legal fee or repair contract, and other apparent attempts at larceny. These skirmishes usually found the league matched against Democrats, not only because they held most county offices but because the Democrats had few other ways of raising campaign funds.

The encounters were sometimes friendly, more often not.

The league, for instance, lobbied through the state legislature in 1945 a bill centralizing all county government purchasing. Then league secretary Crosser invited the county officials to a luncheon to soothe ruffled feelings.

The discussion started on a high plane. Secretary Crosser said he realized everybody present had the public interest at heart and as soon as everyone understood how well centralized purchasing would work—et cetera. The guests listened politely and when their turn came they began to say, one by one, that the bill undoubtedly was well intended but it would end up really costing the taxpayers more money because—et cetera.

County Treasurer Carroll Carter sat through ten minutes of this. He was one of the "class of '32" who had coasted in on the Democratic tide and had held one county office or another ever since. A former barber, Carter had a wife, four children, a trombone that he played competently, and a reputation for wit. He rose and, the spring sun glinting off his glasses and bald head, spoke in a relaxed drawl:

"Gentlemen, gentlemen, suppose we stop kidding each other.

Anybody in his right mind knows that King County will save money if the buying is done by one expert purchasing agent instead of by thirty politicians like me."

He paused to let startled laughter die down.

"But we all know that saving money is not the main point. When we do our own buying, we have a chance to swing a few votes. Votes are our bread and butter. Why pretend we politicians aren't human? We want to keep our jobs, most of us couldn't make a living at anything else. We've got families to support. Now the Municipal League gets a bill through that makes it tougher for us to keep our jobs. Sure, I admit I'm a political hack. But you must remember that in our present system that is a profession in itself. I'm a lousy manager. My office is a mess. But that doesn't matter. I can win elections. And that makes me a success. If I were a good office manager but couldn't win elections, then I would be a failure."

He turned to his host.

"Mr. Crosser, you weren't naïve enough to think you could bring us up here and make us *like* this bill, were you? Why, bless your heart, we'll do everything we can to wreck your centralized purchasing, and we'll do our damndest to knock it out at the next legislature. In the meantime, we'll have to get along the best we can. I'll probably have to ask my employes to kick in an extra dollar a month. Maybe I'll have to put my wife on the payroll again. Don't worry, we'll survive somehow. Darwin operates down at the courthouse, too, you know. Just don't ask us to pretend we like this centralized purchasing. We may be politicians—but we're not hypocrites." [5]

When Carroll Carter sat down, smiling jovially, the room had a purged feeling, all tension gone. And since there was nothing left to say, the luncheon broke up and everybody got back to his office twenty minutes early.

As it turned out, Carter and his colleagues did not knock out the centralized purchasing system at the next legislature or at any other. Instead, the mugwumps knocked out Carter—by mercilessly exposing conditions in his office. He was replaced by a Republican businessman who brought order out of Carter's amiable chaos.

Fates similar to Carter's befell most of the old Democratic

regulars of the "courthouse bunch" during the late 1940s. The league and the newspapers kept them under a constant drumfire of criticism; some were indicted; one county commissioner was convicted of bribery by the Democratic prosecuting attorney (and pardoned by lame-duck Democratic Governor Mon C. Wallgren). Behind the scenes, a group of downtown mugwumps and men of property raised campaign funds for candidates they liked and, when necessary, operated a kind of selective service to draft them into running. While nearly all the members of this informal campaign-supporting group belonged to the Municipal League, the league as an organization had no connection with their efforts.

Sometime during this era, around 1950 or 1952, the league passed through a change of life—whether puberty or menopause has not yet been determined. Its influence had been growing steadily. The membership had passed the three thousand mark in 1946, four thousand two years later, and exceeded five thousand in 1952. Considered merely as a bloc of votes, the group was too big for any official to ignore.

But with greater power, the league found itself forced to speak more carefully. Not only had it outgrown its old role of graft chaser—there were few grafters left in the County-City Building to chase—but the league's broadened membership had led to complications. New points of view demanded a hearing. League committees began to include many parents and teachers wedded to the idea of spending more money on schools. There were newcomers to Seattle who had never known the courthouse bunch of the 1930s and couldn't care less. And while the league membership continued to be overwhelmingly Republican, many bright young Democrats began to join in the 1950s. These college-trained lawyers and businessmen, most of them in their thirties and early forties, had been active amateurs in the local and state Democratic organizations, and they plunged into work on the league committees. The league, too, had developed closer ties with the League of Women Voters, notably in the campaigns for redistricting the legislature and for obtaining a metro government for the Seattle area. And the LWV unit's six hundred women included many outspoken liberals, both Democrats and Republicans.

As a result of all these influences, the Municipal League was pushed increasingly toward a middle-of-the-road, or a middle-of-the-tight-wire, position. To quiet the complaints from the Democratic old regulars that it was biased in its pre-election reports on candidates, the league appointed ten Democrats to its thirty-five-member candidates investigating committee. This did not placate the old regulars—they continued to pass resolutions at county Democratic conventions condemning the league—but it did succeed in getting the league attacked from the other direction as well.

The biggest blast from the right came in 1956. Four years before, Democrat Allan Pomeroy had defeated the mugwump-backed incumbent, Mayor Devin, after ten years in office. Now Pomeroy was running for re-election against a new mugwump entry, boyish-looking attorney Gordon Clinton.

When the league's candidate report (thirty thousand copies plus reprints in the daily press) appeared, it commented regarding Clinton: "Fair knowledge of city problems; active and well regarded in community."

The comment for Pomeroy said: "Some appointments have been subject to criticism; good record as mayor; constructive program on many city problems."

The faint damning of Mayor Pomeroy and the faint praise of their man caused an explosion among Clinton backers. Former officers of the league publicly lambasted the report. The league was accused of permitting a friend of Mayor Pomeroy to sit on the candidates investigating committee. Some long-time league supporters canceled their contributions. More might have, except that the following week Clinton won the election.

League membership, which had been falling off a hundred or so a year since 1952, continued to slide (although that might have resulted from the retirement of its long-time membership secretary, Albert Hull, or from the increase in minimum dues from five dollars to ten dollars a year).

Further evidence of dissatisfaction with the league's middle-of-the-roadism emanated from the conservative Seattle Real Estate Board. It established its own Tax Advisory Study Committee in 1958 to fight for lower property taxes.

The same year, downtown property owners and business firms created the Central Association of Seattle and employed former

Municipal League editor Paul Seibert as manager. Like Chicago's Central Area Committee and the Los Angeles Downtown Businessmen's Association, the new association's purpose was to promote projects and play politics to bolster values in the downtown section.

Some Municipal League members saw these events as signs of deterioration. The league had become too big, too broad. In trying to be all things to all mugwumps it was losing force and direction. Like the potent Los Angeles mugwump coalition of fifty years ago, it had vanquished the common enemy and now had run out of emotional steam.

Other league members disagreed.

It was a healthful sign, they said, that special interests were creating their own pressure groups. This would leave the Municipal League freer to develop itself as a true cross-section of citizens. Already the league, they believed, had gone further than any other citizen agency in the United States to devise a way for the obscure big-city dweller to make his voice heard and his weight felt. Through the league's technique of having staff-gathered facts reviewed by committees of members, reviewed again by the elected trustees and finally issued as recommended policy, the ordinary citizen had a chance to influence public officials, to become more than a civic sheep who could only march dumbly through the voting pens every spring or fall.

The league's assembly-line method of research and committee review had been developed in less than twenty years of trial and error. What had started as largely a weapon for clubbing local grafters and New Deal Democrats had evolved into something more intricate and more far-reaching.

There seemed no reason, its supporters maintained, why the Municipal League in the next twenty years might not hit upon further refinements in the search for ways to make big-city government a responsive instrument, and to save it from becoming as remote from the people, as unreachable as the Atlas Corporation or United States Steel.

12

The Tribal Towns

Boston • St. Louis • Houston

All cities have their factions—something that James Madison (in *Federalist Number Ten*) saw as "sown in the nature of man." To him factionalism was "this dangerous vice" whose yield of "instability, injustice, and confusion introduced into the public councils have, in truth, been the mortal diseases under which popular governments have everywhere perished."

No American city governments have exactly perished, so far as we know, from factionalism. Some, however, are limping badly. In these, for various reasons, the citizens have been unable or unwilling to superimpose a regime of order over the factions. And so the factions multiply and grow.

Every city is plagued with little men who hang around the edges of government, whispering, plotting, arguing. Most cities have developed ways of keeping these small-gauge gentry from positions of power. They are excluded by the presence of more able men holding the power positions, by mugwump organizations that hound them out of city hall, by exposure in the press, by a political boss who keeps them under control, and, perhaps most important, by a traditional intolerance in the community for officeholders who quarrel and connive when there is more important work to do.

In cities that lack these restraints, the little men move in. Each picks up a few followers, constitutes himself a political chieftain, and selects a hunting ground. From then on, his major political goal is to guard this preserve from poachers and to enlarge it whenever he can. A government composed of him and his fellow chieftains has sticky going.

As cases in point: Boston, St. Louis, Houston.

BOSTON—CITY IN SEARCH OF A REVOLT

The story of mugwumps in twentieth-century America is not one of unbroken victories. Among the defeats has been Boston.

Explanations for this defeat are many: the long, slow decline of New England's economy; the Brahmin tradition of freezing family money in trust funds instead of risking it to finance Boston development; the snobbery of the Yankee upper and middle classes who moved to fashionable suburbs to get away from the immigrants, then used their influence to prevent annexation, forcing Boston to become a forty-eight-square-mile compound for low-income Irish, Italians, French Canadians and Jews.

Then there is what some think of as Boston's psychic senility. The city, it is said, passed through a youth of ambition, of ego-hunger, which it satisfied by producing the Adamses, Cabots, Lowells, Lodges, the Concord group, clipper ships, Harvard, Faneuil Hall, the Bunker Hill monument; and having attained the status of hub of the universe, it settled back to a comfortable old age which it has never ended gracefully by dying completely.

Whatever the reasons offered, Boston in the 1960s is a city in trouble.

Its mugwumps look weary, like fighters who have been in the ring too long. They still go through the motions, but their blows have little effect.

The fight began better than half a century ago with a Yankee attempt to turn back the growing power of the Irish Catholic Democrats. Members of six business groups and the Boston Bar Association joined in forming the Good Government Association in 1903. At first the association did not run candidates for city office; it did not even endorse anyone openly. Instead it tried indirectly to influence the voters by issuing brief summaries of candidates' "life, education and experience." This tactic proved to be ineffective. Nearly everyone recognized the association as a front for the Republican Yankees, and they were already outnumbered by the Democrats in Boston nearly two to one.

So in 1907, the mugwumps turned to the Republican-run state legislature a couple of blocks up the street from city hall. Holding the club of state legislative action over the mayor, the mugwumps forced him to appoint a "finance commission" with six members from business groups and one from the Central Labor Union. This commission turned city hall inside out, exposing misdeeds by the Democrats and releasing its reports to Boston newspapers. After nearly two years of this, the finance commission wrote a new city charter giving the mayor extraordinary powers of veto and budget-making, and replacing the large ward-elected city council with a nine-man body elected at large. The finance commission handed this charter plan to the legislature, which in turn submitted it to Boston voters. Despite opposition from many Democratic regulars, the charter squeaked through by four thousand votes.

Buoyed by this victory, the mugwumps organized a Citizens Municipal League of a few hundred members to run candidates for mayor and city council. The league lasted through two elections. In 1910, its candidate for mayor lost narrowly to Democrat John F. Fitzgerald (grandfather of President John Fitzgerald Kennedy). Four years later the margin was greater as handsome young James M. Curley snowed under the Municipal League entry. A brief and strange interlude ensued, with the mugwumps and Mayor Curley turning their charms on each other. The reformers even gave a dinner honoring Curley's fine record his first months in office. Within a year, however, Curley had become the mugwumps' public enemy number one, a rating he held with them until they finally forced him into political retirement in 1951.

Mugwump influence on the city council waned after 1918, although it enjoyed a comeback in 1925, when mugwumps elected nearly half the council. In general, however, the story was one of mugwump weakness—to the point where the real contests took place among the several Irish Democratic politicians, each with his own following. Of these the most colorful was Curley, whose acid tongue dismayed his rivals and delighted newspapermen. When, for instance, Curley learned that former Mayor Fitzgerald was considering running against him, Curley announced to the press that he was preparing "three addresses which, if necessary, I shall deliver in the fall. . . . One of these addresses is entitled 'Graft, Ancient and Modern'; another, 'Great Lovers: from Cleopatra to Toodles'; and last but not least interesting, 'Libertines: from Henry VIII to the Present Day.'" [1]

Fitzgerald made a dignified reply, but he did not run.

The mugwumps and rival Irishmen, among them, defeated Curley six times for mayor; the other four races Curley won. His last defeats came in 1949 and 1951, when wealthy, aging Henry L. Shattuck (one-time Republican legislator and former treasurer of Harvard) and other long-time mugwump foes organized a "youth crusade" against him. They recruited a bright Harvard law graduate, Jerome L. Rappaport, to lead the campaign for their candidate, a conservative Democrat (or in Boston mugwumpese a "decent Democrat"), city clerk John B. Hynes; he had been acting mayor for five months in 1947 while Mayor Curley was serving a mail-fraud sentence in federal prison at Danbury, Connecticut. Rappaport's force of three hundred college students, many of them from modest Irish, Italian and Jewish homes in the city, held rallies, waved placards, rang doorbells and paraded in Pilgrim costumes. Curley, who was then nearly seventy-five, seemed a bit confused by this type of opposition. He lost to Hynes in a close vote.

Two years later James Himself tried a comeback against Hynes, but the Rappaport students, now known as the New Boston Committee and augmented by a hundred or so older mugwumps, helped Hynes crush him 107,000 to 76,000 in the September primary. The New Boston Committee also elected a majority of five men to the nine-seat city council and took four of the five positions on the school committee (school board).

Mugwumps were ecstatic. Articles appeared in national magazines with titles like "A Young Fresh Wind Blows in Boston Town." Speeches were made at the National Municipal League convention. Reform, led by college students, was on the march.

The march proved a short one. The college students became graduates, and then young marrieds with fresh responsibilities. And whereas the campaigners of 1949 and 1951 had been mostly war veterans finishing school under the GI bill, the newer and younger student generation had other things on its mind than municipal politics. As for the older mugwumps, only a devoted few seemed able to stir themselves to any political effort greater than writing an occasional check. And so Rappaport (who had become Mayor Hynes' secretary and then moved to the city legal department) found himself increasingly alone.

He had other troubles. His New Boston Committee endorsed a Harvard professor's suggestion that some Boston schools be closed in neighborhoods that had lost population. The endorsement angered the school administration, the teachers and parents in the school districts involved, and some members of the committee. The latter dropped out. The committee made more enemies by urging that the number of constables be reduced. The coup de grâce came, however, when Rappaport's committee sided with the Boston *Post* (published by high-dealing enterpriser John Fox—the paper folded in October, 1956) in its fight to prevent the city council from granting Sears Roebuck the use of a parcel of city-owned land for customer parking. The *Christian Science Monitor* and other newspapers charged that the *Post* opposed Sears because it refused to buy *Post* advertising space. When Rappaport announced support for the *Post's* position, his New Boston Committee suffered an internal explosion. Eleven directors handed Rappaport their resignations. By 1954, the committee was out of business.

The New Boston Committee, spectacular as it had been, was never more than a side show. Its demise left Boston mugwumps with two long-established organizations.

One is the old Finance Commission. It has been a fixture in Boston politics ever since the Republican-run legislature in 1909 made it a permanent watchdog over the Irish politicians in city hall. The legislature passed a law requiring the City of Boston to appropriate $30,000 a year for expenses of the five-man commission, appointed by the governor, and its staff (the amount later was raised to $60,000 a year). The legislature also gave the commission power to subpoena city records and city officials and to take testimony under oath.

For twenty years the Finance Commission operated as a hard-boiled investigating agency. It curtly summoned city officials to its headquarters, swore them in, and asked questions while a court reporter took down the answers in shorthand. Critical reports poured out in a steady stream. Sometimes the reports had effect, as when the commission exposed that Mayor Curley had rejected a well-known Boston firm's bid of $6,000 for refurnishing the city council chamber and was about to award the job to an obscure company for nearly three times that amount; Curley dropped the idea. Another time the Finance Commission discovered that a Curley-favored contractor had billed the city for the entire cost of tearing up a broken street and repaving it, when he had actually smeared only a few inches of blacktop over the old surface.

Most commission reports, however, merely gathered dust. After a while even the newspapers came to regard the commission as a common scold, and its criticisms received less and less publicity.

Since 1928, the commission has tried to be more sociable with city hall. It has discarded the summonses, oaths and shorthand reporters. The secretary and his three investigators, housed in a rambling old suite of offices across School Street from city hall, confer with officials privately, gathering facts, making suggestions now and then, seldom attacking with a public report.

The new method has made the Finance Commission more popular around city hall, but it has added little to the commission's standing among mugwumps. The commission finds itself described as "inactive," "passive," "not important."

More mugwumps and men of property have swung their support behind another organization, the Boston Municipal Research Bureau. Started in 1932 with famous names like Lowell, Adams and Cabot among its directors, the bureau devoted itself for years to the customary sniping at municipal spending and corruption. Not until the early 1950s did the group discern that the city faces more basic difficulties.

Boston, they saw then, is too crowded. It is too old. It spends too much on day-to-day municipal housekeeping and not enough on capital development, on renewing itself. And too many of its citizens have come to regard such conditions as normal. With an attitude of *que sera sera* that seems out of place in New England, they have accepted for their city a future of complacent decomposition.

Physically, many residential areas present a medieval panorama of red-brick shacks clustered around an occasional church spire.

Many streets laid out a century or more ago are so narrow that fire trucks cannot enter. Old houses fill up the tiny lots, twenty feet or so wide, fifty to sixty feet deep. The city is jammed with nearly 17,000 inhabitants per square mile.

Downtown, a maze of winding streets, reputedly cow paths in colonial days, lends an effect of quaint intimacy as pedestrians amble slowly along—slowly because anyone trying to move fast becomes a public menace. These charming streets unfortunately cut up the downtown into irregular and uneconomical little blocks that discourage rebuilding. As a result, only 20 percent of the office space is in Class A structures, and among these less than 10 percent of the space is air-conditioned.

Financially, Boston's city government has worked itself into a box. Its total general spending per capita is the highest among major American cities; so is its property tax. It has more city employes per thousand population than any city except New York. Its gross city debt per capita is near the top, and so is its rate of spending for schools.

A booming city might be able to absorb this spending. But Boston has not been booming. New taxable construction in the city has been pitifully low, failing to equal the loss of the assessed valuation from land taken for freeways, schools, churches or other tax-exempt use, and from further shrinkage as some property owners are granted reduced valuations on the grounds that their assessments are too high.

A few figures for the postwar years tell the story of Boston's fiscal dilemma: [2]

	1960	Change since 1946
Number of city employes	15,500	Up 17 percent
Property tax levy	$147 million	Up 129 percent
Assessed valuation of property	$1,466 million	Down 4½ percent
Property tax rate (per $1,000 of valuation)	$100.70	Up 140 percent

Fortune magazine in June, 1957, quoted Bostonian Alfred C. Neal, president of the Committee for Economic Development, as saying: "On the basis of tax rates adjusted to full value of property, Boston's taxes are about three-and-a-quarter times as high as the average of twelve cities of about the same size. . . . Our tax system discourages new construction for business purposes."

A small group of Boston mugwumps and men of property have been aware of the grim situation and have attempted to meet it. The *Christian Science Monitor*, which exerts noticeable influence even though it has only 20,000 circulation in Boston, keeps the spotlight on the city's ills. Mayor Hynes in 1957 sought to arouse the leading citizens to action by appointing a hundred of them to a Committee on Civic Progress.

The Municipal Research Bureau and its two-man staff have tried several lines of attack. Allied with the Greater Boston Real Estate Board, it has hammered away at city hall to reduce needless spending—to reorganize, for instance, the fire department whose twenty-four midget districts had been laid out for horse-drawn pumpers; to eliminate the fifty chauffeurs who drove city engineers and park officials around in sedans and half-ton trucks; to make Boston's nineteen city-owned graveyards financially self-supporting; to close down the old Brighton bathhouse where an average of forty persons were taking showers each day at a net cost to the city of $2.50 per shower.

The bureau and its allies sought to shift some of the city's expenses to other branches of government—giving city drawbridges to the state, exempting city vehicles from paying state gasoline taxes, transferring highway mileage within Boston to the Metropolitan District Commission, shifting more library, zoo and welfare expenses to the state government.

Such measures, everyone recognized, were mere aspirin. What Boston needed was massive transfusions of new income. The property tax, running more than $200 for every man, woman and child in the city, had obviously been milked dry. Two other sources of money were suggested. The bureau and men of property wanted a state sales tax with part of the money returning to the cities' treasuries. The liberals of ADA and Harvard, along with most of the regular Democrats, wanted none of the sales tax. They preferred a state graduated net income tax—and the conservatives wanted none of that. The two sides were stuck on dead center.

The impasse illustrated what seems to be Boston's underlying ailment: namely, a confusion of purpose, almost an absence of purpose, among the sundry factions contending for political position.

The lack has long been evident in the general atmosphere around Boston's ancient city hall, an atmosphere of aimlessness and sloth with much telling of stories in the offices, brays of laughter from behind closed doors, secretive conversations in corridors, empty desks with no sign that anyone has worked at them for days or possibly weeks.

Shattuck, the *Monitor*, and other mugwump elements had hoped that Mayor Hynes would fumigate city hall. But, like his contemporary Mayor Kennelly in Chicago, he proved a disappointment. The mugwumps took heart again in 1959 when forty-year-old John F. Collins defeated John E. Powers for mayor. It was one of the city's great political upsets. Collins, a lawyer from Jamaica Plain who had been elected to the legislature, the city council (he almost died of bulbar polio during the 1955 campaign), and as county probate register, had only a pick-up organization of amateurs—mostly young lawyers, real estate men and housewives. Powers, the Democratic leader in the state senate, was endorsed by almost every big name in the Democratic camp, including then Senator John F. Kennedy, House leader John McCormack, most state officials, and forty of Boston's forty-four state legislators. Even Republican Senator Leverett Saltonstall spoke out for Powers.

Collins had two prominent Republican backers—reformer Shattuck and General Robert Cutler, who was White House adviser to President Eisenhower.

Powers comfortably led the five-man field in the September primary. But in the November run-off, Collins, running an underdog campaign from his wheelchair, caught him with 114,000 votes to Powers' 90,000.

Taking office, Collins aroused fresh hopes by cutting some fat from the city budget, adding muscle to the city's feeble urban-renewal program, and starting a campaign to obtain from the reluctant legislature a limited sales tax (exempting food, medicine, children's clothing, rent) to increase Boston's revenue.

Whether Mayor Collins can put together a movement that will

drag Boston up out of its rut remains to be seen. The petty feuds of the Irish political chieftains, the anti-Catholic and anti-Protestant prejudices as immovable as tank traps, the George Apley ineffectuality of some Yankee descendants, the horse-trader mentality of others who would rather make a sharp deal than build a strong community—these have defeated all attempts over the years.

There had been a surge of expectancy in 1945 when native son Joseph P. Kennedy returned from Washington and Wall Street to head Governor Maurice Tobin's "wake-up" campaign in Boston and the state. But nobody seemed to wake up.

The New Boston Committee had defeated Curley, elected Hynes, then petered out like the Children's Crusade.

Hynes himself, with ten successive years in office—longer than any other mayor of the city—proved unable to haul the inert mass of Boston ahead. The Committee on Civic Progress that he named in 1957 to lead a Boston renaissance remained only a hundred eminent names on a letterhead. The five-year-old Conference of Civic and Business Organizations broke up in 1958 when the Chamber of Commerce, retail trade board, real estate board and Municipal Research Bureau fell to squabbling among themselves.

Said one observer, viewing the city from the perspective of Harvard across the Charles River:

> Boston is an economic backwater, like so many parts of New England. That's why people scramble for little advantages and petty graft. Sometimes you hear about the Boston political machines. That's a lot of baloney. It's just chaos. Ethnic and religious splits. There's no dialectic, no political leadership, no leading men. You have to get so many people together to get anything done in Boston. And you can't do it.

Despondency is the fashion in Boston. And yet, for all the town's problems, there is a mugwump element that, like mugwumps everywhere, refuses to give up. They are scattered through the newspapers, the business offices and law firms, the colleges, the unions, and even city hall and the State House. One finds them among the two hundred or so men who, since 1954, have been gathering for the Boston College Seminars, bimonthly dinner meetings to analyze the city's aches and pains. A mugwump cell exists within the Gillette Company (razors), whose board chairman Carl J. Gilbert is regarded as the possible leader of a Boston resurgence, should one ever come.

In its mood of harsh self-examination, Boston may be approaching the frame of mind that Pittsburgh and Philadelphia reached in the latter 1940s. The city could be ripe for revolt against the old order of incompetence and inaction.

Allegheny Conference director Park Martin said of Pittsburgh that it had to feel way down before it could feel way up. Boston in the 1960s is feeling pretty far down. It has only one direction to go.

ST. LOUIS—WITH PUNT AND PRAYER

The fur traders, then the riverboats, the German immigrants, some Irish—and St. Louis by 1870 was the nation's third largest city. But by then the time of youth, excitement and glory was over for cities that drew their vitality from the river. Henceforward St. Louis would work a bit, nap a bit, and let life take its course.

So it was, too, with the city's mugwumps.

They had their high moments. Senator Carl Schurz led the Republican mugwumps nationally in 1884 to block Blaine from the presidency. Two decades later young prosecutor Joseph W. Folk unseated local boss Ed Butler. At the end of World War I other machine politicians were targets of the Civic League, directed by Roger N. Baldwin, who was later to become head of the American Civil Liberties Union, and his assistant Louis F. Budenz, whose interest subsequently turned toward the lot of the proletariat—he eventually became editor of the Communist party *Daily Worker*. (The Civic League itself metamorphosed into the Bureau of Governmental Research in 1922 and the Governmental Research Institute in 1935.)

The better citizens built up a head of steam in the early twenties to put across an $87-million bond issue for street lights, sewers, a courthouse and other improvements. In 1939, they rallied again to outlaw smoky coal, much to the irritation of Illinois mine owners across the river.

Behind these displays, however, lay the undeniable fact of mugwump torpor. While in many cities mugwumps and men of property were taking steps to gain at least partial political control, St. Louis citizens seemed content to let ward hacks (Republicans until 1930, Democrats since then) occupy most of the policy-making positions in local government. As long as the officeholders did not attempt to steal too much—a difficult task with the Governmental Research Institute and the alert *Post-Dispatch* and *Globe-Democrat* looking down their necks—the mugwumps appeared reasonably content. They demanded no large spending programs to improve the city. Rather, they found the city's low bonded debt a source of pride. And so St. Louis moseyed on, unconcerned, into the 1940s.

It is not clear just who first looked in the mirror and discovered that St. Louis had become a frump. By 1950, however, only a blind man could have missed the fact. Nobody had put up a new office building since the era of President Hoover. Nearly half the city's schools dated back to the Spanish-American War. The municipal old-people's home and the workhouse were century-old relics. The 1950 federal census showed 36 percent of St. Louis dwellings as "lacking hot running water, private toilet or bath, or dilapidated." Only New Orleans and San Antonio, among the larger cities, had a higher proportion of slums. In downtown St. Louis, foot traffic had fallen 40 percent since 1930. Property values were dropping, and so were the city's tax returns. In the surrounding county area, trunk sewers, far from being able to handle new industries, were overloaded with the present burden. Firms that wanted to expand their operations were moving out of town.

As in Milwaukee, many leading citizens began to change their ideas about municipal frugality. They approved when the mayor and board of aldermen placed five bond issues on the ballot between 1946 and 1952. They endorsed a new city charter offered to the voters in 1950 containing permission for a city earnings tax. But mugwump blessings did little good. The voters defeated all five bond issues and turned down the charter.

The city's position was moving from bad to desperate. It did not have enough money even to fill holes in the streets. Mayor Joseph Darst called in several eminent citizens (Donald Danforth of Ralston Purina, bank presidents David Calhoun and Arthur Blumeyer, J. W. McAfee of Union Electric, Powell McHaney of General American Life Insurance, former Mayor Aloys Kaufmann, Sidney Baer of Stix, Baer and Fuller, attorney James Douglas, and Ethan Shepley, later chancellor of Washington University) and asked their help in passing bond issues. This was the beginning of Civic Progress, Incorporated.

Meanwhile the *Post-Dispatch* had been hammering away with a series of articles on the theme "Progress or Decay? St. Louis Must Choose." The *Globe-Democrat* added its voice. The Junior Chamber of Commerce started a weekly radio program entitled "Wake Up, St. Louis."

Mayor Darst, seriously ill, did not seek re-election in the spring of 1953. The mugwumps and the press promoted Washington University engineering professor Raymond R. Tucker for the Democratic nomination, which was becoming equivalent to election. With many Republicans "crossing over," Tucker won nomination by a close 1,500 votes despite opposition from Democratic leaders in twenty-three of the city's twenty-eight wards.

The new mayor, facing a hostile board of aldermen, turned to the men who had helped put him in office. At Tucker's request, Civic Progress, Inc., expanded from eight men to eighteen. It began to hold monthly meetings at which the members belabored each other into taking on assignments; and these were not the customary well-bred little chores of holding a luncheon, making a few earnest remarks, and picking up the tab. Edwin Spiegel of Gaylord Container led a campaign that placed the St. Louis Symphony Orchestra on a solid financial base. Edwin Clark of Southwestern Bell Telephone sold dubious businessmen and aldermen on a one-way traffic and no-parking program to relieve congestion on the narrow downtown streets. Insurance firm president McHaney organized a campaign committee that raised $60,000 and, much to the surprise of professional politicians, won voter approval to continue the city earnings tax. Bank presidents Sidney Maestre of Mercantile Trust and Calhoun of St. Louis Union Trust headed the successful drive for an omnibus $110-

million bond issue for streets, hospitals, voting machines, library expansion and many other improvements.

This parade of victories took place within two years, 1953–55. It looked as if St. Louis was on its way. Articles about Civic Progress, Inc., and its deeds appeared in the nation's press. St. Louis, like Pittsburgh, became a port of call for admiring delegations.

Yet a closer look would have prompted caution. The Civic Progress triumphs had been essentially nonpolitical. There had been no opposition and even some assistance from organized labor and the Democratic ward committeemen. Civic Progress' only major opponent had been public apathy, and it had overcome this with the two weapons it had at its disposition—money and smart public relations.

These were wielded by the knowledgeable Fleishman-Hillard agency. In addition to generous campaign funds raised by businessmen, the agency had the personal prestige of the Civic Progress members. This handful of men headed firms that account for a large proportion of the city's payrolls, notably Southwestern Bell Telephone, Ralston Purina, Anheuser-Busch and Monsanto Chemical. These companies could and did provide hordes of volunteer office help whenever needed. Since they represented the biggest advertising accounts in town, a mere hint was enough to insure the cooperation of every advertising agency. Free billboards, full-page advertisements, radio and television time could be had for the asking, donated by business firms.

The majorities it scored at the polls, running as high as six to one and eight to one, seemed proof that Civic Progress had a technique that could not lose. Through well-planned huckstering—or, in a more acceptable phrase, effective use of mass media—a small group of leading citizens could win political campaigns. They needed no mass ground forces, only money and intelligence.

This comfortable concept died on August 6, 1957. On that day the mugwumps had hoped to overthrow the long-entrenched power of the ward politicians. A board of freeholders, aided by the Governmental Research Institute, had written a new city charter cutting the number of wards in the city from twenty-eight to seven, and providing for a board of aldermen of fifteen—one from each of the seven wards and eight elected at large.

The aldermen opposed the charter because it would obviously

deprive most of them of their jobs. The National Association for the Advancement of Colored People opposed it because they feared it would mean the same for the Negro aldermen. The Central Trades and Labor Union joined them in opposition. A similar coalition in 1950 had defeated a mugwump-sponsored charter. This time the outcome was the same. The people rejected the charter by 35,000 votes, a margin of three to two.

Civic Progress and other reformers took their lumps again in 1958 and 1959. A city charter amendment to permit paying the mayor and other top officials more than $10,000 a year met defeat at the polls. So did an ambitious plan to establish a Metropolitan District—a metro government enveloping St. Louis City and St. Louis County, which have been totally separate since 1875. The proposed government would have jurisdiction over sewers (absorbing the metropolitan sewer district created in 1954), area planning, arterial roads, police communications, transit, civil defense and development of industrial sites—something St. Louis woefully lacks.

One reason for the metro district's crushing defeat may have been that the mugwumps themselves were divided. Mayor Tucker had appeared before the freeholders board that was writing the proposed charter, to argue that creating the metro district would merely superimpose a third layer of government on the St. Louis area. He advocated consolidating the city and county governments instead. When the freeholders failed by one vote, ten to nine, to go along with the mayor, he and his adherents decided to sit out the metro district election. The plan lost two to one within the city, three to one in St. Louis County.

The mayor, Civic Progress and other mugwump elements were united, however, on another campaign in 1959—and this one showed a growing political acuteness. The goal was to double the city earnings tax, from one-half percent to one percent. Mayor Tucker sent the board of aldermen four bills. These increased the municipal gasoline tax, property tax, merchandise-and-manufacturers tax, and imposed a rubbish collection charge; each measure carried a rider providing that it would be automatically repealed if a one percent earnings tax were approved by the voters. With the city budget $4 million in the red, it was clear that more revenue had to come from somewhere, and the board of aldermen were happy to shift the decision to the voters themselves. For the voters, the decision was easy. Under the mayor's four bills, they would have to pay all of the tax increases. But if the earnings tax were raised, a third of the added cost would fall on suburbanites who worked in the city. While the commuters fumed, the city dwellers approved the earnings tax by a majority of nine to one.

The mugwumps scored twice again in 1960. Civic Progress members, with a $30,000 campaign fund, won a close vote removing the $10,000-a-year ceiling from city salaries.

Their second victory involved the smaller St. Louis County government, which has jurisdiction over the suburbs. Egged on by the *Post-Dispatch*, the mugwumps, including the League of Women Voters, formed a Citizens Committee and circulated initiative petitions to force a vote on county charter amendments eliminating two elected county officials, the assessor and the tax collector, and taking tax functions away from the elected county clerk; all tax assessing and collecting instead would be handled by a new department of revenue, with an appointed director and a staff under civil service. The change had been proposed three years before by the Governmental Research Institute. In the face of heavy opposition from the courthouse politicians (the change meant they would lose five hundred of their twelve hundred county patronage jobs), the Citizens Committee collected the needed signatures, won a place on the ballot, and saw their proposal adopted by a wide majority. The next day the *Post-Dispatch* said in an editorial:

> Voters struck a blow for efficiency in the patronage-ridden county government. The amendments take the assessing and tax-collection functions out of the hands of the township politicians and provide for their nonpartisan administration under the merit principle. What is good and appropriate for those two functions ought to be equally applicable to the whole range of county government. . . . Perhaps the Citizens Committee . . . would be willing to take on this even greater task.

In other words, St. Louis mugwumps, since they apparently cannot reform their county government all at once as in the defeated metro district plan, might devote themselves to bit-by-bit reform, using the initiative process. They could take a function at a time, placing it under an appointed professional administrator with civil service employes, until they eventually pieced together the type of county government they wanted.

More pressing, however, than housecleaning the county government were the problems of the St. Louis city and school administrations. Here the jobs of twenty-nine aldermen and twelve school directors were traditionally parceled out by deals and jockeying among the Democratic ward committeemen abetted by political-minded union leaders. A reform candidate venturing into this environment had little more chance than a pet rabbit in a jungle.

Reformers in nearly all other ward-run cities during the past seventy-five years have faced a similar dilemma. Either they could try to create a rival ward-by-ward organization able to lick the hack politicians on their own ground. Or they could try to obliterate the ward organizations by winning campaigns for charter changes, providing for city councils elected at large instead of by wards, and creating effective civil service systems.

St. Louis mugwumps briefly considered getting down into the wards and fighting for control of the several Democratic factions. But the unanswerable question always arose, how? The reformers had no manpower in most wards, not even the three or four persons required to set up a minimal ward organization. Most mugwumps live out in the Republican suburbs. They cannot even vote in St. Louis city elections. Hiring political mercenaries in each ward has been a possibility, but an unpopular one. Members of Civic Progress and their allies have shrunk from such open political activity. One put it: "I doubt that we have the right to intervene in a ward where we don't live."

As for eliminating, or at least modifying, the ward system for electing aldermen, the mugwumps tried that with their charter campaigns and were defeated at the polls.

When reformers elsewhere have found themselves in this predicament—outnumbered by the professional politicians running the city, running it rather badly but not badly enough to cause a voter uprising—the reformers have usually been forced to adopt the old Michigan football strategy designed for a team with a weak offense: keep plugging away with a punt and a prayer, and wait for the breaks.

In reform politics, "the breaks" mean an outbreak of scandals so outrageous that they cause the public to blow its top.

Low in manpower as they are, this is the policy that St. Louis mugwumps apparently have had to choose.

The policy yielded dividends in the St. Louis school board election of 1961. For years the board had given off a political aroma. It kept the school administration divided and subservient; instead of having one superintendent, the board had four separate executives who reported directly to it—a superintendent for instruction, an auditor, a secretary-treasurer, and a commissioner for buildings. The buildings commissioner was of special interest to the ward politicians and certain labor leaders because his department had twelve hundred non–civil service jobs to dispense.

In 1960 a circuit court grand jury issued a scorching report on this patronage system in the school buildings department. The grand jury also called upon three school board members to resign, accusing them of using school employes and materials for work on their family homes. One board member did resign, another decided not to file for re-election in 1961, the third chose to fight a citizens' suit to oust him from office.

Soon after the jury reported, the Citizens Association for the Public Schools (CAPS) appeared. This mugwump group announced it would help the three reform-minded men already on the school board by seeing that they gained some allies in the April, 1961, election. As the election neared, CAPS assembled a slate of five reform candidates. Campaigning on the issue of corruption and mediocrity on the board, it elected all five of them. This gave the reformers an eight-to-four majority and with it the promise of long-overdue changes in the board's approach to its job.

Whether the reform majority would last beyond the next school election remained to be seen. Certainly the comfortable margins gained by the CAPS slate in 1961 could not be interpreted as reflecting a sudden, city-wide upsurge of mugwump political strength in general. The results of the mayoral primary held in March, 1961, proved that. In that race for the Democratic nomination, Mayor Tucker barely nosed out the ward politicians' candidate, Democratic national committeeman Mark R. Holloran. He trailed Tucker by only 1,272 votes. (The regulars closed ranks behind the mayor in the general election to turn back Republican Ben H. Lindenbusch.) The board of aldermen emerged from the election with, as usual, a solid anti-mugwump line-up.

The day probably will come when this line-up will crack, giving the reform forces a chance to remake the board of aldermen into a legislative body more in their own image; that done, they can move on to further municipal reforms. At the moment, however, there appears little that St. Louis mugwumps can do, more than they have, to hasten the day. They have drawn plans, made studies, written charters, waged charter campaigns—and lost. That would seem to leave but one alternative: to remain poised, and wait for the other side, through greed or ineptness, to make the big mistakes.

HOUSTON—THE TOUGH CASE

The old cities of the East are congested with more than people and buildings. They are filled with motives, with buried likes and dislikes, ancient calls and fears and wants. Such cities have a feel of complexity, of an involuted tangle of political threads running back into the undecipherable past.

The cities of the Southwest, new and a little raw, have none of this. They give a feeling of openness. The wind blows through them. As yet uncluttered by generations of cultural and psychological accumulation, Dallas, San Antonio and Houston appear simple, direct, unsophisticated. The slick operator is out of place. So is the intellectual liberal with his habit of turning ideas around and around, poking and analyzing. The men who run the Southwest cities have a code of almost Boy Scout ingenuousness: make money and seize power as God gives you the chance; build things; move ahead; roll up your sleeves, and don't expect a valet or hired man to handle things you should handle yourself.

Where Texans differ, however, is in defining what things you should handle yourself. Some believe the rule applies to both making money and local government. Others think it applies only to making money; government is for the hired man.

The rich and near-rich of Dallas and the not-quite-so-rich of San Antonio have intervened in city affairs, studying them, discussing them, shaping them, running men for office and even running for office themselves. They have been not only practicing mugwumps but active politicians.

On the other hand, the Face Cards of Houston, as their detractors call them, have chosen a different role. Like men of property in most places, they have sought only the assurance that local government is in the hands of someone dependable—someone with a friendly ear whom they can reach by picking up the telephone if they feel like it. The Face Cards have had no time for all the political foolishness of research, meetings, statements, issues, debates and campaigns.

This attitude of withdrawal left a little maneuvering room for a young mugwump element that was stirred before World War II by the city-manager campaigns in Dallas and San Antonio. Organized as the Citizens Charter Committee, these business and professional men won voter approval of a city-manager plan in the early 1940s. Many of the Charterites, however, went off to war. In their absence, Jesse Jones' *Chronicle*, the voice of Houston's dinosaur reactionaries, sniped and blasted at the city manager. The besieged manager, John North Edy, lasted two years before the city council fired him.

Determined to wipe the manager plan off the books, the *Chronicle* and others called on the conservatives' old stand-by, Oscar Holcombe, to run for mayor again. During his remarkable career Holcombe had retired and come back more often than Sarah Bernhardt. He first went into office for four terms, 1921–28, then was defeated, returned for two more terms, 1933–37, sat one out, and came back in 1939–40. In 1946 he campaigned on an anti-manager platform and won. The next year, overriding opposition from the returned mugwumps, Houston voted a charter amendment that removed the words "city manager" and substituted "mayor" as chief administrator of the city government.

Defeated at the polls, some mugwumps gathered one evening in the living room of Kenneth E. Womack, Jr., member of a wealthy Texas cotton family, and decided to convert what had been an old taxpayers association into a research bureau. They christened it the Tax Research Association of Houston and Harris County, corraled some funds and employed a staff.

If the founders dreamed that the research association would become the strategy headquarters for a city-manager revival movement (as another new bureau was then becoming under Ed Conroy in San Antonio), they were mistaken. Nobody seemed excited about the city-manager plan any more, and the association gradually developed into what it is today, a statistics-publishing bureau interested mostly in equalizing property assessments within the county.

Instead the fight—or intermittent skirmish—for good government in Houston has come to center about the mayor and the council. The mayor holds unusual authority. Under the 1946 charter revision, he has all the appointing and administrative power formerly granted the city manager. Furthermore, as an elected official, the city council cannot dismiss him. He sits as president and voting member of the council. The only weapon he lacks is the veto.

Any council, even the best, would resent this concentration of power in one of its members. And Houston's council has been far from the best. The posture expected of a councilman, who is elected for only a two-year term, is that of palm outstretched for a campaign contribution. The basic rate, according to city hall sources, is $100, with variations up and down from this figure.

Whatever the council's shortcomings may be, Houston mugwumps have done little to remove them—and "them" refers to both the shortcomings and the councilmen. Except for their largely non-political research association, mugwumps have formed no permanent organization to upgrade the caliber of local administration.

As a substitute, some of them have been active in the Chamber of Commerce; and as chambers of commerce go, Houston has a very good one. It planned the $60-million dam, reservoir and aqueduct project that by the mid-1960s will bring 1.2 billion gallons of industrial water a day from the Trinity River sixty miles away; another fifteen-mile line will carry domestic water from the San Jacinto River. These lines are expected to meet Houston's water needs for the next half-century. The Chamber of Commerce was also prime mover for a new jet airport north of the city. The chamber carefully restricts itself, however, to physical improvements. It does not try to make political ones.

The mugwumps, few as they are, sometimes assemble and set up a temporary organization to help elect a mayor. In 1952, they backed Roy Hofheinz, a forty-year-old attorney who had made a million dollars from real estate and radio stations. Some conservatives lent support. Said one: "Holcombe was getting pretty old. Hofheinz looked like someone who could answer our problem for years to come."

But once in office, Mayor Hofheinz brought great distress to the city council and to many men of property. He proved uncontrollable and unpredictable—a "mustang" was the local term. He infuriated the council by centralizing city purchasing, and he tried to end the practice of each councilman "adopting" certain city departments as his private bailiwick, from which he could draw comfort, headlines and political support. Council meetings became noisy affairs filled with shouts and gavel-banging. The showdown came in a special election in 1955. The councilmen attempted to pass charter amendments cutting Hofheinz down to a "weak mayor" status. In retaliation Hofheinz placed all city offices at stake in the election, including his own; the plan was to liquidate the opposing councilmen. To assist Hofheinz, the mugwumps put together a United Citizens Association, including labor and Negroes.

The voters rejected the council's weak-mayor amendments. But to the dismay of the United Citizens, the voters also let the offending councilmen retain their seats, and they booted out Mayor Hofheinz in favor of the ever-recurrent Holcombe. Hofheinz had won the battle over amendments, but he had lost the war.

Revenge came two years later. Holcombe had been endorsed for re-election by all three newspapers—the *Chronicle*, the liberal Republican *Post*, owned by former Governor W. P. Hobby and his wife, Oveta Culp Hobby, and the smaller Scripps-Howard *Press*. Holcombe's opponent, former city attorney Lewis Cutrer, was backed only by Hofheinz and the thin column of mugwumps. Like Harry Truman in 1948, he had no right to win. But the town's faith in Holcombe and the council had evidently been shaken more than anyone realized by exposure of an intricate deal the year before involving $5 million in Sharpstown water district bonds, some investment bankers, and a loan of $100,000 to a councilman. There was talk of other windfalls to local real estate developers and certain investment bankers when the city, in 1956, had annexed thirty-five other water districts and assumed their debts totaling some $40 million. Election night found Cutrer the winner by a hefty three-to-two majority. Three anti-reform councilmen running for re-election were defeated (a fourth one, who had been indicted in the water-bonds case, had not even bothered to file).

Mayor Cutrer plunged into his new job conscientiously. As financial adviser, he recruited the director of the Tax Research Association to be city treasurer. He leaned over backward to conciliate the councilmen, letting them talk to their hearts' content without lifting the gavel that Hofheinz had swung so freely; as a result, council meetings sometimes lasted until nine o'clock in the evening. He got the Chamber of Commerce's Trinity River water project under way. He appointed an array of citizens committees to advise him on traffic, police, urban renewal, health, parks, metropolitan government and county home rule. There was another committee to study whether Houston should rid itself of one of its quaintest distinctions—that of being the only large city in the United States with no zoning laws.

These committees ranged in size up to one hundred and thirty members. If ever assembled at one time, they would have filled a fair-sized auditorium. Yet they have attempted little and accomplished less. Cutrer's struggle toward better government has been a lonely effort.

Any other good-government mayor in Houston must face the same problem. He can expect slight help from the councilmen. Year in and year out they have shown deep interest in only one goal—to divide the mayor's power over the city departments among themselves, carving out little principalities that each may run like a feudal baron. Their ideal is a return to commission government.

Nor apparently can any mayor expect much help from the city's collection of the usual Texas political factions. There is a "liberal" wing of intellectuals, union leaders (notably of the oil workers and steel workers), Negroes (the Harris County Council of Organizations), and the Harris County Democrats, representing the so-called loyalist element who adhere to the national Democratic party. The "conservative" faction consists of right-wing Democrats and Republicans. Houston also has a radical rightist element that would eliminate the income tax, the United Nations, the United States Supreme Court, labor unions, and half the books in the public library.

All these groups have one thing in common. They ignore city hall and its problems.

The only local battleground they meet on is school board elections. As in Los Angeles during the 1950s, radical right-wingers joust against a liberal element, the Houston Association of Better Schools, for seats on the board. Since the Little Rock furor of 1957, the conservatives have held the majority. At the moment, the liberals—Negro housewife Hattie Mae White and former University of Houston president W. W. Kemmerer—are outnumbered five to two.

When it comes to seats on the city council, however, no citizen organization appears, either to draft able candidates or to keep a watchful eye on those in office. To the Face Cards of Houston, as well as those lower down in the deck, the quality of local government seems a matter of unconcern. This indifference is reflected in the press. One frustrated career official commented: "None of the newspapers is interested in good government. They all give lip service to it. But they won't take an aggressive stand for it."

An oil company lawyer, a mugwump since the city-manager campaigns of two decades ago, lamented: "There's no spirit. Houston has so little capacity for moral indignation. And how do you teach a city that?"

How indeed? The spirit perhaps is not something learned but something caught, like an infection. Tough as Houston is, it may catch the stuff some day. It could come blowing down on the wind from Dallas. Or up from San Antonio.

13

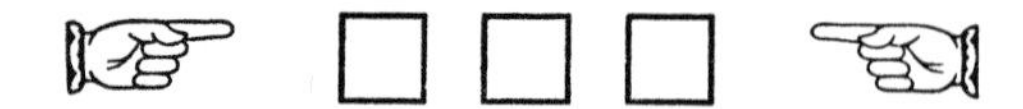

Hell Made Over

PITTSBURGH

Ever since the turn of the century, when Lincoln Steffens took a look at flaming smoke-belching Pittsburgh and called it "hell with the lid off," the city has been described in extreme terms: the most steel, the most dirt, the most monopolies, the most millionaires per capita, and—since World War II—the most dramatic case of urban renewal.

This postwar renaissance has been described in Chapter Six: how the old buildings went crashing down and the new skyscrapers and plazas marched in from the Point, across the Golden Triangle and up the hillside; how a feeling of pride and excitement swept the city, giving it an atmosphere like a college campus with a winning team; how all this was made possible by a remarkable coalition of organized Democrats led by Mayor David Lawrence and wealthy Republicans headed by Richard K. Mellon, assisted by the Mellon group's working tools—the Allegheny Conference on Community Development and the Pennsylvania Economy League.

This coalition is the key to the Pittsburgh story. And it poses to the political observer the fascinating question: Was it an accident that could only happen once, or is it a prototype that can be duplicated by other American cities in this century?

The Pittsburgh juggernaut—for that is what it was, overriding all obstacles—was not built from a blueprint. Nor was its program. The first Allegheny Conference director, Park Martin, confessed:

> In the early years none of us saw clearly the whole road ahead. No over-all program existed. The dependence of one problem to another had not yet been identified, nor its relationship established as part of a broad, comprehensive program. None of the sponsors of the conference were fully aware of the important role they would assume or of the great amount of time they would be asked to give to the program.[1]

What most of the monied gentlemen undoubtedly thought they were getting into was merely another blue-ribbon committee dedicated to the good of Pittsburgh, like the ones their fathers and grandfathers had served on. Before World War I, for instance, the Chamber of Commerce had promoted the Pittsburgh Committee on Planning and the Pittsburgh Civic Commission, which persuaded the mayor to appoint the first city-planning commission (among its members was food packer H. J. Heinz, whose grandson John would be found in the Allegheny Conference).

These committees of the well-to-do were a common device around Pittsburgh—and seemed necessary because of the city's peculiar make-up. As one long-time participant in these affairs described it: "Pittsburgh was always a medieval town. There were the rich and the working poor, and almost no middle class. In order to get something done, the rich had to do it."

The rich and their committees, however, could show little for their efforts. The city steadily sank deeper in grime, smoke and obsolescence. The Mellon brothers, Richard B. and Andrew, helped found a Citizens Committee on City Planning in 1919, but it jogged along through the years without result. Not until the late 1930s, when it was transformed into the Pittsburgh Regional Planning Association and Wallace Richards, formerly with the Green Belt towns, was brought in as director, did the ferment begin that eventually led to the Allegheny Conference.

Probably the conference would have proved only another committee of big names if several currents of circumstance had not chanced to flow together as World War II was ending.

One was the growing backlog of unspendable funds, public and private, that had accumulated during wartime shortages of men and materials. Another was the increasingly obvious dilapidation of Pittsburgh, worsened by depression and war. A third was the alteration of the Pennsylvania Economy League from a 1930-ish penny-pinching taxpayer group into a smartly staffed organization bent on public improvements. And one should not forget Mrs. Mellon and her alleged threat to get out of Pittsburgh unless Richard and his friends did something to clean up the place.

Equally important was Lawrence's decision to run for mayor in 1945.

Pittsburgh had a history of typical hack-ridden government. Now and then a mayor or councilman or other official would go to jail for graft. Petty chieftains competed with each other for political advantage. The old Civic Club of Allegheny County (founded in 1895) and its woman executive secretary tried to improve matters with reports on candidates, proposed charter reforms and studies of state legislation, but they did not get far.

The big industrialists, the millionaires, largely ignored the local government. The lesser business and professional men were almost ludicrously divided. Although Pittsburgh has a relatively compact downtown section, it contained both a Lower Downtown Businessmen's Association and an Upper Downtown Businessmen's Association. They treated the boundary line at Wood Street as an enemy frontier. Once, when a group of citizens and officials urged building a new Pittsburgh civic auditorium on the Point, the Upper Downtown association opposed it because it would be in the territory of the Lower Downtown businessmen.

The factionalism found among the politicians and businessmen extended even to the good-government groups. The city had two rival Leagues of Women Voters. The national organization attempted to end the unique situation by "disaffiliating" one of them, but the ladies declined to disband.

Lawrence himself had never been accused of being a good-government man. He was the tough, effective political boss. In 1920, the thirty-year-old Lawrence began selling insurance and spending his spare time as chairman of the meager Democratic minority in Allegheny County. In 1931, he ran for his first elective office, as county commissioner, and lost by nine thousand votes. After that, he chose the role of power behind the scenes, much as Crump had chosen in Memphis after the humiliation of having to resign as mayor (both men were the same age, forty-two, when they received these setbacks). Lawrence's fortunes changed with the Roosevelt landslide of 1932. Industrial Pittsburgh became Democratic territory, and the Lawrence forces gained control of city hall the next year. Lawrence managed George Earle's winning campaign for governor in 1934; soon after, he assumed command as Democratic state chairman.

In 1945, with the Allegheny Conference one year old, Lawrence announced that he would run for mayor himself, replacing the protégés with whom he had filled the chair since the mid-thirties. Lawrence's motives for deciding to step out front after so many years backstage have been the subject of speculation. Some believe he genuinely wanted to help save decaying Pittsburgh. Others say he was more concerned with saving the decaying Democratic organization that might be wrecked by another weak city administration.

In any event, there was nothing weak about the twelve years of Lawrence administrations that began in 1946. Forming a powerful duumvirate with the Allegheny Conference, he handled the political side of the renaissance with no-nonsense dispatch. If the law required the city council to pass an ordinance for a project, it passed it; the words "the mayor wants it" were enough to assure that. If action was required by the three county commissioners, it took place a little more slowly but just as surely. When state legislation was called for, he and the Allegheny Conference Republicans between them could round up the needed support.

Lawrence, however, was not a true organization man. He was a virtuoso. Like Franklin D. Roosevelt, he built no line of succession behind him, and when Lawrence was elected governor in 1958 and left for Harrisburg, the political climate started to change. Within two years the city council began occasionally to balk at approving new redevelopment projects. The three labor members of the nine-man council especially took to questioning any action that would dispossess home owners or small businessmen.

The board of county commissioners got a new chairman—an anti-Lawrence Democrat, dentist William D. McClelland, who had lost to Lawrence's candidate George Leader in the gubernatorial primary in 1954. The board that had once cooperated fully with Lawrence's full-steam-ahead approach on major projects now switched to a go-slow attitude. Dr. McClelland advocated holding up large-scale programs until the voters could approved them in popular referendums. The board also balked and haggled over such matters as contributing $80,000 toward the city's 1959 bicentennial celebration, $250,000 for removal of the old Point Bridge, and additional funds to help construct a city-county sports stadium on the city's North Side.

These actions chilled relations with the Allegheny Conference. The rah-rah spirit went out of the Pittsburgh renaissance. The Mellon family foundations and other private fund-givers began to avoid projects that might be bogged down in controversy before the city council or the county commissioners.

The conference's bonds with the retail business community frayed too. For several years the Mellon group maintained a kind of united front with the retailers by means of the Pittsburgh Civic-Business Council, a central body that raised $450,000 a year for the conference, the Regional Planning Association, the Better Business Bureau, the Chamber of Commerce, and the Pittsburgh Convention Bureau. In the late 1950s, however, this joint fund-raising effort ceased. Now the Allegheny Conference members provide about $240,000 a year just for the conference and its technical arm, the Regional Planning Association.[2]

Mellon opened up another urban renewal front after 1956. He and his aides formed ACTION-Housing, Incorporated, to promote apartment-building within the city. Like the Cleveland Development Foundation, it established a $2-million loan fund for private developers. The first, relatively small Spring Hills project opened in 1959—slightly over 200 apartments renting at $77.50 to $97.50 a month. One fifth of them were set aside for Negro tenants. The larger East Hills development was planned with nearly half the 1,400 units scaled for renters in the $4,000 to $7,000-a-year bracket, the remaining apartments for those with higher incomes.

Plans for more apartments and other projects are on the drawing boards. The Pittsburgh renaissance has slowed, but it has not stopped.

In late 1957, after a visit to the city, the author jotted down this note to himself:

> Is the political partnership that created the renaissance a basically solid alliance of forces that can last year after year—or is it the chance result of a few strong men getting together? Have the men of Pittsburgh created a set of political institutions—"offices" in a sense—that are peculiarly adapted to the needs of a metropolitan center in this era and so will endure while the men in them change? Or have they merely assembled a combination like the Washington Senators of pitcher Walter Johnson's heyday, a fine team as long as the individual performers are around?

We now have part of the answer. Mayor Lawrence's departure in 1959 left a hole that no other politician or group of politicians has yet filled. Would the loss of Richard Mellon be a final crippling blow to the renaissance? Or even if Mellon stays on the job for many years to come, will the effort bog down for lack of political direction in city hall and the county government?

Pittsburgh has entered into its second revolution without ever quite finishing its first one. The atmosphere of old-time hack politics still clings to portions of its government. Side by side with municipal operations run by able professionals are other operations surrounded by stogy smoke and hunched shoulders. Policemen, firemen and city planners are protected by civil service, but employes in public works, lands and buildings, and the water department are not. A quarter of the city's five thousand jobs are dealt with as patronage. The week in October, 1960, that the author revisited Pittsburgh, a city councilman, an assistant superintendent in the lands and buildings department, and a private contractor were indicted for allegedly faking bills for "phantom" repairs to city, county and school property.

As long as Lawrence was around, the Pittsburgh rebuilders could overlook some such shortcomings in city hall. Lawrence kept the little men in line. But for the long pull, Pittsburgh may conclude that it will be better to finish the job of professionalizing its government, relegating the little men to the periphery where they cannot undercut public confidence in the government, and cannot obstruct every proposal for change.

With the pace of the renaissance slackened for the moment, Pittsburgh now has a breathing spell in which to finish its first revolution. That done, perhaps it can regain momentum in its second.

The Allegheny Conference may recoil from the idea of heading a reform movement to professionalize city hall. To lend the conference members' weight to such a campaign without seeming to impose a company-town type of domination over the city—that presents a nice political problem.

But the conference has handled difficult problems before. And in Pittsburgh the practical question is: If the Allegheny Conference does not take the lead, who will?

14

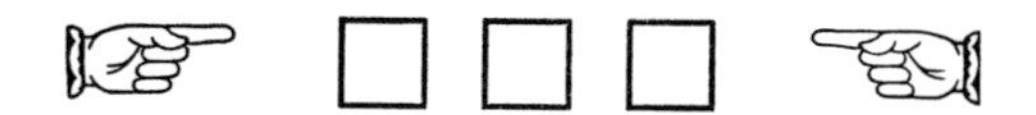

Labor's Love Lost

Minneapolis • San Francisco • Detroit

The mugwump's relations with organized labor have seldom been good. He has found the union man, at times, an unkempt agitator who should be suppressed—if necessary, by force. Again, the mugwump, embroiled in a passionate crusade, has found the unionist indifferent to his cause—plainly a bad citizen. Yet again, when the union man has shed his indifference and entered politics in strength, the mugwump has seen him as a dangerous invader clearly bent on subverting the public welfare.

Samuel Gompers is credited with leading the early American labor movement out of the poppy fields of utopianism and political reform, and down the rocky trail of straight trade unionism. Most unionists have been content to follow this path ever since. A union, as they see it, is for getting more pay and better working conditions. Reform politics is for other people.

Not all early unionists stayed on the straight and rocky trail. When Eugene V. Debs and Victor L. Berger launched the Socialist party at the turn of the century, many unionists gave it their support.

The Socialists, whose intellectual forebears had fled to the New World after the unsuccessful 1848 revolutions in Europe, denounced the captains of industry and the malefactors of great wealth in much the same terms as the Progressive mugwumps. The mugwumps, however, never regarded the Socialists and their labor allies as anything but crackpots and arch-rivals for political power. As the Socialist vote grew before World War I in Los Angeles, New York, Milwaukee, Buffalo and other cities, the ranks of business and professional men hardened against them, and municipal campaigns became bruising affairs.

The Socialists reached their high-water mark in the municipal elections of 1917, probably because of their anti-war platform; their candidates received nearly 20 percent of the vote in Cleveland, 12 percent in Cincinnati, 35 percent in Toledo, 25 percent in Buffalo; in New York City, Morris Hillquit got 90,000 more votes for mayor than the Republican entry but fell behind the winning Democrat. Thereafter the Socialist movement, like its contemporary, the Progressive movement, ran out of gas. Today hardly a trace of the once potent Socialists remains in big-city politics except for a few aging followers in Milwaukee and in New York's Liberal party.

The withering of the Socialists after World War I left their union followers with no intellectual leadership except the conservative pork-choppers who headed the American Federation of Labor. These plodding men, unconcerned with political ideology, had seen their ranks expand under wartime conditions from two million members in 1914 to over four million in 1920. Then came the conservative reaction of the twenties, the open-shop drives by business organizations, unfriendly Republican administrations in Washington, a blizzard of anti-labor injunctions from the courts. AFL membership plunged to 2½ million in 1932, only slightly more than it had been twenty years before. The New Deal and its pro-labor legislation reversed the trend. Rising employment during World War II took union membership up with it. After the war, anti-union forces marched again, but despite some gains like the Taft-Hartley Act, they failed to decimate labor as they had in the twenties.

Throughout these vicissitudes, the average union leader's approach toward city government changed little. His wants were few: don't use police to break our strikes, keep municipal wage scales up, let public employes join our unions. And since the building trades' unions usually dominated the central labor council in each city, labor officials showed a special concern with the city building code and its effect on the fortunes of organized carpenters, electricians, plumbers, bricklayers, sheet metal workers, plasterers and other construction craftsmen.

Politically, the unions were generally satisfied if a token number of their people were named to the park board, police board, school board—this for the sake of prestige rather than power. Rarely did they contend for a major political advantage such as the mayor's office or a majority of seats on the city council. Even more rarely—except in New York and Philadelphia—did unions take an active part in reform crusades.

In a few cities, however, labor has broken from this pattern. In one, a labor party seized control of the government for nearly a decade, then was pushed to the side lines where it now stands. In another, the Central Labor Union battles doggedly with mugwumps who are trying to end its fourteen-year rule. In a third, a giant union draws closer to the power it has never been able to gain.

All three stories are different, but all have a common beginning. In violence.

MINNEAPOLIS—LEGACY OF A STREET FIGHT

Minneapolis had always been an open-shop town and little argument about it, until that day in 1934. The businessmen with their Citizens Alliance had taken care of every attempt to unionize local workers. But the Dunne brothers, four itinerant sons of a poor Irish immigrant, were more determined than the others. The four—Miles; Fenton; Vincent, who looked like actor Humphrey Bogart; and Grant, nervous and pain-ridden from a World War I gassing—were confirmed Trotskyites, much to the displeasure of their older brother Bill, a Stalinist, who edited the *Daily Worker* in New York.

The four Dunne boys organized a band of Minneapolis truck drivers into Teamsters Local 574. Then they threw a picket line around the city's produce warehouses, and the "better people" decided the time for direct action had come.

Some seven hundred regular policemen were mobilized. In addition a thousand young men, many from good families, were sworn in as deputies. It was something of a lark to be wearing boots and pistols and carrying hickory ax handles. Had the respectable elements guessed the political repercussions to come, they would undoubtedly have kept their young men at home.

The police and deputies tried to smash the picket lines by force. Vincent Dunne, using reserves like a military commander, sent hundreds of labor men in from side streets. One labor group was led by Congressman Francis Shoemaker. While an estimated 25,000 citizens watched from the sidewalks and rooftops, the two forces clashed one afternoon and the following day. Injuries ran into the hundreds. One deputy, a well-known young manufacturer, was found dead. State militia restored an uneasy truce, but on July 20 violence broke out again. This time the police were heavily armed with shotguns. Two men died, fifty others were hurt, most of them with buckshot wounds in the back. Martial law returned, and after thirty stormy days the teamster strike ended.

The political effects, however, had just begun. Depression-plagued farmers supported the teamsters, helping them win concessions from the employers. The bloodletting had not only unified labor elements in the city but had won sympathy for labor from many white-collar citizens. In 1935, a year after the street battles, Minneapolis elected its first Farmer-Labor mayor and council, after they campaigned against using city police in labor disputes.

The Dunne boys continued to organize Midwestern truck drivers, and by the late thirties their locals had spread across eleven states. Then they made a fatal mistake. They threatened to lead the entire Teamsters Union, nationally, out of the AFL and into the young CIO. Teamster president Daniel Tobin dispatched three hundred organizers to Minneapolis and sent his lieutenant, Dave Beck of Seattle, to take over Local 574 as receiver. Tobin also called on his good friends in the White House for aid, and the federal Justice Department soon had the Dunne boys and twenty-six other teamsters indicted under the Smith Act, charged as members of the Socialist Workers party with plotting "armed revolution against the government of the United States."

Grant Dunne, the war gas victim, shot himself before the trial in 1941. Miles was among those acquitted, Vincent and seventeen others were convicted. To complete the Dunnes' overthrow, Governor Harold Stassen's state labor conciliator, given extraordinary powers by the legislature, certified without a vote of the Minneapolis Teamsters that Tobin's AFL local was their legal bargaining agent.

With the Dunnes and their Trotskyite colleagues gone, the political mantle fell on the Central Labor Union composed of the city's AFL locals. The CLU's influence grew steadily during the 1940s, although it lost the spotlight from 1945 to 1948 during Mayor Hubert Humphrey's vigorous reform administration. A crusading liberal, Humphrey drove crooks and racketeers from the city, tried to modernize the municipal machinery, helped combine the state's weak Democratic party with the agrarian Farmer-Labor party to create what became Minnesota's version of the Democrats—the Democratic-Farmer-Labor party, known locally as the DFL.

When Humphrey left for the United States Senate, the Central Labor Union moved back in, stronger than ever. It soon controlled the mayor, city council, school board, county commissioners, civil service commission, board of public welfare, charter commission, planning commission, building commission—that is, virtually the entire mechanism of city and county government.

Meanwhile the mugwumps had begun to pull themselves together. Still a bit groggy from their knockout in the thirties, they started during World War II with a loose organization called the Good Government Group made up of sixty bankers, lawyers and small businessmen. As an early experiment, they promoted several state-level gimmicks including a legislative research council, a Little Hoover Commission, and a convention to revise the state constitution.

Locally they had backed Mayor Humphrey's attempt to rewrite the city charter. Humphrey had brought in the Public Administration Service of Chicago for a $40,000 survey of the rambling city government. The voters were electing a mayor, city comptroller, city treasurer, twenty-six aldermen from thirteen wards, twelve park board members, six library directors and two members of the board of estimate and taxation. Four bodies—the council, park board, library board, estimate board—could levy taxes. They, as well as the welfare board, adopted their own budgets, hired their own employes, and set their own salary scales. Thus the city government had five separate budgets, and five personnel systems with varying rates of pay. In addition, the council, park board and estimate board could borrow money on their own.

The Public Administration Service recommended discarding this unusual conglomeration and replacing it with a conventional strong mayor-council form of government. When the proposal finally reached the ballot in 1948, the Central Labor Union opposed it. The new charter, needing a 60 percent majority, obtained only 42 percent of the vote.

Growing more sure of themselves despite this setback, the Good Government Group agreed they would try to amend the charter piece by piece. They concentrated first on reducing the city council from twenty-six members, two from each ward, to half that size. The CLU balked again, but this time when the proposition went before the voters in 1951, it passed decisively. The CLU, it appeared, could be beaten after all.

The encouraged mugwumps began serious talk of founding a permanent organization. They called on the town's major men of property at Pillsbury and General Mills, Minneapolis Honeywell, Northern States Power Company, the *Star* and *Tribune*, Dayton Company department store, and the larger banks. Some thirty firms pledged to furnish a total of $25,000 a year for three years. A steering committee debated whether to establish a research bureau, or a citizens league with broad membership and limited political activity as in Seattle and Cleveland, or an outright municipal party as in Cincinnati and Kansas City. They settled on the Seattle-Cleveland model. The Citizens League of Minneapolis and Hennepin County was formed on February 14, 1952. Within six months it had a thousand members; five years later, with 3,500 members, it was, next to Seattle's, the largest such citizens organization in the country.

Minneapolis mugwumps decided they had to go further. While the league and its ally, the League of Women Voters, were keeping close watch on city hall, and the city's newspaper monopoly, the *Tribune* and *Star*, both published by John Cowles, gave full coverage to their findings, the Central Labor Union still controlled the municipal offices. So the mugwumps moved openly into politics.

Their chances seemed bright because of a split within Democratic ranks brought on by a CLU blunder.

Ever since Humphrey's departure in 1949, the CLU had been, in effect, the Democratic Party in Minneapolis.* And the CLU meant, politically speaking, its president—a forceful gentleman with receding hair and dark pencil-thin mustache, Walter Cramond. Like George Johns of the San Francisco labor council, Cramond had differed from the general run of labor leaders by showing an intense interest in local government. Minneapolis mugwumps must have prayed many a night that the CLU president would develop less interest, but those prayers obviously have gone unheard.

Cramond offers a case study in how effective a labor official can become in city affairs if he devotes time and energy to them. The instrument through which he has operated, the Central Labor Union, consists of six hundred delegates elected by seventy thousand union members. These six hundred delegates in turn choose a nine-man executive board. For political chores, the CLU has its separate Committee on Political Education (COPE). This twenty-five-man group sits as a screening committee on candidates, giving or withholding support, including campaign funds. The CLU collects three cents a month from union members for political purposes; this fund of approximately $25,000 a year was appreciably higher before the CLU, in obedience to action by

* The political alignment in Minneapolis, as in many cities, is basically Republican versus Democrat, but, as elsewhere, these labels are not always used. In Milwaukee, for instance, the Democrats on the city council and school board are called Progressives, the Republicans are known as Nonpartisans. The Minneapolis label situation is more complex. The Democratic-Farmer-Labor members are called Liberals and have been for many years. The Republicans, however, were known as the Conservatives until 1953, when they became Progressives; in 1957 they renamed themselves Independents—a series of changes that has had even many Minneapolis citizens confused.

the national AFL-CIO, expelled 26,000 of James Hoffa's teamsters in the late 1950s.

CLU's domination over the city council was nearly complete for several years. Cramond and his lieutenant, David Roe of the building-trades council, usually attended the council meetings held every other Friday. They would gather with their Liberal majority of aldermen for a briefing session beforehand, and if something unforeseen came up during the meeting, the Liberals might ask a recess and adjourn to another room with Cramond and Roe to decide how to vote.

Trouble arose in 1955 when several independent-minded young Liberals, the oldest of them thirty-three, became part of the CLU majority on the council. Two vacancies had to be filled on the school board—the members had died—and the CLU executive board sent the city council the names of the two replacements it wanted the council to appoint. The council members did not care for the suggestions, especially one of them, an old buddy of Cramond's from the linoleum-layers union who had never finished grade school and seemed completely unqualified. The council grudgingly approved the pair, but they revolted a few months later when the Central Labor executives proposed another crony to head the city's bond-reviewing committee. The council rejected him, eight to five, with three Liberal aldermen siding with the opposition.

Cramond decided to crack the whip. The eight Liberal aldermen were summoned to the Labor Temple, handed copies of a new loyalty pledge and told to sign. All had signed a pledge before, more or less as a formality, just as all labor-endorsed candidates had been doing since World War I days. But the new version was tougher, binding the aldermen to accept a unit rule in their Liberal caucus before council meetings; thus the five "loyal" aldermen could outvote the three "disloyal" ones in caucus and then go out into the full council meeting with a solid eight-vote majority.

Seven of the Liberal aldermen signed the pledge. The remaining one, Kent Youngdahl, nephew of federal judge and former Minnesota Governor Luther Youngdahl, took his unsigned copy to the *Star* and *Tribune*. It appeared the next morning on the front page for all the citizenry to read:

> I hereby agree that if I receive the endorsement of this [Central Labor Union] committee, I pledge to actively support the program and platform formulated by the labor movement on city, county, state and national issues; that I will join a caucus of all other labor-endorsed candidates which is pledged to abide by unit rule on all matters of organization or on basic labor issues; that I will work and cooperate with all other endorsed candidates to the fullest extent in making this program effective; that I will clear all campaign literature through this committee and will cause to have distributed only that which is approved; if it is found at any time that I have failed to meet the obligation outlined above, I agree that I forfeit this labor endorsement.[1]

Public reaction came quick and strong, and the mugwumps had their issue for the next election: independence versus The Pledge.

The mugwumps planned to make their move against the CLU in the coming school board contest. For years, school employes in the Federation of Teachers, the janitors union, the painters, carpenters and truck drivers—all members of the Central Labor Union—had screened candidates for the school board and had handed their recommendations to the central body. This became the CLU slate and was nearly always elected. Mugwump attempts to upset this system through a Citizens Committee for an Independent School Board in 1953 had failed; in 1955, the committee managed to elect one candidate to the seven-man board. After the ruckus over the pledge, mugwumps believed they might do better in the 1957 election. That March, twenty liberal Republicans opened a small office, persuaded fifteen Democrats to join them, and announced the formation of CORG (Citizens Organized for Responsible Government). Raising $15,000 they helped the Independent School Board Committee campaign for three seats on the school board and won all of them; the CLU, which had controlled five of the board's seven members, found itself reduced to two.

That June election day in 1957 held more bad news for the CLU. Its mayor for eight years, former housepainter Eric Hoyer, lost by a narrow margin to forty-two-year-old attorney P. Kenneth

Peterson, who had been state Republican chairman. In the council races, Youngdahl and three other rebel Liberals beat the CLU candidates, while the five Independent (that is, Republican) incumbents held their seats. Cramond, left with almost no one on the council he could call his own, ceased attending the Liberal caucus before council meetings.

He was far from finished, however. In the 1959 city primary he had the pleasure of seeing his entry, printing firm executive Gerald R. Dillon, eliminate the disobedient Youngdahl in a three-way race for mayor. Dillon lost in the run-off to incumbent Mayor Peterson.

A bigger moment came in June, 1960, when Cramond helped deal the mugwumps a major defeat. For nearly two years the reformers had been working on a new city charter. They had assembled fifty-six representatives from the Citizens League, the League of Women Voters, the Chamber of Commerce, and the DFL and Republican parties to form a Joint Charter Review Committee.

It soon became clear what they were working toward—a strong-mayor form of government such as Humphrey had sought and failed to get a decade earlier. Cramond and the CLU, as before, wanted none of this. Labor in most American cities has traditionally distrusted strong mayors or city managers or any other form of centralized authority; unionists prefer that power be divided among many elected officials, feeling that these are easier to approach and persuade. Labor in Minneapolis represents an aggravated case of this suspicion. The CLU presumably would like almost every municipal employe above the rank of clerk-typist to be elected, if that could be arranged.

Cramond and his cohorts in city hall were not worried at first by the charter review committee. It was an unofficial group with no authority. When the committee finished writing its charter and handed it to the official charter commission (a standing body of fifteen members appointed by the district judges), the official commission received it politely and filed it away. That was supposed to be that.

Attorneys among the reformers, however, had found a legal provision that the charter commission could be compelled to place the matter on the ballot if 8,500 voters petitioned for it. The drive for signatures gained 15,000. A special election was set for June.

The campaign developed into a bitter one. Siding with the reformers were top members of the DFL organization, including Governor Orville Freeman, state senators Donald M. Fraser and Jack Davis, and state representatives Sally Luther and Robert Latz. The *Star* and *Tribune* newspapers pounded away in favor of the charter revision. Dillon, whom Cramond had backed for mayor the year before, was co-chairman of the reformers' campaign committee.

Ranged against them were Cramond, the CLU, an American Legion Post, several business associations, ultra-conservatives in We the People, Inc., and the Minneapolis Property Owners Association, and almost everyone in city hall, including supposedly pro-reform members of the city council. The council employed a press agent to work against the charter, appropriating city funds to pay him. These opponents charged that the Cowles-owned newspapers would dominate the mayor and run the city. Policemen in uniform went from door to door carrying anti-charter signs and asking permission to stick them on lawns. Billboards appeared bearing a picture of President Lincoln and reading: "100 Years Ago Abe Lincoln Warned the Workers Against This Kind of Charter Proposal. Vote NO June 7th."

On June 7 the people did vote no. And in almost the same proportion as they had in 1948. The "anti" vote had totaled 58 percent then. This time 56 percent rejected the charter.

After his victory, Cramond and the CLU let it be known they would not forget Governor Freeman and others who had sided with the reformers. The CLU passed a resolution declaring:

> Be it resolved that in the future we deny endorsement to any person seeking political office who is in league with the monopoly press in denying the right of the people to vote for their representatives in public office. . . . We in the Minneapolis labor movement find grievous fault with any Democratic-Farmer-Labor officeholder or legislator who endeavored to take away representation from the people.

Meanwhile, the mugwumps' candidate-running organization CORG was having mixed luck. In 1958 its candidate for county commissioner lost. But in 1959 both its candidates for the school board won, giving the mugwumps a six-to-one majority over the CLU; two of the four CORG candidates for the library board won; both its candidates for the park board lost; and on the city council, incumbent alderman Allan Anderson won re-election but his running mate, University of Minnesota sociology professor Arnold Rose, lost by 118 votes. CORG's final score for 1959 was five won, five lost.

These figures seemed to reflect the over-all political situation that has evolved in Minneapolis. Both sides, the Cramond-led CLU and the mugwumps, appear in the early sixties to be at something of a stand-off. The CLU, which in the early 1950s controlled all the tangled branches of local government, has been shaken loose from some of them. It still holds others firmly.

Among the reformers there has been a degree of confused milling. The charter setback in 1959 was hard to take. CORG, which was supposed to become another Kansas City Citizens Association or a Cincinnati Charter Party, does not seem to be moving in that direction. Instead of swelling into a powerful corps of two hundred influential men as planned in 1957, it has dwindled to a dozen who carry the load of finding candidates (they often can't) and collecting campaign funds. The Citizens League, after zooming in its first five years to 3,500 members, has declined to fewer than 2,500.

Some big businessmen wonder out loud whether nonpartisan organizations like the league and CORG are the answer; maybe, they say, we should put all our effort into building a strong Republican party organization in Minneapolis and use that to rout Cramond and the CLU.

As they reappraise where they are going and how, Minneapolis mugwumps and men of property may decide to experiment with new instruments of reform, modified to meet the city's unique political structure. One possibility mentioned is a local variation of the Allegheny Conference that would include a few university intellectuals along with the top business leaders.

Whatever political instruments may emerge, one thing is reasonably sure. They will not include pistols and hickory ax handles.

SAN FRANCISCO—THE TRUE AND THE TROUBLED

Los Angeles, an agricultural village that grew into a quiet city on its way to giantism, acquired its mugwumps easily. They arrived steadily from the East and Midwest bringing neat ready-made bundles of Protestant ethics and attitudes with them. But San Francisco, the roaring gold camp and seaport, erupted into cityhood. Its steep hills and polyglot population provided poor soil for mugwump institutions.

Certainly few mugwumps were in evidence as James Bryce visited San Francisco in the 1880s. Of the city and California he wrote:

> . . . It grew up, after the cession by Mexico and the discovery of gold, like a gourd in the night. A great population had gathered before there was any regular government to keep it in order, much less any education or social culture to refine it. The wildness of that time passed into the blood of the people, and has left them more tolerant of violent deeds, more prone to interferences with or supersessions of regular law, than are the people of most parts of the Union . . .
>
> The scum which the westward moving wave of emigration carries on its crest is here stopped, because it can go no farther. It accumulates in San Francisco, and forms a dangerous constituent in the population—a population perhaps more mixed than one finds anywhere else in America, for Frenchmen, Italians, Portuguese, Greeks and the children of Australian convicts abound there, side by side with Negroes, Germans and Irish. Of the Chinese one need not speak; for though they number some 12,000, have a large quarter to themselves and have given rise to the dominant question in Pacific coast politics, they do not themselves join in any political movement, but mingle as little with the whites as oil with water.
>
> California, more than any other part of the Union, is a coun-

> try by itself, and San Francisco a capital. Cut off from the more populous parts of the Mississippi valley by an almost continuous desert of 1,200 miles across which the two daily trains move like ships across the ocean, separated from Oregon on the north by a wilderness of sparsely settled mountain and forest, it has grown up in its own way and acquired a sort of consciousness of separate existence. San Francisco dwarfs the other cities, and is a commercial and intellectual centre, and source of influence for the surrounding regions, more powerful over them than is any Eastern city over its neighborhood. It is a New York which has got no Boston on one side of it, and no shrewd and orderly rural population on the other, to keep it in order . . .
>
> Large fortunes are swiftly made and not less swiftly spent. Changes of public sentiment are sudden and violent. The most active minds are too much absorbed in great business enterprises to attend to politics.[2]

Yet even as Bryce wrote, a mugwump element was taking political shape in San Francisco. It grew as a reaction to the motley crews who in succession gained control of city hall—the Workingmen's party born in the hard times of 1877 and loud-spoken against the Southern Pacific Railroad, Nob Hill millionaires and the Chinese coolie laborers; the Democratic regime in the eighties of the "blind boss," saloon-keeper Chris Buckley, who fled the state ahead of a grand jury indictment; and his successor, Republican boss Daniel Burns, whom the mugwumps forced from office three years later with a trial for graft.

The moves against Buckley and Burns, however, were mere preliminaries for the main event—the fight against organized labor.

San Francisco already had numerous unions when the first of the great waterfront strikes broke out in 1886. As other unions came to the aid of the dock workers, the waterfront employers retaliated by forming an association. A broader group of the city's businessmen, the Board of Manufacturers and Employers, appeared in 1891. The lines were hard drawn by 1893 when the second major dock strike occurred. This ended with a bomb blast on Christmas Day outside a strikebreakers' boarding house. It killed eight men and injured many more. Amid strong public disapproval, the union cause collapsed.

For the next six years the mugwump-business coalition held control. Mayor James D. Phelan, a socially prominent young reformer, promoted a new city charter; it contained a favorite mugwump gimmick of the day aimed at corrupt utilities, a section permitting the city to operate the street railway, water, gas and electric systems.

By 1901 the unionists felt strong enough for a comeback. The Central Labor Council launched a drive to make San Francisco a closed-shop town. Walkouts began in May, and soon half the city's firms were closed. The employers' association raised a $200,000 fund, imported strikebreakers and hired special police. For the next three months they and the regular police of Phelan's reform government ranged the streets and docks hunting for strikers, while the strikers hid and waited their chance to catch "scab" workers unprotected. After three months of this guerrilla warfare five men had been killed, uncounted hundreds beaten, stabbed and wounded by gunfire. The union forces signed a surrender agreement in October.

But the victory of the businessmen and mugwumps turned out to be a Pyrrhic one. The strong-arm methods used to beat down labor had alienated the citizenry, just as labor's violence had done six years before. When city elections were held a month after the October surrender, the newly formed Union Labor party swept the ticket. Installing a friendly police chief, the unions proceeded to organize San Francisco into one of the nation's tightest closed-shop cities. And thus it remains to this day.

The architect of the Union Labor party was a lawyer and onetime reformer, Abraham Ruef. His successful candidate for mayor was a dignified bassoon player, Eugene Schmitz. They and their followers were to bring San Francisco politics one of the wildest decades in what, as Bryce had observed, was a city already given to wild political swings.

It was the mugwumps' and men of property's turn to regroup their scattered forces. They sat out the 1903 election, and the Ruef-Schmitz ticket won by a larger edge than it had two years before. Victory, however, made some of the winners careless.

They took to selling utility franchises and collecting police payoffs on the notorious Barbary Coast as openly as the Bay fishermen peddling their catch. The huge three-story sporting house at 620 Jackson Street acquired the nickname of the Municipal Crib, since most of its profits ended up in city hall.

Fremont Older's San Francisco *Bulletin*, aided by former Mayor Phelan and other businessmen, entered an anti-graft slate in 1905, but Ruef and Schmitz overwhelmed them at the polls. Undeterred, Older persuaded Phelan and a liberal-minded young millionaire, Rudolph Spreckels, to put up $100,000 for an investigation fund. They hired the William J. Burns agency to collect evidence, after ascertaining from District Attorney William Langdon (a Ruef man but an honest one) that he would call a grand jury if the evidence warranted it. A trip to Washington gained President Theodore Roosevelt's promise that United States Attorney Francis J. Heney would be released from his duties in San Francisco, if needed to serve as special counsel.

The prolonged graft trials that followed made San Francisco history. The first casualty was the Union Labor ticket in the 1907 election. It lost decisively to a slate backed by the mugwump-business coalition's Good Government League. The second casualty was the mugwump-business coalition itself.

The wreck could be blamed on the mugwumps' failure to understand how few and weak they were, and their mistaken belief that the driving impulse behind the reform coalition was a common desire for honest government rather than a desire to smash the unions.

The men of property applauded the trials as long as Union Labor politicians were on the stand confessing to bribes. But when Ruef confessed, he implicated leading businessmen at Pacific Gas and Electric Company, Home Telephone, Pacific States Telephone and Telegraph, Parkside Realty Company and others. The two biggest fish on the hook were William F. Herrin, head of Southern Pacific's political bureau, and transit company president Patrick Calhoun (grandson of South Carolina's John C. Calhoun and a downtown hero since he had brought in 1,200 strikebreakers, barricaded the car barns and beaten the streetcarmen's union).

One condition that the unorthodox Spreckels had attached

to his contribution toward the $100,000 investigation fund had been that no one should be spared, no matter how prominent. Prosecutor Heney pressed ahead accordingly with indictment of Calhoun and the others.

Businessmen exploded with indignation. The graft trials, they cried, should be stopped. When Older, Spreckels, Heney, Phelan, Hiram Johnson and other Progressive mugwumps entered a slate in the 1909 city election, seventy major businessmen formed a committee and helped the erstwhile enemy, the Union Labor party, to win back control of the mayor's office and the city-county board of supervisors.

The trials dragged on for two more years before sputtering out. Despite the hundreds of indictments and wide publicity, only one man was sentenced to prison—Ruef for fourteen years. Higher courts set aside three other convictions, but none of the businessmen charged with giving bribes was convicted. Calhoun's first trial ended in a hung jury; he was finally acquitted four years later. Aside from Ruef, the most notable victim of the trials was prosecutor Heney. He was shot and critically wounded in the courtroom by an assailant who later died mysteriously in his jail cell.

The 1909 election brought home to the little mugwump band that they were not too popular in San Francisco. Organized labor could not forgive them for taking the employers' side in the bloody anti-union conflicts. The business community looked on them as traitors to the middle class for their prosecution of Calhoun and other champions of the open shop. And the reformers' strait-laced concern with right and wrong, with good and evil, was out of step with the city's mood.

In 1909, while the mugwump candidate was talking reform, his opponent, P.H. "Pinhead" McCarthy, was campaigning on a platform to make San Francisco "the Paris of America." Pinhead won substantially. He was followed as mayor by "Sunny Jim" Rolph, a westernized version of Jimmy Walker. Sunny Jim campaigned in a silk hat and high-top boots, never discussed a serious issue, blew the siren on the Ferry Building or led a parade up Market Street at the least provocation, and won ten elections in a row, finally becoming governor of California.

To the south, once-rural Los Angeles had overtaken San Francisco in population and went racing ahead. But the Bay City told itself it had something better than mere size. It had a swashbuckling history, it had color, cable cars and ferry boats, painters, writers, culture, restaurants, hills and a skyline, it had bohemianism, it had spirit. There appeared a breed known as the True San Franciscan, who loved all this and wanted to preserve it forever.

In this setting the reformers did what they could. It was not much.

A church-led element undertook a drive to clean up the Barbary Coast, culminating in a gigantic police raid in February, 1917, that closed eighty-three brothels and sent more than a thousand soiled doves packing.

Another group, working through the real estate board, founded a Bureau of Governmental Research in 1916. Following a middle-of-the-road course during the 1920s, the bureau plugged doggedly for a new city charter that would remove at least some power from the Irish Catholic politicians in city hall. The effort succeeded in 1931, when the voters approved a charter reducing the number of elective offices (to organized labor's enduring displeasure) and providing for a chief administrative officer to manage a dozen of the city departments. Since then the bureau has had two main concerns: to protect the charter against labor- and politician-sponsored attempts to increase the number of elective offices, and to support economy-minded officials in successive administrations. The bureau, as mentioned in Chapter Six, has become the working staff for the downtown economy bloc—the Municipal Conference—representing the Chamber of Commerce, the junior chamber, the real estate board and six other organizations of downtown merchants, property owners, hotel and apartment managers.

During the 1930s and 1940s, the economy doctrine was endorsed by the entire business community. In the 1950s, however, this front cracked. The division deepened after dairy magnate George Christopher, a Republican, became mayor in 1955. On one side stood the economy-forever group, which for years had been led by the bureau and the Municipal Conference. On the other were the mayor and those who believed that colorful old

San Francisco must clear out thousands of its colorful old buildings and erect something new in their place.

The mayor gained powerful allies for urban renewal when the Blyth-Zellerbach Committee, named for securities man Charles R. Blyth and James D. Zellerbach of the Zellerbach Paper Company, was formed in 1957. Blyth, Zellerbach and nine other big-business people met and agreed that the city's decrepit "produce row," with its warehouses and vegetable trucks, should be moved from the valuable land it occupied north of Market Street so the area could be used for a $60-million Golden Gateway redevelopment project. The morning after their meeting, the eleven men sent in checks totaling $55,000; with this, planning studies for the Golden Gateway began.

The mayor also accomplished a much needed overhaul of the city redevelopment agency. As his appointees became a majority on the agency board in the late fifties, they replaced almost the entire redevelopment staff.

For added political leverage, the San Francisco Planning and Urban Renewal Association was established with a two-member staff and a $50,000-a-year budget. The chairman of its board was Jerd Sullivan, big fund-raiser for the Republican party and for the Volunteers for Better Government, the candidate-running organization that has sponsored, at one time or another, most of those on the city-county board of supervisors.

Many elements in the Municipal Conference and the research bureau also became converts to the doctrine of rebuilding the city.

With this alignment behind it, San Francisco's urban renewal program picked up speed. By the mid-1960s the city expects to have 2,200 new apartments ($110 to $300 a month) and thirteen acres of office buildings in the Golden Gateway; 7,000 new dwelling units and a three-block-long Japanese Cultural and Trade Center in the Western Addition project strung between Van Ness and Divisadero Avenues, west of the downtown section; and, in the Diamond Heights project, another 8,000 people living in houses and tower apartments on the south slope of 900-foot-high Twin Peaks—a huge expanse that has always been vacant because early land platters laid it out inanely on a grid pattern calling for streets so steep only a mule could have climbed them.

Again in late 1960 Mayor Christopher turned to the Blyth-Zellerbach Committee, now composed of twenty-five corporation board chairmen, for another helping hand—and this time the assignment was a delicate one. Worried by the steady rise of 5 and 6 percent a year in the city budget while city revenues panted to keep up, the mayor wanted to know if big-business experts could find ways to hold the budget level without damaging municipal services. Did the city have needless employes? Where else, if anywhere, was it wasting money?

No politician would have taken on the assignment, but the Blyth-Zellerbach group did. Leading firms, including Pacific Telephone and Telegraph, Standard Oil of California, Pacific Gas and Electric, Bank of America, Wells Fargo–American Trust Bank, Crocker-Anglo Bank and Zellerbach Paper Company detached one or two executives apiece to serve on the fifteen-man Mayor's Committee for Municipal Management; with them sat a representative from the mayor's office and from the governmental research bureau.

The committee decided on a pilot study among the thirty-five city departments, and chose the medium-sized recreation and parks department with its 870 employes. The Standard Oil executive loaned to direct the study said: "We're proceeding just as we do when we have an ailment, usually dropping profits, in one of our companies. We find out everything the company does and match it with what it is supposed to do. In the process we generally learn what is wrong and propose changes to bring the company back to health."

The mayor's committee represented a brave attempt to defy the Parkinsonian thesis that all bureaucrats build empires, all staffs expand, and work expands to fill the time available to do it.

If the committee should actually propose cuts in overgrown work crews, cuts in inflated pay scales, or firing superfluous executives, it can expect brickbats from all directions. They will come, of course, from many parts of city hall, and will undoubtedly come from organized labor.

In San Francisco, as elsewhere, labor officials habitually resist any attempt to reduce pay scales or the number of jobs, whether the attempt is made within their jurisdiction or somewhere far removed. They react according to the principle that higher wages anywhere tend to bring higher wages everywhere, and the elimination of jobs for some hurts all.

This reaction is fortified in San Francisco by the long history of conflict between Montgomery Street businessmen and the unions. The head-splitting clashes that led to the Union Labor party at the beginning of the century have not returned, except briefly along the waterfront in the mid-1930s. The Union Labor party itself, although it is still in existence, has become a pale copy of the rampaging Ruef-Schmitz model of 1905. Less than half the city's unions have representatives in it, and it does little more than endorse pro-union candidates in city elections every two years. Organized labor's real weight around city hall is felt more from the central labor council and its secretary, George Johns, one-time president of the city's board of education. Johns keeps a close eye on municipal affairs and sounds the alarm to other labor leaders when anything threatens their interests.

Since one of their prime interests is in city pay scales, and since they distrust the downtown economy bloc and its influence, the labor men have forced through amendments to the city charter embedding various wage formulas in that already bulky document. For instance, the amendment covering municipal transit operators specifies they must be paid the average of the two highest wage scales in the United States among cities having at least a half-million population and a transit system with four hundred or more operating employes.

Plainly, labor leaders who want this sort of thing in the city charter are going to give a rough reception to any suggestions for efficiency from the Mayor's Committee for Municipal Management if the proposals mean fewer jobs or lower pay. And organized labor so far has been able to wield an effective veto power at city hall when it wants to.

The mayor, however, has some weapons at his disposition, too. He prepares the annual city budget, in which he could make reductions suggested by his management committee; and the board of supervisors may not legally add items that the mayor has not included. The mayor also has authority to fill vacancies on the board of supervisors by appointment, and in San Francisco this means a great deal. Most supervisors first get a place on the board through the mayor's appointment (San Francisco supervisors have a habit of resigning to accept a judgeship or a state office, or to return to private life). Running in the next city election as an incumbent, the appointee nearly always wins. Thus over the years, the mayor's original appointments can heavily influence the composition of the board.

If the mayor should choose to fight for an "efficiency movement" within city hall, he would find another type of ally—the serious young men, most of them aged thirty-five to forty-five, who are moving in growing numbers behind the administrative desks. Their sober approach to their jobs still seems a bit out of place among the lilts of Irish laughter, but the newcomers have already brought a noticeable air of responsibility to the high-ceilinged offices.

All these—the big businessmen's revolt against economy-at-any-price, the housecleaning of a do-nothing redevelopment agency, the sudden drive behind the Golden Gateway, Western Addition and Diamond Heights undertakings, the talk that more, much more, of the city should be leveled and built again, the intent young men grown impatient with the traditional ways at city hall, echoes of their impatience along Montgomery Street—all these add up to a deep-running dissatisfaction in the city by the Golden Gate.

It was fine to be the Paris of America, just as it was grand for Boston to be the Hub of the Universe. Yet old glories cannot sustain a city forever. The complacent True San Franciscan is still far from extinct, but a new breed is emerging—the troubled San Franciscan, who thinks the romantic past was fun, but it is time to get on with the future.

DETROIT—BETWEEN MODELS

Detroit appears, to the outsider, to be a composite of other cities. It has the basic vitality of a New York or Los Angeles. It has a colony of corporate wealthy like Pittsburgh. It has a new city hall and other gleaming slabs rising at its civic center like New Orleans. Its mugwumps are sharply alienated from labor, as in Minneapolis and San Francisco. The air contains a faint raw scent of the jungle, like Chicago.

Yet there are differences. Detroit's vitality is dulled by chronic unemployment, a standing army of 100,000 or more, existing side by side with millions of square feet of empty outmoded factories. The wealthy, unlike those of Pittsburgh, pour little of themselves into their city. While they often contribute generous sums to civic projects, the gesture somehow suggests nobility flinging out alms during a quick ride through the streets.

In Minneapolis, mugwumps wrestle forward and back with union leaders to control local government. In Detroit, mugwumps exert quiet influence trying not to disturb the preoccupied giant, the United Auto Workers Union, as it gazes off toward Lansing and Washington.

For Detroit mugwumps, remaining quiet is not too difficult, because they don't do too much. Like mugwumps in Los Angeles, Houston and a few other cities, they find themselves at loose ends. They seem to be groping for a new militant credo that will make it worth while to go out and crusade again.

There was a time when Detroit reformers did more than their share of crusading. In fact, one of the early models for the mugwumps' first revolution took shape there. Long before Henry Ford put the first Model T on the road, a millionaire shoe manufacturer named Hazen S. Pingree demonstrated, while reformers around the country watched in fascination, how to clean up a corrupt city.

The Republican leaders in 1889 had chosen Pingree as a safe, solid candidate for mayor who would disturb nothing. Fifty years old, he had never been in politics, had hardly ever voted. But churchgoer Pingree took his oath of office seriously. Aided by a staff of ex-newspapermen and others whom he paid largely from his own pocket, Pingree discovered that the private transit and electric-power utilities were fleecing the public through franchises granted by a bribed city council. Pingree exposed them, then started a municipally owned electric system. He threatened to do the same with the streetcar company.

Hearing rumors that the school board was accepting graft from textbook publishers and makers of school furniture, Pingree set detectives on their trail. When the evidence was complete, the mayor arrived with a squad of police and a paddy wagon at an evening meeting and publicly arrested almost the entire Detroit board of education.

During his seven years as mayor, Pingree found himself opposed by most of the men of property and their allied newspapers; just as similar elements a decade later were to fight Tom Johnson as Cleveland's reform mayor and the California Progressives as they tried to clean up San Francisco.[3] Pingree, the shoe man who knew nothing about politics, beat his opponents at every turn. He swept four successive elections. When the newspapers conspired to give him the silent treatment by never mentioning his name, the mayor prepared huge bulletin boards and hung them outside the city hall, giving his version of what was happening in Detroit and calling the publishers various kinds of rascals. With lines of citizens gathering all day to read the bulletins, the publishers decided they had to reply to Pingree, and the embargo was dropped.

Just as Mark Hanna used the Ohio legislature to harass Mayor Johnson in Cleveland, so the utilities used the Michigan state government to undercut Pingree. His riposte was to file for governor in 1896. He won and in 1898 was re-elected for a second two-year term. By the time he retired in 1900, worn by ten years of constant infighting, Pingree had laid down the lines of battle that most big-city mugwumps were to follow throughout the Progressive era.[4]

Pingree's reform administrations, however, were essentially a personal *tour de force*. Good citizens, unorganized, gave him their support, but when he passed, reform passed with him. The old crowd of hacks returned to run city hall undisturbed for more than a decade.

Then in 1912 Detroit mugwumps revived, led by sixty-nine-year-old Henry M. Leland, president of Cadillac Motor Company and one of the few auto pioneers, along with Ford and R. E. Olds, who would never touch a drink in the old Detroit Athletic Club. Aided by prohibitionist Pliny Marsh, Leland started the Detroit Civic Uplift League, which two years later changed its name to the less stuffy-sounding Detroit Citizens League.

The mugwumps proceeded to run up an impressive string of triumphs, including the Scott-Flowers "clean election" law of 1915, the junking of the large ward-elected school board in favor of a seven-man body, and a Michigan state prohibition law in 1916. That spring the mugwumps also augmented their Citizens League by founding a Bureau of Governmental Research and employing Lent D. Upson of Dayton as its director.

Soon Detroit had modern budgets for the city and county governments, centralized purchasing and other management improvements. But the reformers' greatest victory was the new city charter that went into effect in 1919, four years before the mugwumps in Cleveland and seven years before those in Cincinnati succeeded in obtaining reform charters. The Detroiters considered and rejected the city-manager plan, then only a few years old, choosing instead a strong-mayor form with a nine-man council elected at large, like the plan that Boston mugwumps had sold to their city in 1909.

The first mugwump mayor was James Couzens, a courageous, humorless, quarrelsome fellow who had put up $2,500 to help Henry Ford start his auto company in 1903, became general manager, started having differences with Ford in World War I days, and finally bowed out when Henry handed him a personal check for $29,300,000. Couzens went into office in 1919 backed by a mugwump majority of six to three on the council. Like Pingree, he charted an independent course. He took obvious delight in defying Detroit's business leaders, especially on the issue of municipal ownership, over which the town was sharply split. Couzens at last pushed through city purchase of the street railway system, realizing Pingree's old dream.

Later that year, 1922, Couzens resigned to accept appointment to the United States Senate. About the same time Leland retired at the age of seventy-nine after ten years as president of the Citizens League. Their departures signaled the end of the Progressive reform era in Detroit.

That era no doubt seemed turbulent to those who experienced it, but it was mild indeed compared with the two tension-wracked decades that lay ahead. Detroit in the twenties had its share of the nation's general giddiness, plus a special giddiness of its own marked by three simultaneous booms—in auto making, in real estate, and in bootlegging. All had their political effects, both on the way up and, after 1929, on the way down.

The most serious tensions, however, took the shape of anti-Catholicism, anti-Negroism, and anti-unionism. The anti-Catholic feeling, which had showed its head before World War I, grew abruptly in the mid-twenties, stirred up by the Ku Klux Klan and some members of the Masonic order. The Catholics, in turn, solidified their lines; the Hearst newspaper, the *Times*, became their chief spokesman. Most mugwumps tried to keep clear of the religious controversy, but with a strain of anti-Catholicism running far back into the mugwump past, it was inevitable that traces of antagonism should appear. The Citizens League disparaged both the Klan and the Catholic forces. When Hearst's *Times* took to blasting city hall corruption and helped get Judge Frank Murphy, a Catholic and a Democrat, appointed to investigate conditions as a one-man grand jury, mugwumps dismissed his findings as "almost farcical" and noted in the *National Municipal Review* with thinly veiled approval that Murphy's opponents were gathering evidence for his impeachment. Later, in 1930, when the voters recalled an incompetent mayor and elected Murphy to serve the remaining year of his term, the Citizens League grumbled that the people of Detroit had not greatly improved their situation.

The mugwump camp was feeling somewhat put out, anyway, at the time. Their influence at city hall had shrunk since their long-time spokesman in the city council, sedate John C. Lodge, had been elected mayor in 1927, then had been humiliatingly defeated in the primary when he sought re-election two years later.

Murphy, skilled politician that he was, assuaged the mugwumps by consulting them about appointments. He even named Chester Rightor of the Governmental Research Bureau staff as city controller. Before he left in 1933 to accept President Roosevelt's appointment as governor general of the Philippines, the mugwumps had decided Murphy was a pretty good fellow after all.

The labor tension that gripped Detroit in the mid-1930s found the mugwumps, as was to be expected, ranged against the upstart CIO and its drive to unionize the auto workers. (John L. Lewis was the ogre of the moment, not Walter Reuther, then an obscure organizer.) Detroit had always been an open-shop town where union agitators, when detected, received a back-room pummeling, then were fired and black-listed. This order of things was overturned with a violence that outdid the Minneapolis teamsters' strike in drawing nation-wide attention.

Throughout this and the other battles of the twenties and thirties, some leading mugwumps attempted to keep the Citizens League and the Bureau of Governmental Research out of the firing line and occupied instead with their regular business of municipal betterment. This they succeeded in doing moderately well. Bureau director Upson, who by this time was recognized as one of the best research-bureau men in the country, played a leading part during the late twenties in developing the first system of uniform crime reports, a system later taken over by the FBI. The research bureau also attempted to ease racial tension by releasing a study in 1927 showing that the arrival of Negroes in Detroit neighborhoods had not lowered property values.

As for dynamite-laden issues like municipal ownership and labor relations, Upson advocated neutralism. Giving his opinion on the matter some years later, he said:

> How are bureaus to avoid partisanship, avoid becoming the agents of reaction or of alleged reaction? My answer is this: stay away from those social questions in which there is danger that . . . the opinions of yourself, your trustees or your contributors may be substituted for facts. . . . Research bureaus and taxpayer organizations are on dangerous ground if they become involved in what highly controversial functions a government undertakes beyond the point of insisting that any new function be soundly organized and financed. . . . A civic agency fast enough acquires a reputation for conservatism by exposing crackpot schemes to the test of facts, without aggravating that reputation by taking unsupported stands on economic and social issues.[5]

By the 1950s, maintaining neutrality was no longer an acute problem for Detroit's mugwump organizations. Some issues, like anti-Catholicism and municipal ownership, had faded. The Negro problem had simmered down, everybody hoped permanently. Unionization had been accepted as a fact of life, albeit reluctantly. Conservatives no longer thought in terms of using local government as a weapon to crush organized labor.

The United Auto Workers, on the other hand, had called off their attempts at a frontal assault on city hall. Three times they had attempted to elect a labor mayor, and three times the mugwumps, men of property and newspapers had beaten them. After 1949, the UAW stopped trying.

Besides, union leaders had other matters to worry about during the late 1940s and '50s. With the postwar conservative swing bringing the Taft-Hartley Act, the Landrum-Griffin Act, and a flock of state right-to-work laws, leaders of the UAW and other big unions fought for their lives. They had little time for expanding their role in municipal government.

That defensive psychology still prevails. Said an executive in the UAW's Citizenship Department (political department): "We have not spent as much time and effort at city hall as we should have. City government is a housekeeping government, an administrative government. It doesn't make policy that affects us the way state and national government does."

This indifference is not total. When the National Association for the Advancement of Colored People complained that Detroit police were being brutal to Negroes, the UAW made an inquiry. When the city council was considering a net, graduated income tax with exemptions for low-income Detroiters, the UAW favored it. When the proposal was changed to a flat one-percent earnings tax without exemptions, the UAW successfully brought pressure on the mayor to veto it.

At city election time, the UAW, like most unions elsewhere, endorses a slate of acceptable candidates. These endorsements evidently have a high correlation with success at the polls. In the 1957 city primary, for instance, sixteen of the eighteen nominated for city council had labor endorsement; the only two who did not, ran fifteenth and seventeenth. From this one can only conclude that labor's seal of approval swings many votes—either that, or UAW leaders possess an uncanny ability to pick winners.

An analysis of the same primary indicates that the labor endorsement carries more weight than that of the Detroit Citizens League. The league gave its highest "preferred" rating to eight council candidates; of these, seven were nominated, and all were labor-endorsed. The UAW had not endorsed the single "preferred" entry who failed nomination. The Citizens League gave its second highest rating of "qualified" to sixteen candidates. The seven among these who were nominated all had labor endorsement; among the nine not nominated, only one had labor support.

Despite its obvious influence on elections, the UAW has never controlled the city council as the Central Labor Union has done in Minneapolis. The Detroit council is about evenly divided between pro-labor "liberals" and business-oriented "conservatives."

As for the mugwumps and men of property, they are not much more excited about the city government than the unionists. They seem, on the whole, satisfied with its professional competence. Not since a blowup in 1940 that sent the mayor and scores of policemen to jail for graft has there been a scandal. The Board of Commerce keeps a closer eye than anyone else on the council and city departments. The Citizens Research Council of Michigan (formerly Upson's Bureau of Governmental Research) also has an observer in evidence, especially when the city's chronic need for more revenue comes up for discussion.

The mugwumps show greater concern about reforming the government of Wayne County, an area which includes Detroit and is the industrial heart of the state. While the United States contains many weird contraptions called county governments, few can equal that of Wayne County. Its legislative body is a massive board of one hundred and fifteen supervisors (a few years ago it was only a hundred, but every time a new city is incorporated, it gets a supervisor, and since the law provides that Detroit must always have a majority on the board, Detroit gets another supervisor, too). The county's executive is supposed to be a board of three elected auditors; however, most county departments are independent of them, under an elected prosecuting attorney, sheriff, county clerk, treasurer, register of deeds, and drain commissioner, so that the board of auditors can do little except propose the annual budget. The county has been going in the hole at the rate of $4 million a year for the past several years. And in 1959 it gained the distinction of having, according to the National Municipal League, the longest ballot in the world; it listed candidates for fifty-three separate offices.

The mugwumps believe they could reduce the Wayne County government to manageable proportions if they were free to write a new county charter, but the state constitution forbids that. Detroit reformers have been fighting for thirty years, until they are arm-weary, to remove this restriction and obtain county home rule.

A ray of hope appeared in 1960 after the state League of

Women Voters and the state Junior Chamber of Commerce collected approximately 300,000 signatures and forced onto the state ballot a proposition making it easier to call a convention to revise the state constitution.[6] The amendment, which the voters approved in November, 1960, also breaks the rural areas' written-in strangle hold on any constitutional convention that might be called; instead of having three delegates from each state senatorial district, the new amendment provides that a convention shall have one delegate from each senatorial district and one for each representative in the legislature, thus giving a slightly better break to the cities with their larger number of representatives. Detroit mugwumps hope that any future constitution written by a convention and approved by Michigan voters will contain a section permitting Wayne County to write a home-rule charter modernizing its government.

Aside from a county charter, Detroit's mugwumps and men of property seem most concerned these days about "economic growth." Name-studded committees have sprung up with the announced goal of creating a climate in which business will prosper and unemployment disappear. William M. Day, president of Michigan Bell Telephone, has headed two of these groups—Michigan's Committee for Economic Development and the Southeastern Michigan Metropolitan Research Corporation. Detroit Mayor Louis C. Miriani added a Mayor's Committee for Economic Growth, with Detroit Edison president Walter L. Cisler as chairman.

Another blue-ribbon committee, led by banker Joseph M. Dodge, handed in a study on local government finances in 1957. The Citizens Research Council did most of the staff work.

Laudable as these efforts have been, they have been undertaken in what could hardly be described as an atmosphere of pulsating excitement. Prominent committee members have served dutifully rather than zealously. The spirit that powered such crusades as that for the 1919 city charter has not revived.

For a while, downtown spirit reawakened for the city's celebration of its 250th anniversary in 1951. This put new energy behind completion of the long-planned $110-million civic center along the Detroit River (a $5½-million Veterans Memorial building, a $26-million City-County Building, a $5½-million Ford auditorium for which the Ford family and Ford dealers across the nation put up a third of the money, and the dramatic $54-million Cobo Convention Hall and Exhibit Building). This surge of downtown activity included the erection of a block-square bus terminal, an equally large National Bank building, and a thirty-story Michigan Consolidated Gas Building.

City planner Charles Blessing and his ninety-man staff during the 1950s enthusiastically turned out plans and models for remaking nearly every inch of downtown Detroit, but their enthusiasm did not infect the business leaders. The Gratiot-Orleans downtown slum-clearance project was stalled for years until in 1954 a mortgage banker went to Walter Reuther and asked if he could do something. Reuther persuaded the mayor to appoint a citizens committee of ten labor and business leaders, and they soon set the legal and financial wheels turning. In late 1958, tenants started occupying the first of two thousand middle-income apartments in the park-like development. In general, however, Detroit's men of property showed no compulsion toward large-scale rebuilding. As one spokesman said, "Some day? Yes, we'll have to tackle it sooner or later. But there's no sense of urgency now."

Sooner or later, of course, something will come along to jar Detroit's leaders into a sense of urgency. It may come in a batch of statistics. Or in a sudden sense of falling behind as other major mets and super mets move ahead faster into the second revolution.

The goad may even prove to be Reuther and the UAW. Bemused as they have been with distant places, the unionists may have time, with the friendlier Kennedy administration in Washington, to relax and putter around home for a while. Urban renewal, new low-income housing and redevelopment of industrial sites could claim increasing attention, affecting as they do thousands of UAW members. Once involved in this set of local problems, union leaders are likely to find themselves drawn into others, until finally they are poking around in all corners of city hall.

A few leaders within the UAW have felt for some time that the union should keep more closely informed on what is happening in Detroit and Wayne County government. This feeling led to formation of the UAW's Metropolitan Research Bureau in 1958. So far it is a modest $20,000-a-year operation with a youthful director and a secretary, producing academic-sounding reports for the private consumption of UAW officials. It may be a significant first step, however, toward ending the downtown mugwumps' monopoly on the research device as a means of influencing local government.

The increased presence of the UAW around the City-County Building would be sure to build a fire under the Board of Commerce, the Research Council and the Citizens League. The fire would become a roaring blaze if the labor men should start a movement to amend the city charter so as to have partisan city elections instead of nonpartisan ones—something that UAW spokesmen have said they would like to do. With Detroit heavily Democratic and the UAW the leader of the Democratic coalition, this attitude is normal enough.

On the other hand, an alliance between the UAW and the downtown mugwumps and men of property, a limited type of alliance, is not outside the realm of possibility. Both sides stand to gain from comprehensive redevelopment of the city, which is now in a state of economic flux.

That, however, seems to be some way off. The time of action has not arrived. No fire burns under the Detroit mugwump. He moves slowly, reflectively, like a man turning something over in his mind. Or a man looking for something to turn over in his mind.

Being a mugwump, he is impatient for a crusade. But he can't, for the life of him, think of anything worth fighting for. The mugwump philosophy, the old objectives and beliefs, that served to move him a generation or more ago are worn out. He is temporarily out of a cause, and it is taking him a while to fashion a new one.

In Detroit parlance, he is not out of business. He is just retooling.

15

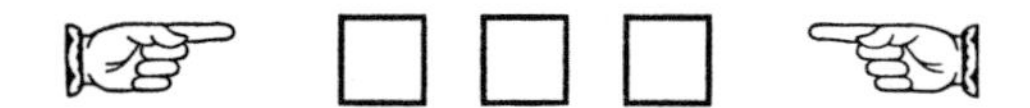

Prognosis

As the political tourist finishes his trek through mugwumpland, he discovers that each of the twenty cities where he browsed has its claims to uniqueness.

New York's egghead alliance of mugwumps, social workers, labor leaders and intellectuals is a reform bloc unduplicated anywhere else.

Dallas has been the city tightly controlled by a score of big mugwumps, a control now beginning to crumble from old age.

Minneapolis has been the only major United States city of this era run by a labor government.

In New Orleans a thirty-four-year-old war veteran got elected reform mayor, then built a political machine that outdid the professionals.

Pittsburgh is the grimy waif to whom a multimillionaire Republican and a Democratic boss played Pygmalion.

Chicago can boast the most powerful political machine and the busiest Crime Commission.

Philadelphia has its improbable good-government coalition of reform Republicans, reform Democrats, big newspapers, the ADA and the AFL-CIO.

American cities' uniqueness extends to their mugwump institutions. None is the exact duplicate of any other, no two operate in precisely the same way. Some proceed quietly and effectively, like the Milwaukee Citizens Governmental Research Bureau. Others wage campaigns and fling charges, like Cincinnati's Charter Committee. Some are open to all citizens and arrive at decisions through relatively democratic procedures, like the Seattle Municipal League. Others resemble exclusive clubs, like the Pennsylvania Economy League.

Some cities have intrinsically strong mugwump agencies, like St. Louis with its Governmental Research Institute and its Civic Progress, Incorporated, aided by fighting newspapers, yet are dominated by ward politicians. In a city like Los Angeles, mugwump organizations are puny, but city hall is largely free of party hacks.

Diversity, of course, is to be expected, since each city was born individually and grew according to its own intake of immigrants. It thrived or weakened as the nation's changing economy found use for automobiles instead of riverboats, oil instead of cordwood. Each acquired its own political history.

Although this diversity has inevitably affected the cities' reform institutions, giving them varying shapes, nearly all these institutions have fallen into one of two basic patterns: the candidate-running municipal parties that try to elect good men to office; and the research agencies that avoid personalities and concentrate on issues, policies, procedures and laws.

Which of the two is the stronger instrument? Which in the long run leads to better government? On this the debate has never ended.

To many mugwumps the municipal party has had powerful appeal. If there are crooks and crumbs in city hall, then take them on in open combat, lick them at the polls, and keep licking them whenever they challenge. It seems the logical, direct way to attain good government. What is more, it provides the thrill of a sporting event. There is the planning, the campaign, the clash on election day, and by nightfall, victory or defeat. If defeated, the reformers, like Rutgers, can always look forward to next year. If victorious, then there is celebration because virtue has triumphed and good government is assured.

If it were only that simple. But unlike a television Western, municipal administration involves more than good guys versus bad guys. Election results, no matter who wins, cannot assure good government. Admittedly, when a municipal reform party has taken over city hall, it has generally brought improved government, especially if its predecessor has been a hack political machine. The reformers put men in office who will not steal money or sell jobs. But there are other ways of misgoverning.

Just as a government controlled by a party machine tends toward cronyism, corruption and incompetence, so a non-machine professionalized government tends toward remoteness from the people, toward introversion, dogma and bureaucratism. A government of bureaucrats is capable of wasting as much of the people's money as a machine of political hacks. The hack takes it in the form of graft. The bureaucrat takes it legally with unneeded programs and empire-building.

Somebody must be around to curb and criticize the bureaucrat just as somebody must be around to expose the grafting hack. Therein lies the weakness of the municipal party as an instrument of reform. It has failed as a critic.

Like any other political party, it has tended to defend its own. If it persuades men to run for office and helps elect them, it will not turn on them the next week or next month with public, or even private, rebukes. Rather, it supports them and protects them in office and leaves them alone to handle their duties. This hands-off attitude has characterized candidate-electing organizations in Kansas City, Dallas, San Antonio, San Francisco and elsewhere; only the Cincinnati Charter Committee maintains regular contact with its councilmen through weekly luncheons, and any policy differences arising there are settled within the family.

In a city saddled with a Pendergast, a Hynicka, a Long or a Crump, there has apparently been no way to dislodge him except by a citizen uprising led by a reform party. Unfortunately, the parties have tended to become permanent. Reform leaders usually declare they dare not lay aside the power they have created, because if they do the bad politicians will seize it again. And so they have become perennial runners of candidates and defenders of their administrations. In addition, leading newspapers are usually allied with the good-government party. And so the press, too, largely abdicates its traditional role of critic and becomes an apologist for city hall.

Some mugwumps believe the ideal solution is to have what editor Meeman of Memphis calls "a strong right arm and a strong left arm"—that is, both a candidate-running organization and a research agency.

This is theoretically possible. San Francisco, in fact, has both types of agencies; they remain, however, somewhat behind the scenes compared with similar organizations in other cities, and each has a slightly different base of support. In general, no city seems big enough for both a strong municipal party and a strong research bureau. There is an inherent contradiction between the two types of agencies, and the mugwumps in a city evidently must choose which type they want to support.

Kansas City's long-established research bureau lasted only two years after mugwumps there defeated the Pendergast machine in 1940. Thereafter the reformers put all their energies into their candidate-running Citizens Association, never questioning the administration of their city manager Cookingham. The research institute was revived only after the Citizens Association met defeat in 1959.

In Cincinnati, the Charter Committee has dominated the reform movement for nearly forty years, totally overshadowing the local research bureau. The story is the same in Dallas; indeed, the research bureau there became dormant following the death of its director in the late 1950s. Memphis mugwumps have let their Civic Research Committee fade away, expending their time and money instead on their campaign organization, the Citizens Association. In Seattle, the Municipal League got off the ground in the late 1930s only after the candidate-running Cincinnatus group folded. From these cases one might conclude that there is some kind of Gresham's law among reform agencies to the effect that candidate-running organizations drive out research organizations; the former with their excitement of periodic face-to-face combat seem to have a stronger attraction than the research agencies with their less dramatic, intellectually more demanding day-after-day grind of fact-gathering and analysis. As a corollary, one could add that research agencies tend to flourish only where candidate-running organizations have failed or have never been tried. (Since, however, the candidate-running municipal parties have failed rather often in major cities, they are now outnumbered by the research agencies approximately three to one.)

Although there has been little open quarrel between them, what is actually involved here are two fundamentally unreconcilable concepts of reform.

One might be called the "personal" concept, the belief that good government derives from good men in office. Therefore, the best possible government results from putting the best possible men into office and letting them manage public affairs. Reform consists of ejecting low-quality men from power and replacing them with high-quality men.

The other concept of reform could be called that of the "skeptic" or "gadfly" school. Those who subscribe to this—and the author confesses himself among them—admit that able, honest men are preferable in government to bumblers and frauds. But the skeptic makes the further assumption that government can *always* be improved, that the public interest is *never* totally served, and that there is a basic conflict between the officeholder and the citizen. The citizen can never leave public affairs entirely to the good sense and good intentions of the official. Instead, the citizen must continually act to protect himself against tyranny; if not tyranny, dishonesty; if not dishonesty, officiousness; if not officiousness, sloth; and if not sloth, stupidity. This attitude found expression with Wendell Phillips nearly a century ago:

> Republics exist only on the tenure of being constantly agitated. . . . Every government is always growing corrupt. Every Secretary of State . . . is an enemy to the people of necessity, because the moment he joins the government, he gravitates against that popular agitation which is the life of a republic. A republic is nothing but a constant overflow of lava. . . . The republic which sinks to sleep, trusting to constitutions and machinery, to politicians and statesmen, for the safety of its liberties, never will have any.[1]

All mugwumps, whether municipal-party men running candidates for office or skeptics agitating for impersonal reforms, have couched their appeals to the public in similar terms, in those of morality. Their arguments have followed the formula: this is wrong, it must go—that is right, we must do it.

To many a hardened politician, accustomed to making his sales pitch in terms of benefits—who gains from this and how much—the mugwump's harping on right and wrong, good and evil, justice and injustice, has sounded amateurish. Those are just words.

But the mugwump, even if unwittingly, has been playing the most astute kind of politics. He has constantly sought the strong moral position on public questions. Groping by instinct and conditioning rather than by reasoned calculation, he and his fellows have tried to reduce every issue to right and wrong, placing themselves on the side of right. The mugwump may not always have succeeded in his quest, but he has known enough to search.

What he has sought in each case is not the "true" moral position, one that a committee of logicians would agree fits that description. He has sought the *practical* moral position, one that the majority of people in the society involved—the city, county, state or nation—can accept as the moral position because it squares with their precepts of right and wrong. By so doing, the mugwump has won their votes at critical moments and has gained political influence out of all proportion to his numbers.

During the past century the mugwump has succeeded in pinning the label of evil on the spoils system, Tammany Hall, Boss Tweed and scores of other political sultans, bribe-proffering utility companies, bribe-taking public officials, saloons, crooked cops, ward politicians, decentralized purchasing, oversized city councils, weak mayors, long ballots, partisan elections, and many other objects. Identifying these evils, devising methods to eliminate them, and campaigning until the methods were adopted—these have comprised the first revolution of the cities.

In the second revolution, it is reasonable to expect that the mugwump will proceed in much the same way—discerning what he believes are the most serious evils threatening the cities, labeling the evils as such in the public mind, advancing proposals for correcting the evils, and lobbying until the proposals are put into effect.

Even the most cursory glance at the American scene reveals the major issue to which the mugwump will most likely address himself in the coming decades. This is the question of whether the large American city shall be saved as a place where the ordinary citizen can work and live, or whether it shall be permitted to degenerate into a huge blighted slum of factories and deserted store fronts, inhabited only by the poor and the criminal. It is the question of whether the United States metropolis shall be subjected to extensive internal and external plastic surgery to keep it alive, healthy and attractive. It is also the question of whether it will move submissively toward the time when, in the economist J. K. Galbraith's phrase, "either people awake one morning and find they cannot get into the city, or there comes that climactic evening when they can't get out."

For some people such questions are not pressing. They believe the American city is doomed, and the best thing to do is stop worrying about it. They would apply to every crowded, aging metropolis the advice Frank Lloyd Wright had for Pittsburgh: abandon it. In the words of a Detroit automobile executive: "The city's an anachronism. It's sinking like a mastodon in the mire."

The mugwump does not accept this answer. He finds it immoral to contemplate abandoning 500 billion dollars' worth of urban property to decay, and half the country's population to an increasingly squalid, undignified existence. A young Seattle lawyer, one of the Northwest's vigorous reformers, declares:

> Our goal could be called a search for the four freedoms of urban life—freedom from congestion, freedom from pollution, freedom from blight, and freedom from confusion.
>
> Freedom from congestion means freedom from strangled traffic, vehicular and pedestrian, and from blocks to communication and movement of all types. Freedom from pollution means freedom from polluted air as well as polluted water. Freedom from blight means freedom from ugliness and waste in all its forms. Freedom from confusion means freedom from confused and contradictory physical developments, and more importantly freedom from confusion in the web of local government activities and their impact on the individual.
>
> The goals of urban freedom should be an objective second in importance only to our effort to survive as a nation in a troubled world.[2]

Part of the mugwump's job in the second revolution will be to issue and reissue statements like this, defining and redefining the ultimate purpose of the crusade. It is the task of creating the dream.

A second task entails translating the dream into specific plans and legislation needed to make the dream come true.

A third assignment is to promote within each major city an alliance composed of the men of property, public officials, labor leaders, Negro leaders and anyone else of political importance—an alliance whose members, overlooking their differences on other matters, agree to work together toward realizing the metropolitan dream.

A fourth necessity is a nation-wide system of intercommunication among these local coalitions—meetings, correspondence, publications, visits—so that coalition members in all cities reach eventual agreement on objectives and on political strategy to employ in Washington and the state capitols.

If the second revolution is to succeed, this intercommunication will have to go well beyond private conferences, easily passed resolutions and discreet lobbying. The promoters of the metropolitan dream must reach out to the public and there build broad, deep support. A new wave of civic patriotism must materialize, a feeling of home-town pride that has little to do with economic interest. To the jaded city dweller of today, the idea of such a surge of feeling may seem fantastic. Yet townsmen in the Middle Ages poured their hearts and their silver into another prodigious effort, the erecting of their Gothic cathedrals for the glory of God and their city. Conceivably, modern townsmen may be moved to excitement and even wonder as they catch the vision of their communities shedding drabness and rising as places of beauty.

Urban Americans, for all their apparent rootlessness, hunger for something to be loyal to, and a populace that can take vicarious pride in the Los Angeles Rams or Antoine's Restaurant is undoubtedly capable of being stirred to devotion to the city in which it lives.

Such a ground swell of feeling could be hastened by a change in an American attitude that seems to be taking form in the 1960s. Walter Lippmann, Galbraith and other intellectuals have been leading a growing criticism of America's worship of the Gross National Product. The country, they declare, has gone overboard in its production of consumer goods; it has been frittering away its strength and resources in an endless stream of bechromed cars, pushbutton stoves and electric foot warmers, while starving the country's public needs for schools, hospitals, research, transportation, conservation and welfare services. These critics propose a change in the nation's sense of values. In their view, the obsessive drive to forever fatten the GNP regardless of what goes into it has been leading society down a dead end. This high-level grumbling conceivably could filter down and infect the general citizenry. There was a noticeable wave of response to President Kennedy's 1961 inaugural address asking the people to sacrifice private comfort for the country's welfare. A surprising number of United States citizens might be ready to agree that necessary public spending is more important than frivolous personal acquisition.

In such a climate, the movement for remaking America's cities could find easier going. For clearly the creation of livable major mets and super mets will absorb huge public subsidies coming from public taxes. These will go into mass transit systems, new streets, sewage networks and disposal plants, clearance of commercial and residential slums, the building of low-income housing, improved schools, recreation centers, public clinics, and a dozen other demands.

Just as clearly, these subsidies, probably equaling each year the combined billions the federal government has been donating to farm growers and foreign aid, will be approved only after sweeping political changes in Congress and in state legislatures. The prevailing coalitions of rural and business conservatives will have to be overthrown by coalitions of progressive Republicans and progressive Democrats, supported by the metropolitan bloc. The grotesque figure of malapportionment in legislatures must go—and it will, once big-city forces make up their minds that it must.

Merely getting the subsidies will not be enough. Somebody must be given power to plan and execute their spending—somebody legally superior to the present hodgepodge of independent cities and special-purpose districts found in every large population center. This somebody may prove to be either the metropolitan-area kind of government exemplified by Toronto, Canada, and Dade County, Florida, or—and this seems more probable—

reformed state governments with full-time (and possibly unicameral) legislatures responsive to big-city demands, and professionalized state agencies assigned to handle metropolitan problems.

The mugwump's place in the second revolution will be more than that of promoter of these changes. He will also have to serve as watchdog. The possibilities of corruption and abuse, especially in using the power of eminent domain, are enormous. Each program must be subjected to scrutiny and questions must be asked. Will it enrich a few at the expense of the many? Does it demand sacrifices from one group, no sacrifices from another? Does it grant special privilege to some and deprive others of equal opportunity?

The mugwump no doubt will keep a narrow eye on such urban-renewal devices as the "writedown"—a procedure by which the local redevelopment authority, using federal and city funds, buys a slum area, then resells it for a fraction of the cost to a private redeveloper. This has come under heavy attack in several cities, including New York, where some redevelopers in the 1950s used the device for obtaining control of several blocks of slum tenements with a small payment, then milking the tenement dwellers of rents for years without erecting a single new building. In Boston, the redevelopment agency paid $5.40 per square foot for twenty-two acres of slums in the New York Streets area, cleared the land and sold it to a redeveloper for only 70 cents a square foot. While the project had the announced objective of attracting new industry to Boston, its occupants ended up being three firms already in town—the Boston *Herald-Traveler* newspaper, the Graybar and Westinghouse electric companies; the *Herald-Traveler* put up a large brick building, the electric firms built two smaller warehouses. The project was also supposed to increase the assessed value of the land and the tax revenue from it. Yet the area, as a slum, was assessed at $4.99 a square foot; and after redevelopment and the investment of some $4.8 million of public funds, the most highly developed section, which contained the new *Herald-Traveler* plant, was assessed at $3.34 a square foot—a third less than it had been in its slum days.[3]

The writedown device also came in for sharp comment at California Governor Edmund G. Brown's state conference on housing in 1961. One speaker, state assemblyman Samuel R. Geddes, said:

> For the first time in history our tax money is being used for programs of slum clearance for the benefit of the well-to-do. Vast areas, usually containing much lowpriced housing, are bulldozed to make way for luxury units at fantastic rents. The displaced people are simply shoved out of the area into already overcrowded sections, where their presence pushes up rents even more for those least able to afford them.

There is an obvious need during the second revolution for the mugwump to keep under constant surveillance such experimental gadgets as the writedown (already the Committee for Economic Development is intimating that the writedown might be eliminated).[4] As the revolution gains momentum, the mugwump may be expected to step aside as a promoter and give greater attention to detecting blunders, oversights and wrongdoing, then heckling others to adopt the needed remedies. That historically has been the role in which he is most at home.

All this, of course, is pure speculation. The American big-city mugwump in the 1960s, '70s and '80s may be concerned with far different issues and a far different program from our projected second revolution—even though it is difficult in the logic of events to imagine what greater demand will arise.

But one thing is sure. The mugwump will be concerned about something. A compulsive meddler in public affairs, he can no more still his voice than Gauguin could lay down his brush. Nor does he wish to. The mugwump has not the least doubt that his constant intervention in government, his endless advocacy of change during past generations has worked to the general good.

Let us add this hope: that in his intervention and advocacy, the mugwump will be a less solitary figure than he has been.

The mugwump, limited like any man by his prejudices and his background, should not appear as lone counsel for the public interest. He should be joined by other men with different backgrounds and different prejudices—men of labor, of the soil, of the church, of the great corporations, of the dark minorities.

These can learn much from the mugwump.

And the best hope for the American future lies in the prospect that they will develop an equal devotion to what, in their eyes, is the public good, an equal willingness to sacrifice their time and energy for that ideal. From this clash of devotions may come an eventual understanding by all sides that the others mean well, too; and this understanding in turn will yeld the atmosphere of mutual tolerance and respect and compromise that, in the long run, can spell the difference between survival and decline for America's democratic processes.

The all-important thing is a willingness to work, to consider facts, to think, to speak, and to do this with a mind as divorced from selfish interest as is possible for the human animal.

The mugwump has had this willingness. Thus the secret of his political rise in this century is really no great secret at all. It has consisted largely of an attitude that any group can appropriate for the taking.

Nowhere is it more clearly laid out than in the closing paragraph that a stiff-collared, precise New York mugwump, aged eighty, wrote in his autobiography a few years before his death.[5] He concluded:

> Those who read this book will mostly be younger than I, men of the generations who must bear the active part in the work ahead. Let them learn from our adventures what they can. Let them charge us with our failures and do better in their turn.
>
> But let them not turn aside from what they have to do, nor think that criticism excuses inaction. Let them have hope, and virtue, and let them believe in mankind and its future, for there is good as well as evil, and the man who tries to work for the good, believing in its eventual victory, while he may suffer setback and even disaster, will never know defeat. The only deadly sin I know is cynicism.
>
> Henry L. Stimson

Notes

2: THE SETTING

1. Bryce, James, *The American Commonwealth*, Commonwealth Publishing Company, New York, 1908, Vol. II, pp. 742–3.

3: ACTIVISTS, MEN OF PROPERTY AND MUGWUMPS

1. Adams, Henry, *The Education of Henry Adams*, Modern Library, Random House, New York, 1931, p. vi, Introduction.
2. *National Municipal Review*, July, 1927, facing p. 427.

4: THE CURIOUS BANNERS

1. Bryce, *op. cit.*, pp. 423–4.
2. *Ibid.*, p. 183, footnote.
3. Hofstadter, Richard, *Age of Reform*, Alfred A. Knopf, New York, 1955, p. 183.
4. Stimson, Henry L., and Bundy, McGeorge, *On Active Serv-*

ice in Peace and War, Harper & Bros., New York, 1947, 1948, p. 22.

5. *Ibid.*, p. 81.

6. This sketch is not based on a scientific study of the Municipal League membership (none has ever been made) but on the author's personal acquaintanceship with league members during his three years on the league staff. The "graph" is merely a visualization of one observer's impressions.

7. Schlesinger, Arthur Meier, *Rise of the City, 1878–1898*, Macmillan Company, New York, 1933, p. 353.

8. *National Municipal Review*, January, 1919, p. 1.

9. *Ibid.*, March, 1919, p. 197.

10. Bryce, *op. cit.*, p. 553.

11. *National Municipal Review*, March, 1917, pp. 205–6.

12. The Hare system of proportional representation works roughly as follows. A winning candidate needs to gain not a majority or plurality of votes but a "quota" of votes. The quota is calculated by dividing the total number of valid ballots cast by one more than the number of vacancies to be filled, then adding to this figure one vote; thus, with 6,000 votes cast and five vacancies to fill, the 6,000 is divided by 6 (five vacancies plus one), giving 1,000—so the quota for election becomes 1,001. The voter marks his ballot in order of his preference; that is, a "1" for his first choice, a "2" opposite his second, and so on for as many as he wishes on the list of candidates. The ballots are sorted according to the first choices marked on them. Anyone reaching a quota of first-choice votes is declared elected. His above-quota ballots are counted according to the second choices marked on them. After this, the trailing candidate with the fewest votes is eliminated, and all his ballots are likewise redistributed according to their second choices. This process of eliminating candidates and redistributing their ballots according to the next choice continues until enough candidates have reached the quota, or until only the number to be elected are left.

13. *National Municipal Review*, September, 1918, p. 459.

5: RESEARCH: THE GIMMICK THAT WORKED

1. *Atlantic Monthly*, October, 1908, p. 459.
2. *Outlook Magazine*, August 28, 1909, p. 1054.
3. Gill, Norman N., *Municipal Research Bureaus*, American Council on Public Affairs, Washington, D.C., 1944, p. 16.
4. Bryce, *op. cit.*, Vol. I, p. 699.
5. The quotation is from Lester Velie's *Labor U.S.A.*, Harper & Brothers, New York, 1959, p. 103.

6: FOUR INSTRUMENTS OF POWER

1. Quotations such as this, appearing throughout the book, are taken from the author's interviews.
2. Address before the annual conference of the Governmental Research Association, Detroit, December 15, 1945.
3. Upson, Lent D., *Organized Citizen Concern with Government*, Governmental Research Association, New York, Special Pamphlet Series No. 2, May, 1946, pp. 5 and 7, rearranged for logical progression.
4. Geise, John, *Man and the Western World*, Harcourt, Brace and Company, New York, 1940, p. 540.
5. From Citizens Union questions on city policy for candidates for mayor, board of estimate and city council, August, 1957.
6. In the Seattle and Minneapolis leagues, most committee members get started up the ladder by sending in a "committee preference sheet." This sheet, mailed out to every member each year, briefly describes the fifteen or twenty standing committees and asks the member to indicate which ones he would like to join. From 10 to 15 percent of the Seattle members mail back their preferences; the Minneapolis response has been about half that large. The Cleveland league in 1957, for the first time, tried the preference sheets—postcards, actually, since Cleveland has only five standing committees—and received a surprising 12 percent response, half of it from members who had never before served on a league committee.

The work load for committees in six citizens leagues looked like this in a typical year, 1957 (compiled from the author's interviews and from a survey by the Seattle Municipal League in 1958; auditing, nominating and other committees dealing with purely internal affairs are not included):

CITIZENS UNION, New York—thirteen committees; most important are the fiscal affairs and management committee (it watches the city budget, purchasing, etc.), local candidates committee (it prepares pre-election reports on candidates) and the legislative committee (it studies bills introduced in the state legislature which affect New York City).

Number of committee meetings held during the year	135
Members attending two or more committee meetings during the year	225

MINNEAPOLIS CITIZENS LEAGUE—fifteen committees including city budget, county budget, education, elections and candidate review, forms and structures of local government, metropolitan government, and others.

Committee meetings held during year	175
Members attending two or more meetings	400

SEATTLE MUNICIPAL LEAGUE—sixteen committees including candidates investigating committee, county planning, city planning, metropolitan problems, port committee, public schools, law enforcement, and others.

Committee meetings held during year	215
Members attending two or more meetings	430

CLEVELAND CITIZENS LEAGUE—five committees (candidates, taxation and finance, judicial administration, county government, city government) plus special committees as required.

Committee meetings held during year	50
Members attending two or more meetings	200

DETROIT CITIZENS LEAGUE—a candidates committee; twenty members and six meetings during the year.

CIVIC CLUB, Pittsburgh—five committees on city and county budget, legislative committee, county reorganization, voters' directory (candidates report) and the committee on exceptionally able youth (for awarding college scholarships).

Committee meetings held during year	40
Members attending two or more meetings	125

7. Upson, *op. cit.*
8. Reprinted in *The Reporter Reader*, Doubleday & Co., Garden City, New York, 1956, p. 17.
9. *The Exploding Metropolis*, editors of *Fortune*, Doubleday Anchor Books, Garden City, New York, 1958, p. 79.
10. Address reprinted in *Greater Cleveland*, Cleveland Citizens League publication, May, 1957.
11. Pirenne, Henri, *Medieval Cities—Their Origins and the Revival of Trade*, Frank D. Halsey's translation, Princeton University Press, Princeton, N. J., 1925.

7: THE SECOND REVOLUTION

1. Dr. Luther Gulick jarred even the most enthusiastic urban renewers by estimating the cost of building and rebuilding United States cities in the next twenty years at $250 trillion. He was addressing the 1958 National Conference on Metropolitan Growth in Washington, D.C.
2. Author's computation, from U. S. Census Bureau figures on revenue and expenditures for 1952 and 1953, quoted by the Advisory Committee on Local Government in its report to the President's Commission on Intergovernmental Relations, U. S. Government Printing Office, June, 1955, p. 13.

8: FRIENDS AND FOES

1. Faulkner, Harold U., *American Political and Social History*, F. S. Crofts & Co., New York, 1940, p. 413.

9: THE OLD PROS' LAST STAND

1. A leader of the reform group, attorney Irving M. Engel, chairman of the New York Committee for Democratic Voters, takes exception to the wording in this paragraph. He declares: "We are not seeking to gain control of the party organization, but rather to open it up to control by a majority of the Democratic

voters. The chief figures in the reform movement—Senator Lehman, Mrs. Roosevelt, Mr. Finletter, Mr. Edelstein and [I] do not have the slightest interest in gaining control of Tammany. We could not care less who is county leader so long as he is democratically chosen and does not possess the autocratic powers which the county leader has exercised in the past."

2. The state assembly district leader is elected directly by the voters in some New York counties; in others he is chosen indirectly by the party's county committeemen. In Manhattan, the Democrats elect their assembly district leaders directly; the Republicans choose theirs through the county committee.

3. *University of Pennsylvania Law Review*, Philadelphia, Vol. 106, No. 2, December, 1957, p. 284.

4. The next year, 1948, Arvey topped his state ticket with two other mugwumpish candidates, Professor Paul H. Douglas for United States senator and Adlai Stevenson for governor.

5. "Chicago's Machine Gun Politics," *Nation*, March 15, 1952.

6. For more on this era see: Merriam, Robert E., and Goetz, Rachel M., *Going into Politics*, Harper and Brothers, New York, 1957.

7. Liebling, A. J., *Chicago: The Second City*, Alfred A. Knopf, New York, 1952, p. 106.

8. This issue was picked at random; however, it may have been a worse than typical day for Chicago's police.

10: THE "GOOD" MACHINES

1. The only other reform administration during Cox's long reign was that of Mayor Edward J. Dempsey in 1905–6.

2. A good description of the early years of the Charter Committee appears in Charles P. Taft's *City Management, the Cincinnati Experiment*, Farrar & Rinehart, New York, 1933.

3. A Charter Committee spokesman, previewing the manuscript, took strong exception to this explanation. He wrote: "The paralysis was inflicted by the combination of building and loan interests, metal trades industries, the gas company and Republican 'do-nothingness' which kept the auto industry out of Cincinnati

and has always gagged over spending money."

4. Cincinnati's first bureau of governmental research was founded in 1909 but later went out of existence.

5. The expressway bond issue was resubmitted to the voters in January 1961, and this time carried comfortably, 40,800 to 23,800.

6. The most complete analysis that the author has seen of San Antonio political and voting patterns was done by Mitchell Grossman of the San Antonio College political science faculty: *Multi-Factional Politics in San Antonio and Bexar County, Texas,* 1959, unpublished. Some of the information in this section is based on his study.

7. From *The Watchdog of Law Enforcement and Criminal Justice,* publication of Metropolitan Crime Commission of New Orleans, September, 1959, pp. 2, 3, 4.

11: THE TIDY TOWNS

1. For more about this period, see Richard Maher's section on Cleveland in *Our Fair City,* edited by Robert S. Allen, Vanguard Press, New York, 1947.

2. More on the politics of Los Angeles and San Francisco during this period may be found in George E. Mowry's *The California Progressives,* University of California Press, Berkeley, 1951.

3. Two of the departments—Library, and Recreation and Parks—were totally independent. The others required approval of their annual budgets by the city council and the mayor, but otherwise operated, for practical purposes, as autonomous units.

4. Seattle mugwumps, like those in San Francisco, at first opposed the anti-Chinese agitators of the 1880s. Following street riots and shootings in 1885, Seattle mugwumps formed a law-and-order group, the Loyal League, that ran leading pioneer Arthur A. Denny for mayor. He lost by forty-one votes to the candidate of the anti-Chinese "People's Party." Eight years later Denny led in forming the Municipal League, which obtained legislation placing city police and firemen under civil service, then disbanded.

5. Quotations taken from the author's shorthand notes made at the luncheon.

12: THE TRIBAL TOWNS

1. *National Municipal Review,* May, 1926, p. 253.
2. Author's computation from statistics provided by Boston Municipal Research Bureau.

13: HELL MADE OVER

1. Address to U. S. Conference of Mayors, September 11, 1957, New York City.
2. A spokesman for the Mellon organization complains that this paragraph is "a bit severe." He adds: "Actually, this was a case where at long last the planning phases of the redevelopment here in Pittsburgh were separated from the purely business phases. This is a clear-cut case of letting business concerns support matters that were purely in their own self-interest and placing the planning function on a separate fund solicitation."

14: LABOR'S LOVE LOST

1. Minneapolis *Star,* December 30, 1955.
2. Bryce, *op. cit.,* pp. 439 to 443.
3. Among the lobbyists the utilities brought to Detroit to outmaneuver Pingree was Tom L. Johnson of Cleveland. Pingree so impressed Johnson that he went home a converted reformer and became Cleveland's famous reform mayor.
4. A colorful chapter on Mayor Pingree appears in Malcolm W. Bingay's *Detroit Is My Own Home Town,* Bobbs-Merrill Co., New York, 1946, pp. 229–43. Other good material is in Leo Donovan's section on Detroit in *Our Fair City, op. cit.,* p. 148 et seq.
5. Speech before the annual conference of the Governmental Research Association in Detroit, December 15, 1945.
6. The key provision making it easier to call a constitutional convention provides that the proposition needs approval only of a majority voting on the question itself; previously a majority of

all those voting in the election was required. Many voters, of course, never get down to marking ballot propositions. Thus in 1948 a proposal for calling a constitutional convention received 855,000 yes votes against 799,000 no votes, but it failed to carry because it needed 1,057,000 for a majority among those voting in the election. In 1958 a similar proposal got 821,000 yes and 608,000 no votes, but it required an affirmative majority of 1,171,000.

15: PROGNOSIS

1. Quoted by Hofstadter, *op. cit.*, p. 138.
2. Ellis, James R., "The Time of Decision for Urban Areas," *Municipal News,* publication of Municipal League of Seattle and King County, January 7, 1961, p. 2.
3. Taken from *Assessed Values, Real Estate, Downtown Boston, 1959,* Greater Boston Real Estate Board.
4. CED's actual phrasing was: "Resale of publicly acquired sites without writedowns should be thoroughly explored." *Guiding Metropolitan Growth,* Committee for Economic Development, New York, August, 1960, p. 8.
5. *On Active Service in Peace and War, op. cit.*, p. 672.

Directory of Mugwump Organizations

This listing includes mugwump and promoter organizations that have significance in the government and politics of the twenty cities discussed in this book. Names and addresses, given here as of 1961, are subject, of course, to frequent change.

BOSTON

BOSTON MUNICIPAL RESEARCH BUREAU, 294 Washington Street. Joseph Slavet, executive secretary; assistant; researcher; two clerical. Budget $46,000 a year plus research studies made under contract; 300 contributors; thirty-nine directors and officers.

FINANCE COMMISSION OF THE CITY OF BOSTON, 24 School Street. Thomas J. Murphy, executive secretary; Anthony J. Young, chairman; three investigators; two clerical. Appointed commission of five members. Budget $60,000 a year, paid from city treasury.

AMERICANS FOR DEMOCRATIC ACTION, 6 Beacon Street. Melvin Warshaw, executive director; one clerical; 2,500 members in Boston area, paying dues of $5 ($7.50 per couple).

CHICAGO

THE CIVIC FEDERATION, 69 West Washington Street. Harland C. Stockwell, executive secretary; five researchers; three clerical. Budget $120,000 a year from 1,000 individuals and corporations.

CHICAGO CRIME COMMISSION, 79 West Monroe Street. Virgil W. Peterson, operating director; twenty-five court observers, investigators, statisticians and clerical employes. Budget $165,000 a year from 1,900 contributors.

LEAGUE OF WOMEN VOTERS OF CHICAGO, 67 East Madison Street. Two office employes; 1,300 members, budget $24,000 a year. Associated with CITIZEN INFORMATION SERVICE OF METROPOLITAN CHICAGO, and LEAGUE OF WOMEN VOTERS OF ILLINOIS in same office. Citizen Information Service has two office employes, a $30,000 budget from foundations, corporations and individuals. League of Women Voters of Illinois has three office employes, $49,500 a year from local league pledges.

INDEPENDENT VOTERS OF ILLINOIS, 14 East Jackson. Julian Klugman, executive director; two clerical. Budget $25,000 a year, plus campaign expenses up to $25,000 a year; membership varies from 1,000 to 3,000, with dues at $7.50 a year ($10 for couples). Affiliated with Americans for Democratic Action national headquarters in Washington, D.C.

BETTER GOVERNMENT ASSOCIATION, 343 South Dearborn. George E. Mahin, executive director; assistant; one clerical. Budget $45,000 a year from 600 firms and individuals.

CITIZENS OF GREATER CHICAGO, 8 South Dearborn. Miss Sarah Mildren, acting executive director; one clerical. Budget $15,000 a year.

CITY CLUB OF CHICAGO, 189 West Madison Street. Miss Elsie T. Micholson, assistant to the president. Budget $18,000 a year from 750 members.

CINCINNATI

CITY CHARTER COMMITTEE, Carew Tower. Forest Frank, executive director; Mrs. Everett W. Hobart, director, women's division; two clerical. Budget $32,000 for office, plus $30,000 and up for election campaigns every other year; 75 percent of budget from 700 donors giving $25 to $1,000 each; remaining fourth from 1,000 smaller contributions.

CITIZENS DEVELOPMENT COMMITTEE, Union Central Building. George C. Hayward, executive secretary and treasurer; one clerical. Budget $30,000 a year for office, plus up to $25,000 a year for special studies and services; most of funds from a hundred firms giving $50 to $4,000 each, a small fraction from 200 individual members at $2 and $10.

BUREAU OF GOVERNMENTAL RESEARCH, 812 Race Street. Robert D. Van Fossen, acting director; Calvin Skinner, consultant; woman assistant; two field men; stenographer. Budget $35,000 a year, from 250 firms and individuals, plus funds for contract studies.

HAMILTON COUNTY GOOD GOVERNMENT LEAGUE, 4 West Seventh Street. Mrs. Iola Hessler, executive secretary; legal counsel. Budget estimated $10,000 a year.

CLEVELAND

CITIZENS LEAGUE OF GREATER CLEVELAND, 1010 Euclid Building. Estal E. Sparlin, director; two researchers; membership-public relations secretary; three clerical. Operated in conjunction with CLEVELAND BUREAU OF GOVERNMENTAL RESEARCH, in same office. Citizens League budget of $30,000 a year from 3,000 members; Research Bureau budget of $25,000 a year from 300 firms, plus $25,000 from Cleveland Development Foundation for metropolitan-government research.

CLEVELAND DEVELOPMENT FOUNDATION, Midland Building. Upshur Evans, president; assistant; one clerical. Budget $100,000 a year for office, plus cost of engineering, architectural and legal services, contributed by ninety Cleveland corporations. Board of thirty-six trustees.

DALLAS

DALLAS CITIZENS COUNCIL, No office. Assistant secretary is Mrs. Lillian McDonald of Watson Associates public relations agency, Greater National Life Building. Expenses $12,000 a year contributed by 230 members.

CITIZENS CHARTER ASSOCIATION, No office. Chairman of reorganization committee is W. H. Cothrum, 2116 North Field Street. Campaign funds of $30,000 to $35,000 for city elections (held in odd-numbered years) contributed by businessmen.

GREATER DALLAS PLANNING COUNCIL, 2021 Fidelity Union Tower. Mrs. Mary Greding, secretary; Woodall Rodgers, president; approximately 1,000 members. Not active since death of manager Granville W. Moore.

DETROIT

CITIZENS RESEARCH COUNCIL OF MICHIGAN, 1526 David Stott Building. Robert E. Pickup, executive director; five researchers; three clerical in Detroit office, plus three researchers, one clerical at state capital, Lansing. Budget $220,000 a year from major corporations and the Relm Foundation.

DETROIT CITIZENS LEAGUE, 1119 Dime Building. William H. O'Brien, executive secretary; two clerical. Budget $28,000 a year, half from 2,400 members at $5, $10, $25, other half from 200 firms (most give $25 to $100).

GREATER DETROIT BOARD OF COMMERCE, 320 West Lafayette. Willis Hall, secretary-manager; Arthur Hinkley, city hall representative.

HOUSTON

TAX RESEARCH ASSOCIATION OF HOUSTON AND HARRIS COUNTY, Continental Bank Building. James E. White, Jr., executive director;

researcher; two clerical. Budget $40,000 a year, from 650 members and contributing firms.

HOUSTON CHAMBER OF COMMERCE, 914 Main Street. Marvin Hurley, executive vice-president; four staff members assigned to city and county government affairs.

KANSAS CITY

CITIZENS ASSOCIATION OF KANSAS CITY, Board of Trade Building. Carl B. Short, Jr., executive secretary; part-time woman assistant; one clerical. Budget $25,000 a year for office, plus $100,000 every fourth year for election campaigns. Executive and advisory committees of seventy members; some 6,000 informal members.

CIVIC RESEARCH INSTITUTE, Railway Exchange Building. C. E. Curran, executive secretary; Cliff C. Jones, Jr., chairman; pollster; half-time secretary.

KANSAS CITY CRIME COMMISSION, 400 Waltower Building. Curtis Thatcher, managing director; investigator; two clerical.

LOS ANGELES

PROPERTY OWNERS TAX ASSOCIATION OF CALIFORNIA, 132 West First Street. W. A. Pixley, chairman; Paul Sheedy, executive vice-president; researcher; one clerical.

LOS ANGELES CHAMBER OF COMMERCE, 404 South Bixel Avenue. Harold Wright, general manager; James L. Beebe, chairman, state and local government committee.

CALIFORNIA TAXPAYERS' ASSOCIATION, 750 Pacific Electric Building. J. Roy Holland, assistant general manager, and Richard Winter, director of local activities, give some time to municipal affairs.

DOWNTOWN BUSINESSMEN'S ASSOCIATION, 743 Subway Terminal Building. Robert M. Shillito, general manager; researcher; public relations; two clerical. Budget $100,000 for office, plus $50,000 for study projects, contributed by 300 firms.

MEMPHIS

CITIZENS ASSOCIATION OF MEMPHIS AND SHELBY COUNTY, P.O. Box 6752; no office. J. W. Ramsay, president; Edmund Orgill, first vice-president; 900 members.

CIVIC RESEARCH COMMITTEE, Eighty One Madison Building. Mrs. Hubert C. Stroupe, secretary. Budget $4,500 a year, from 600 members and Meeman Foundation.

MILWAUKEE

CITIZENS' GOVERNMENTAL RESEARCH BUREAU, 125 East Wells Street. Norman N. Gill, executive director; three researchers; two clerical. Budget $45,000 to $50,000 a year from business sources.

GREATER MILWAUKEE COMMITTEE, 110 East Wisconsin Street. Rudolph A. Schoenecker, director; Einar Gaustad, consultant; one clerical. Budget $40,000 to $50,000 a year from 150 members.

MILWAUKEE DEVELOPMENT GROUP, 626 East Wisconsin Street. Chairman Edmund Fitzgerald. Annual underwriting $110,000; normal expenditures $20,000 to $30,000. Twenty-one members.

MINNEAPOLIS

CITIZENS LEAGUE OF MINNEAPOLIS AND HENNEPIN COUNTY, 545 Mobil Oil Building, 84 South Sixth Street. Verne C. Johnson, executive director; research-editor; membership-finance secretary; public relations man; four clerical. Budget $60,000 a year from 2,300 members and 450 firms and organizations.

LEAGUE OF WOMEN VOTERS, 414 Mobil Oil Building, 84 South Sixth Street. Mrs. S. P. Coombs, executive secretary; assistant. Budget $19,000 a year; 1,150 members.

CITIZENS ORGANIZED FOR RESPONSIBLE GOVERNMENT (CORG), 227 Foshay Tower. Mrs. Hayle Cavanor, director; Philip Sherman (of

Pillsbury Company legal department), chairman. Budget $8,000 a year for office, plus $15,000 to $25,000 for election campaigns each year or two, raised by 100 members from business sources.

NEW ORLEANS

BUREAU OF GOVERNMENTAL RESEARCH, 822 Perdido Street. Val C. Mogensen, director; two researchers; two clerical. Budget $40,000 a year, from 800 members and 160 contributing firms.

METROPOLITAN CRIME COMMISSION, 1325 National Bank of Commerce Building. Aaron M. Kohn, managing director; one clerical. Budget $30,000 to $35,000 a year, from 100 members and other contributors.

VOTERS SERVICE, Room B E 11, City Hall. Mrs. Edgar B. Stern, president; two women employes. Budget $25,000 a year raised by Mrs. Stern and eleven-woman committee.

NEW YORK

CITIZENS UNION OF THE CITY OF NEW YORK, 5 Beekman Street. Milton M. Bergerman, chairman; George H. Hallett, Jr., executive secretary; Samuel D. Smoleff, counsel; three research and clerical, plus two part-time. Budget $69,000 a year; 3,800 members.

CITIZENS BUDGET COMMISSION, INC., 51 East 42nd Street. John M. Leavens, executive director; four researchers; public relations man; five clerical; Harold Riegelman, counsel. Budget $150,000 a year from 750 corporations, plus foundation grants for special studies.

LEAGUE OF WOMEN VOTERS, 461 Park Avenue South. Five clerical employes; 3,300 members. Budget $40,000 a year.

WOMEN'S CITY CLUB, 277 Park Avenue. Mrs. Jerome L. Strauss, president; executive secretary; four clerical; 950 members. Budget $50,000 a year from members' dues.

CITIZENS COMMITTEE FOR CHILDREN, 112 East 19th Street. Mrs. Joseph P. Lash, director; nine professionals; nine clerical; 130 women members. Budget $155,000 a year.

REGIONAL PLAN ASSOCIATION, 230 West 41st Street. John P. Keith, executive director; fifteen professionals; ten clerical. Budget $225,-000 a year plus grants for studies; half of funds from 650 members, half from foundations.

AMERICANS FOR DEMOCRATIC ACTION, 136 Fifth Avenue. Jacques Wilmore, executive director; fund-raiser; two clerical; 1,900 members in New York City area. Budget $38,000 a year.

LIBERAL PARTY, 160 West 44th Street. Ben Davidson, director. Allied with INTERNATIONAL LADY GARMENT WORKERS UNION, 1710 Broadway; Gus Tyler, director, Political Education Department.

NEW YORK COMMITTEE FOR DEMOCRATIC VOTERS, 145 East 52nd Street. Irving M. Engel, chairman; Julius C. C. Edelstein, secretary; Richard A. Brown, executive director; two clerical. Co-ordinating body for anti-Tammany Democrats.

PHILADELPHIA

PENNSYLVANIA ECONOMY LEAGUE (EASTERN DIVISION), in association with BUREAU OF MUNICIPAL RESEARCH, 1321 Arch Street. Lennox Moak, director; ten to fifteen researchers; ten clerical. Budget $225,000 to $275,000 a year, mostly from major industries, retailers and banks.

GREATER PHILADELPHIA MOVEMENT, Western Savings Fund Building. William H. Wilcox, director; assistant; four clerical. Budget $50,000 a year plus approximately $30,000 for research contracts.

COMMITTEE OF SEVENTY, 1202 Land Title Building. Harry K. Butcher, executive secretary; two investigators; two clerical. Budget $50,000 a year from 750 contributors.

AMERICANS FOR DEMOCRATIC ACTION, Southeast Pennsylvania Chapter, 20 South 15th Street. Leon Shull, executive director; part-time assistant; part-time researcher; three clerical. Budget $32,000 a year from 1,000 members.

PITTSBURGH

PENNSYLVANIA ECONOMY LEAGUE (WESTERN DIVISION), Union Trust Building. Howard Stewart, director; ten to fifteen researchers; equal number clerical. Budget $300,000 a year, includes contributions to offices in state capital, Harrisburg, and in nine other western Pennsylvania counties.

ALLEGHENY CONFERENCE ON COMMUNITY DEVELOPMENT, Civic Building. Edward J. Magee, executive director; assistant; planning engineer; legal counsel; two clerical. Budget $130,000 a year from 125 sponsors. Affiliated with PITTSBURGH REGIONAL PLANNING ASSOCIATION (budget $107,000) in same building; Patrick J. Cusick, executive director.

ACTION HOUSING, INC., J. Stanley Purnell, board chairman; he is assistant to the president, T. Mellon and Sons, 525 William Penn Place.

CIVIC CLUB OF ALLEGHENY COUNTY, 225 Penn Sheraton Hotel. Mrs. Helen Baird La Monte, executive secretary; one part-time clerical employe. Budget $10,000 a year from 650 members.

ST. LOUIS

GOVERNMENTAL RESEARCH INSTITUTE, 1016 Arcade Building. Victor D. Brannon, director; assistant; three researchers; fund raiser; two clerical. Budget $70,000 to $75,000 a year, from 430 firms and individuals (range from $25 to $1,500, median subscription approximately $100).

CIVIC PROGRESS, INC., No office. Secretary is Harry B. Wilson of Fleishman-Hillard public relations agency, 407 North Eighth Street. Expenses $7,500 a year, plus special assessments ranging from nothing up to $35,000 a year, contributed by the twenty-six members.

SAN ANTONIO

GOOD GOVERNMENT LEAGUE, No office. Chairman is Harold Herndon, Milam Building. Raises $10,000 to $60,000 to campaign for city council slate and for bond issues in city elections. Campaigns have been handled by Ellis Shapiro agency, Insurance Building.

RESEARCH AND PLANNING COUNCIL, 118 Broadway. John F. Willmott, executive secretary; two clerical. Budget $31,000 a year, plus special study fund of $10,000 a year, from membership of 300 firms and individuals.

SAN FRANCISCO

SAN FRANCISCO BUREAU OF GOVERNMENTAL RESEARCH, 58 Sutter Street. Alfred F. Smith, director; assistant; one clerical. Budget $42,000 a year, from 300 individuals and firms.

SAN FRANCISCO VOLUNTEERS FOR BETTER GOVERNMENT, No office. Current president is Hunt Conrad, Kern County Land Company, Pacific Mutual Life Building. Thirty to thirty-five young (under forty) business and professional men. Raise $30,000 to $35,000 and enter slate of three or four candidates for city-county board of supervisors elections in off years.

CIVIC LEAGUE OF IMPROVEMENT CLUBS AND ASSOCIATIONS, 859 Flood Building. Philip F. Ringole, president; Elmer Robinson, chairman of advisory board. Mrs. Augusta Haas, secretary. Budget $20,000 a year for office, plus $20,000 to $25,000 for recommended-candidates mailing before local elections.

SAN FRANCISCO PLANNING AND URBAN RENEWAL ASSOCIATION, 126 Post Street. John Hirten, Jr., executive director; one clerical. Budget $50,000 a year, from 500 members.

LEAGUE OF WOMEN VOTERS, 1215 Hotel St. Francis. One clerical. Budget $10,000 a year, from 800 members.

SEATTLE

MUNICIPAL LEAGUE OF SEATTLE AND KING COUNTY, 431 Lyon Building. C. A. Crosser, executive secretary; research-editor; membership secretary; three clerical. Budget $70,000 a year, from 3,600 members and 550 contributing firms.

LEAGUE OF WOMEN VOTERS, Vance Hotel. Part-time secretary. Budget $8,000 a year; 650 members.

CENTRAL ASSOCIATION OF SEATTLE, Suite 222 Olympic Hotel. Paul Seibert, executive vice-president; two clerical. Budget $40,000 a year, contributed by downtown businessmen.

Index

ABOUT THE AUTHOR

After graduating with a degree in journalism from the University of Washington, LORIN PETERSON was a reporter for the Seattle *Post-Intelligencer,* wrote for Seattle radio stations KOMO-KJR, and taught at the University School of Journalism while working for his M.A. in political science. He has also been editor and later research director of the Seattle Municipal League; community relations officer of the University of Washington Division of Adult Education; and principal author of *Living in Seattle,* which has been a Seattle school textbook since 1951. He has written many reports and studies, including two major reports for the California legislature.

Lorin Peterson writes: "I am one of those newsmen who decided to do a book. At the time, I was working for the American Broadcasting Company newsroom in Hollywood and I was forty-one—just about the same age as my father when he decided to quit being a chiropractor in a southeastern Minnesota farming village and bundled the family off to a coal-mining town in the Cascade foothills of Washington, where he set up shop as a weekly newspaper publisher. There must be some slow-maturing gland in the Peterson males that sends them off on strange quests just when they should be settling down to solid respectability."

Mr. Peterson's particular quest has been three years of first-hand research in mugwumpland, from Boston to San Francisco. He now lives in Santa Monica with his wife, Joyce, who is a political reporter, and their young son, Thair.